SLUMS ARE FOR PEOPLE

# SLUMS ARE FOR PEOPLE

The Barrio Magsaysay Pilot Project
in Philippine Urban Community Development

**by Aprodicio A. Laquian**

East-West Center Press                     Honolulu

To my Father    —who knew how it was;

and

to Agnes Helen    —who may never know how it is.

# Contents

ILLUSTRATIONS

TABLES

# Foreword

In recent years the spectacular growth of urban populations in the poorer countries of the world has caused anxieties and even despair among those committed to helping human welfare and social development. The accelerating rate of urban migration, propelled by distress in the countryside and pulled by the attractions of the cities, has raised the specter of teeming, anomic masses, crowded into unlivable slums, whose inevitable frustrations can produce only a rising level of violence, both criminal and political.

A few scholars have questioned this nightmare view of urbanization in the new states and have pointed to indexes and statistics that suggest that new city dwellers are not necessarily so prone to crime or radicalism. In this book Aprodicio A. Laquian takes us by way of his disciplined but humanely understanding research into Tondo, the toughest and most troubled district of Manila, and shows us that "Slums are for people" and that those who live in them have life styles that are informed by reason and valued sentiments. His remarkable capacity to blend sensitivity with objectivity gives him the ability to explain why people may choose to live in such crowded conditions; how they are applying traditional practices and attitudes to facilitate their social and psychological adjustments in their transition to modernity; and why public policies, to be effective and appreciated, must be responsive to the very real sense of community legitimacy of slum people.

This book is more than a partisan defense of the human virtues of downtrodden peoples, for Dr. Laquian is equally sensitive and understanding of the complex relationship between research and action programs, between the scholar's quest for knowledge and the officials' need for policies and commitment. This book is therefore more than a research report; it is a rare account of how research can fit into a larger program of action and maintain its independence, while providing self-conscious guidance to both scholar and official. The same capacity for awareness of the many dimensions of human relations that makes Dr. Laquian so understanding of the dynamics of slum life also makes him equally understanding of the problem of organizational relations and interagency cooperation in the elite world of officialdom.

In bringing together what have been the academically separate fields of political development, urban studies, and public administration, Aprodicio A. Laquian has demonstrated that the analytical approaches of the social sciences do not have to violate the full integrity of what is studied but are in fact consistent with a holistic view of man and society. His highest contribution is that he has shown how the social sciences can be successfully used both to explain human behavior and to guide public policies, and in both cases in the fullest spirit of humane values.

It was a noteworthy act of innovation when the Philippine government, which had pioneered in devising community development programs for rural villages, decided that the concept of community development and the principle of self-help could and should also be used in dealing with urban problems. Fortunately, this experiment in transferring rural development techniques to the city included an appreciation of the potential value of social science research, for it has resulted in a valuable addition to our understanding of the urban scene in the developing countries.

Lucian W. Pye

*Department of Political Science*
*Massachusetts Institute of Technology*

# Preface

The College of Public Administration, University of the Philippines, seeks to focus attention on current administrative and political problems through its researches and publications. In previous works, the CPA faculty and staff have made studies on community development, fiscal policy, technical assistance, and local governments. Lately, attention has been shifting to urban development and the problems that attend it.

This book, *Slums Are for People*, reflects this trend.

Indeed, as the Philippines progresses, our problems will be shifting from the rural to the urban areas. Already, the two main metropolitan areas in the Philippines, Manila and Cebu, are going through varied difficulties arising from high density living caused by large scale migration from the rural areas. Urban changes in the Philippines as in other developing countries, call for administrative and political innovations. Studies like this book would help greatly in the evolution of such planned changes because they do not only shed light on the problem; they propose concrete solutions as well.

Like most pilot projects, the Barrio Magsaysay study should be seen as a rich lode of insights rather than a tight program approach to the solution of urban problems. While it proposes certain approaches that have been found useful on a pilot scale, the study's value rests more on its theoretical formulations that are designed to stimulate thinking and debate. Dr. Laquian provokes in this book, as in his former writings, certain issues and ideas, the resolution of which may mean a great deal to urban studies in this part of the world. For example, to what extent is his proposition that cities are really composed of small primary group communities true and empirically verifiable? Or on a grander scale, how feasible are his ideas on "planned urban slums" and how will they affect the planning and development of future cities already plagued by the problem?

It is significant that urban community development, an approach advocated by Dr. Laquian in this book, has its theoretical basis on a program already tested in the rural areas. The Philippines, together with India and the Republic of China, has contributed a great deal to the theories and practices of community development. Urban community development is something new. As such, the findings in the Barrio Magsaysay study may help in understanding this process further.

It is in the effort to find the right mixture between administrative theory and practice that this study typifies the work being done at the College of Public Administration. The Barrio Magsaysay pilot project combines both action and research. It was done under field experimental conditions in an effort to understand the process of planned social change. At the same time, concrete action programs were carried out in the community and detailed accounts of the methods used were made. Thus, not only were insights gained in the study—practical guides on how change may be carried out have also been devised.

The Local Government Center, a unit of the College of Public Administration, was set up to perform the four-fold task of research, consultation, training, and publication. This work of Dr. Laquian embodies these goals. His field research was done while he worked as a consultant to the Presidential Arm on Community Development and engaged in training personnel from various cooperating agencies in the skills and abilities needed for urban community development. As the reader will find out, the combination of these activities has greatly enriched the content of the book.

Carlos P. Ramos

*Dean, College of Public Administration*
*University of the Philippines*

# Acknowledgment

In an effort as extensive as this pilot project, it is inevitable that the organizers would owe a great debt of gratitude to many persons. The author is especially grateful to Secretary Ernesto M. Maceda, secretary of Community Development, who saw the need for, and the promise of, urban community development. Mr. Raymond V. Johnson of the Asia Foundation, aside from so kindly approving the grant for this study, shared with the author his thoughts and impressions on the subject, not to mention all the clippings, books, and materials that he thoughtfully labeled "For your reference." Mr. Oscar J. Arellano, president and managing director of Operation Brotherhood International, was a constant source of ideas, insights, stimulation, and challenge. It is to his credit that in spite of the tight personnel situation at his office, he agreed to send OB teams to participate in the project.

It is a mark of the scholarly interests of Dean Carlos P. Ramos, of the College of Public Administration, that he allowed the author to undertake this project even as the University rules and regulations specifically stated that the author can work "provided he does not devote more than ten per cent of his time" to the project. Director Raul P. de Guzman of the Local Government Center, friend and *kumpadre,* was not only a source of ideas—he also gave the author full support.

The advisory panel for the project composed of Mary R. Hollnsteiner, Mercedes Concepcion, and Richard Poethig was most helpful in pointing out research and operational implica-

xvi    *Acknowledgment*

tions of the project activities. The author is also most grateful
to Director Tito Mijares, of the Bureau of the Census and
Statistics, for the punching of the survey data on IBM cards;
to the University of Hawaii for the processing of the cards;
and to Fr. Frank X. Lynch, S. J. for handling this arrangement
with the University of Hawaii. If the project data were tabulated by hand, it would have been an extremely difficult and
tedious job. To Mila Abad, too, goes the author's special
thanks for all the statistical computations and smiles of joy
for each significant chi square correlation.

To the action and research teams who were participants in
this pioneering effort goes the commendation for a job well
done. The purpose and methods of the project may have been
blurred at times, but their diligence and patience kept the
project on the right track. Miss Belinda A. Aquino, serving as
co-discoverer, critic and general Girl Friday, contributed to
this final product in more ways than she can ever guess. The
staff of the Operations and Field Training Division, PACD,
led by Eduardo Bigornia, was a constant source of support.
Linda S. Pabellano, by faithfully working on the manuscript
beyond ordinary hours, and Nelia G. Baga, who assisted her,
made the early publication of the report possible. To the
leaders and residents of Barrio Magsaysay who often wondered what college kids and professors were doing in their
community, we hope this work will provide the answers.
Finally, to my wife, Eleanor, who has also wondered what
her husband did on weekends, I hope this work can be a
partial explanation.

Aprodicio A. Laquian

*Manila*
*6 January 1968*

SLUMS ARE FOR PEOPLE

# Introduction

When *Slums Are for People* was first published in 1968, it was intended primarily as a report on the experiment in urban community development which was known as the Barrio Magsaysay Pilot Project. The policy orientation of the study was clear. It concluded with an appeal for a wider coverage of urban community development in the Philippines and the setting up of a nation-wide program that would go beyond the pilot stage. The book also gave specific proposals on workable approaches, desirable projects, and feasible programs.

Because of the unique methodology used in the Barrio Magsaysay Pilot Project, however, the study also yielded certain new concepts and insights that are of special relevance to scholarly research. The carefully monitored situation wherein Community Development workers entered an urban slum community provided case studies and generalizations that are of significance to theories of induced social change. The special relationship between the research personnel and the action workers gave the researchers a great deal of insight on the mutual benefits that can arise from this more "applied" use of the social sciences. Finally, the codification of this research-action project in the Philippines provides new data and information that would be most useful in the growing literature on comparative urban development. For the slum and squatter problem is not unique to the Philippines. It is shared by practically all developing countries and the highly developed ones.

Compared to other countries, slums and squatters in the Philippines are relatively new. There is, in fact, no vernacular term for slum or squatter in the country, unless one regards the mongrelized term "iskwater" as part of the language. The closest thing to a slum area in the Philippines is the *looban,* which literally means "interior" and denotes a neighborhood not directly accessible from a main thoroughfare. As commonly understood, however, the term *looban* does not carry the negative connotation of slum. On the contrary, the term implies a sense of neighborliness, cooperative efforts, primary groups, and a lively sense of community.

In India, where slums have been known for centuries, there are many words for them. Among these are *bustees, jompris, juggies, ahatas, cheris, katras, chawls,* and lanes.[1] Similarly, in Latin America, slum and squatter communities are common and are variously referred to as *jacales* or *colonias proletarias* in Mexico; *favelas, mocambos, algados, or vilas de malocas* in Brazil; *callampas* in Chile; *villas miserias* in Buenos Aires; *barrios clandestinos* in Colombia and Peru; and *ranchos* in Venezuela.[2]

Slums in the United States are quite common, though historically, squatters have been a rural rather than an urban phenomenon. Because, in this land of affluence, slums can be embarrassing, several polite words or "terms of a genteel nature," have been used to refer to them. These include "blighted area," "renewal area," "deteriorated area," "gray area," "lower class neighborhood," "low income area," and "inner core area."[3]

In the rapidly expanding cities of Southeast Asia, slums and squatters have formed colonies in both the core and the periphery of the city. The extent of the problem in the great cities of Southeast Asia is comparable to the situation in Manila, where about one-third of the metropolitan area population is composed of squatters and slum dwellers. In 1961, about 25 per cent of the population of Djakarta was made up of squatters and slum dwellers. The same situation existed in Kuala Lumpur, where about 100,000 people lived in the slums and squatter areas. Singapore had about 26 per cent of its population also made up of squatters and slum dwellers.[4]

The prevalence of slums and squatter areas in most of the cities of the Third World calls for specific approaches and programs that could promise to meet the problems they entail. Such programs, however, require a correct understanding of the processes and events that lead to the formation of such unorganized urban settlements. I hope that *Slums Are for People,* as a careful account of a research-action program in a squatter–slum community, may add to this understanding.

## Slums and the Urban Problem

The growing concern with the problems raised by slums and squatters has revealed that they are merely indexes of socio-economic dislocations arising from the nature of growth processes in the developing countries. These societies in transition are faced with many serious problems, the most important of which is rapid population growth. Somehow, the interaction between the developed and the underdeveloped countries has contributed to this problem. With the introduction of environmental sanitation, anti-biotics, sulpha drugs, DDT, and other wonders of modern technology, the death rate in the new countries has gone down drastically. Since in most of these societies, traditional practices and institutions favored large families, the rate of population growth in the developing countries has rapidly risen.

The population problem manifests itself in many ways, the most worrisome one being the rapid growth of cities and towns in the Third World. Hauser has concluded that the developing countries are "overurbanized," because compared to developed countries at similar stages of growth, they have a larger share of their population living in cities—an urban population that can hardly be justified by the levels of agricultural and non-agricultural productivity existing in these countries.[5] McGee has estimated that in the last decade, population growth in the cities of the Third World has contributed almost 200 million to the 342 million of the world's urban population increase. Citing Davis, McGee sets the average gain in the proportion of urban population in the emergent countries at 20 per cent, compared to a 15 per cent growth rate in the developed countries during their period of most rapid growth.[6]

There is some doubt, however, whether this rapid growth of cities and towns in the developing countries is really urbanization. McGee believes that it is not and calls it a process of *pseudourbanization.* His arguments center around the fact that the cities of the Third World are growing at a rapid rate, but that this growth is not accompanied by economic, political, and psycho-social changes that are the characteristics of true urbanization. Industrialization and manufacturing in these countries lag behind the growing needs of the people. Agricultural productivity is not developing at a fast-enough rate. Thus, people are being pushed away from the farms, not because agricultural efficiency has achieved high production making it possible for a smaller share of the labor force to be devoted to agriculture, but because of the harshness of life in the rural areas.

The migrants from the rural areas, therefore, are the most important elements in the rapid growth of cities and towns in the Third World. Since they move to the city with few or no skills, possessing low education and meager income, they have to stay in the slums or squat on somebody else's property to be able to survive. Psychologically, they are driven by the same fatalism and blind trust in Fate that has made rural life acceptable. Socially, they cling together and form primary group associations to make life in the city more bearable. These rural-urban migrants, therefore, are the real transitionals. Within a short time, they have to make the attitudinal and behavioral changes that would enable them to live in the rapidly modernizing urban community. If they successfully manage to go through this transition without grave dislocations to the society, their accelerated modernization may add to the pace of economic and political development. However, if the system is not able to accommodate their demands successfully, they may add to the disruptive instabilities that characterize growth in the developing countries.

## The 'Rurban' Slum as 'Zone of Transition'

The only lasting solution to the slum and squatter problem, therefore, is to hasten the transition of both the squatters and slum dwellers as persons—and the slum and squatter areas as communities—from their present disruptive state to a more developmental level. The transition of the rural-urban migrant from a personality type characterized by authoritarianism, dependence, fatalism, low achievement motivation, and other configurations typical of traditional people to a personality type possessing other-directedness, independence, saliency, efficacy, and high achievement motivation should be hastened. This process will help to make the migrant an asset rather than a liability to the urban society which he has joined. Correspondingly, the run-down shacks and hovels occupied by the squatters and slum dwellers must give way to homes and tenements less prone to fire, sanitation, and other hazards. In this process, however, the organization of community life must remain intimate, relevant, and participatory. Changes in the people's personalities, their physical environment, and their way of life must occur in such a way that the spirit of community and citizen involvement must be maintained.

There have been many proposals on how this transition of the rural person to a truly urban man may be achieved. In countries with a more bureaucractic orientation, this transition has been experimentally entrusted to "transitional way stations" where migrants from the rural areas are first asked to reside in communities for transients and are instructed and trained to adjust to urban life. In these communities, the migrants are taught certain occupational skills, enabled to familiarize themselves with the gadgets and instruments involved in urban life, and instructed on personal and group behavior norms expected of city people. After their "orientation and training" program, the migrants are placed in specific jobs for which they have showed skills and correct aptitudes; they are provided housing; and are integrated into the urban community.

Needless to say, this type of structured programs for the transition of rural-urban migrants is possible only where certain conditions are present. First, there must be a means of controlling the internal movements of people, which involves complex means of identification processes. Second, there must be ways and means of supporting the rural-urban migrants while they are undergoing the transition process, which entails subsidy for the program. Third, the whole economy and polity must be planned so that the placement of the migrants to their proper jobs, residences, recreational groups, and political communities would be effectively and efficiently done. Finally, this program assumes the availability of instructional, training, and educational methods that would make it possible to transform a rural person to an urban person. It is obvious that in the free-wheeling politics of the Phillippines, the institution of such control measures is difficult to conceive. Even where the technical and pedagogical means are available, the politicians and the strong power of the underprivileged people will make it extremely difficult for such a scheme to succeed.

In fact, even a variant of the "transitional way station" approach which has been introduced in the Philippines in the form of the Central Institute for the Training and Rehabilitation of Urban Squatters (CITRUS) has not met with too much success. As planned, CITRUS would operate a training center for urban squatters in the relocation site of Sapang Palay and other places. Because in Metropolitan Manila squatters and slum dwellers are already in the city, the plan is to decongest the slums by relocating some of the squatters to this training site. At the site, the former squatters and slum dwellers would be sorted out, given training in skills along their aptitudes, and later placed in jobs and localities. Trainees with an aptitude for farming would be made better farmers and urged to go back to agriculture. Those with aptitudes in industry would be trained in certain skills and placed in proper jobs. The CITRUS plant, therefore, is seen as a conveyor belt where former squatters and slum dwellers may be given a chance to lead a new life by training. It is hoped that, when the slum and squatter areas within the city have all been decongested, the training course may be offered to new rural-urban migrants.

Even a cursory knowledge of political traditions and norms in the Philippines will show that too structured a program such as the "transitional way station" will be met with great difficulties. The dependence of politicians on votes, the bartering of squatter and slum-dweller votes for specific favors, and the welfare-consciousness that makes people identify quickly and emotionally with the underprivileged—all these militate against the "transitional way station" program in its bureaucratic form. And yet, it is obvious that something must be done to hasten the personality and social changes that would make former rural inhabitants urban citizens. This book suggests that this approach may be found right in the slum communities themselves.

The argument that slum and squatter communities may in effect act as the transitional way stations where people may be able to change without the rigorous and sometimes artificial instructional methods of the bureaucratized approach is based on the research finding that slum and squatter communities are really "rurban" human settlements where social norms and patterns of behavior still possess both rural and urban characteristics. More specifically, this argues that (1) the economics of slum life enable slum dwellers to save and thereby improve their chances for economic and social mobility; (2) community life in the slums, retaining as it does many primary group relationships characteristic of rural community life, is found hospitable by slum dwellers and squatters in transition; and (3) political life in the slums, featuring organized politics, machine activities, and intensive participation, tends to instruct squatters and slum dwellers in political roles necessary for their integration into the polity. The findings in this study support the arguments posed above. Other studies conducted in various parts of Manila point to similar findings.

For example, tentative findings from a study on adjustment of squatters and slum dwellers to the urban environment made by Angangco and Arcinas [7] revealed that adjustment was not much of a problem to these people although many of them (73 per cent of the sample) migrated directly from the provinces. Two factors were found conducive to easy adjustment by the study: the presence of relatives in the area and previous experience in squatting of some of the respondents. Adjustment was also greatly facilitated by maintenance of contact with relatives through visiting and correspondence and by the formation of new friendships in the community. It was found that physical propinquity was a strong factor in the formation of new primary groups. This factor was found to be much stronger than ethnicity in the creation of closer social interactions in the squatter area.

My own research in another older slum area shows that the growth of community spirit bridges local community fragmentation through time. When Isla de Kokomo was first studied in 1963, it revealed the presence of two distinct communities—an older rural barrio that had been swallowed up by the metropolitan sprawl but that has remained essentially intact, and a new community of former squatters who built their shacks in what were once the ricefields of the old community. A re-study of the area in 1967, just four years later, revealed that interactions among the residents of the two communities had intensified to such a degree that politically, they were, in fact, members of a larger community. The achievement of this political integration, rapidly being supported by socio-cultural factors, reveals the dynamics of processes that may be of great importance in the attainment of metropolitan-wide integration in the future.

It is, of course, too much to expect that all squatter and slum colonies in Metropolitan Manila would, willy nilly, become natural communities. Even with a dynamic urban community development program, there are certain areas that would find the sense of community difficult to achieve. One such area in Metropolitan Manila would be the railroad right of way which has been occupied by squatters.

One difficulty with the railroad squatters is the fact that the physical shape of the land they are squatting on makes it extremely difficult for them to develop social and personal interactions that would contribute to community formation. Stretched all the way from Caloocan City to Taguig, Rizal, some 17,680 squatter families on the railroad tracks have no hope of developing a community identity of their own. A survey of these squatters made with the assistance of the Social Welfare Administration, People's Homesite and Housing Corporation, the City of Manila's Department of Social Welfare, the Presidential Assistant on Housing and Resettlement Agency, the Presidential Arm on Community Development, and others revealed that many of the social factors that make for community life were barely perceptible. Only a little more than 12 per cent of the squatters were members of organizations, according to the survey. Urban services were greatly lacking (only 27 per cent had their own sources of drinking water, more than half had no toilets, and only 4.2 per cent used electricity for cooking). Cooperative work habits and community leadership was also not too evident among these squatters.

Another place where the sense of community may be difficult to achieve is in old core city slums. Though no studies of old slums in the center of Manila have come to my attention so far, there are indications from the experience in other countries that such slums may reach a point of social disorganization, making it extremely difficult to rehabilitate them with urban CD techniques. To some extent, this may be due to the outmigration of successful and more ambitious slum dwellers, which would most likely leave a leadership vacuum. As the lack of cooperative efforts and community control becomes evident, the inner core slum would tend to attract antisocial elements and society's dropouts. This has been the pattern in industrialized countries. So far, Manila's slums have not followed this pattern because of the "rurban" nature of the migrants. With this, however, the growth of the disorganized slum in the core city would inevitably come. I hope that the housing and other conditions in the urban area will have been improved before that day.

## The Philippine Scene

Many things important to urban development have happened since this book came out in January 1968. In the field of housing and urban development, the most important seems to be the increased attention given to the problem of squatters and slum dwellers. The government and the mass media have contributed to this growing concern. In 1968, President Ferdinand E. Marcos announced that housing and urban development would be one of the most important fields his administration would emphasize. He created a committee to study the housing and urban development problem and caused to be set up a National Housing Corporation to provide low cost housing. The Philippine Senate conducted hearings on the housing problem through its committee on housing, urban development, and resettlement. Through news items, serialized articles, editorials, and columns, the newspapers voiced the public apprehension over the growing squatter and slum problem, describing the situation as distressing, critical, and even explosive.

The heightened official and public concern has some basis in fact because the slum and squatter problem in Metropolitan Manila has become increasingly worse. The latest survey of the extent of the problem in April 1968 revealed that there are about 127,852 squatter families (767,112 persons) and 55,907 families (335,442 persons) living in slums, a total of 183,759 families or 1,102,554 persons. The distribution of these squatters and slum dwellers in the metropolitan area is shown in an accompanying table.[8]

There are indications, too, that the rate of migration to urban centers from the rural areas is increasing. A survey showed that 28 per cent of a sample of squatters moved to Manila from 1961 to 1965 and that 9 per cent migrated to the urban center from 1966 to 1967. A more recent survey of new migrants on the railroad tracks revealed that 40.3 per cent of the sample were from the Visayas (29.3 per cent from Western Visayas and 11.0 per cent from Eastern Visayas). Of greater concern, however, is the survey finding that 12.38 per cent of the 17,680 families squatting on the railroad tracks claim to be natives of Metropolitan Manila. This means that a second generation of squatters is now contributing to the already serious problem, even as the rate of rural to urban migration is mounting.

As in the past, the government's solution to the squatter problem has been through relocation and low cost housing. In 1968, some 5,000 squatter families were evicted from the Quezon City Park site and relocated to Carmona, Cavite and Sapang Palay, Bulacan. A smaller group of squatter families were also relocated from the Development Bank of the Philippines site in Makati and transferred to San Pedro Tunasan. In these relocation centers, the new concept of "core housing" was tried for the first time. As in previous relocation efforts, however, there were still serious lack of planning, coordination, and the provision of such essential services as water, transportation, and food.

The government's low cost housing scheme has produced only 250 units in the Zabarte Project of the People's Homesite and Housing Corporation, with another 310 additional houses contemplated. The phhc has also constructed a five-storey tenement building in its North Avenue subdivision in Quezon City, but the 32 dwelling units in the tenement have not been awarded. In both the Zabarte and the North Avenue projects, the phhc has experimented in pre-fabrication techniques. The North Avenue project is especially noteworthy because it introduces a new concept in design and uses materials proposed by a Japanese architect. After thorough tests (the building withstood the big earthquake of 1968), the phhc is planning to build nine more tenements in its North Avenue subdivision. However, because of the phhc's financial difficulties and because of the fact that its corporate lease on life has only seven more years to go if it is not extended, it remains to be seen if the additional projects it has planned would be pushed through.

Another venture in low cost housing was started in 1968 with the joint efforts of the Social Security System and the Land and Housing Development Corporation of Bancom. With sss financing and lhdc management, 500 dwelling units were constructed in Marikina, Rizal, and another 500 are currently under construction. Even with the limit placed on the costs of these houses, however, the expensive land, building materials, and labor in Metropolitan Manila are still pricing them outside the ability of the average slum dweller.

The most ambitious effort of the Marcos administration to meet the housing problem was the creation of the National Housing Corporation. Unfortunately, this attempt has been bogged down by charges of anomalies and irregularities. The very nature of the corporation has been challenged, and its negotiations with a German firm for a low-cost housing factory has been seriously questioned. The NHC had planned to manufacture pre-fabricated homes costing ₱ 6,000 or less each and to sell these at long-term installments to low income families for as low as ₱ 42.42 a month payable in 25 years. It had hoped to cut down costs by mass production and to tap the resources of government lending institutions for long-term loans to homeowners. The cloud of suspicion that has engulfed the corporation, however, would most likely prevent it from doing something tangibly beneficial in the near future.

All in all, in the field of urban development, the first three years of the Marcos administration have been significant in that attention has been called to urban problems, especially low cost housing and squatting. However, the initial efforts introduced during this time have been small scale and faltering. The one big attempt to provide low cost housing has been tainted with graft charges. The forecast for the solution of the urban problems faced by the country, therefore, is still the same: things are likely to get worse before they get better.

# CHAPTER 1

# Slums and Squatters

To the average reader of Manila newspapers, the name of Barrio Magsaysay in Tondo is almost synonymous with riots, gang wars, pier pirates, and thrill killings. Although the barrio is a new part of the city's first district (being a squatter colony that grew up in the reclaimed foreshore lands), it is already fast acquiring the reputation generally applied to Tondo.

The image of Tondo as a tough and troubled district is part of Manila's lore. One may say, however, that there are really two Tondos. There is, first of all, the old Tondo of the writers—the proletarian mystique, Katipunan and Bonifacio, the poor boy made good, the fierce identity, and pride. This rather self-conscious image is apparent in the writings of Andres Cristobal Cruz (*Tondo by Two*, and *Ang Tundo Man, May Langit Din*), Amado V. Hernandez, Pacifico Aprieto, and even Epifanio San Juan, Jr. This is the Tondo of the proud poor, sneering at Society, zesty, taunting, tough, and challenging. Too often, however, this is the Tondo of nostalgia, a happy-sad life of angry youth and lost loves of mellowed memories penned by now socially acceptable former Tondo residents who have achieved mobility.

There is, however, the Tondo of the too real present—of slums, poverty, and misery. This is the Tondo of the social worker, the policeman, and the politician. Tondo has the highest density of settlement in Manila, the worst sanitation problem, and the highest crime rate. This is the Tondo of tattooed police characters, of dope pushers, of *matadero* killings, and of Oxo-Sigue Sigue gang wars.

Barrio Magsaysay belongs to this Tondo of today. It is new enough to have all the problems of the present. It has not quite achieved the image and the character of the older Tondo. The Barrio may be developing a self-image and a character of its own, but there has been only partial success in this. Newcomers and visitors to the place call it a squatter area, a slum. Its residents, however, call it their community. To them, it is home.

This study of Barrio Magsaysay raises certain questions that are only beginning to be raised among those interested in urban affairs. What, in reality, is a slum? What physical, social, and psychological factors mark an area as a slum and another as a quaint run-down, but viable community with character? What value judgments do we express when we say that an area is an urban slum, and how do these value judgments affect our ability to do something about the slum problem?

Too often, indeed, the idea of the slum carries with it certain unstated values and preconceptions that are uniquely Western. To most modern urban people, slums are evil. The slum is a poverty area, run-down, overcrowded, inhabited by persons who are not welcome to other residential areas. The slum is characterized by unsanitary conditions, high death and sickness rates, crime, delinquency, and vice. The way of life in slums makes inhabitants strangers to one another and wish to be; there is a high rate of mobility among the people but relative permanency of slum neighborhoods. The appearance of the slum is its universal mark—"neglect and disorder with respect to buildings, yards and streets ... structural overage and decline." [1]

This negative idea of slum life, essentially a Western viewpoint, has been transported elsewhere, even where climate, society, and culture demand new conceptualizations. The United Nations, for example, defines a slum as:

... a building, group of buildings, or area characterized by overcrowding, deterioration, unsanitary conditions or absence of facilities or amenities which, because of these conditions or any of them, endanger the health, safety or morals of its inhabitants or the community.[2]

Most people who have given us a definition of the slum, as noted by Anderson, have "loaded it with various evil connotations." [3] Remembering perhaps, the wastes and excesses of the Industrial Revolution, which have spawned slums, the characteristic reaction to slums in Western countries is to wipe them off the beautiful face of the city.

The same negative attitude toward slums is evident in Western man's picture of the squatter. Squatting, in legal terms, means the occupancy of a piece of land or building by people without the expressed consent of the owner. As such, it is closely tied up with the notion of private property. The squatter is unjust because he is denying the property's use to its rightful owner.

As urbanization becomes a world-wide phenomenon, slums and squatting become common in developing countries. The push of the poor countryside and the pull of the urban center send people flocking to cities at unprecedented rates. The results, especially during periods of political or natural upheavals and calamities, are choking and overcrowding of the cities.

The city in developing areas is closely linked to Western civilization. In former colonies, especially, administrators and politicians, who are most likely to be Westernized because of education and training, react to slums and squatting with a strongly negative tone. Urban sociologists and psychologists, with their Western orientation, join in the condemnation of the slum dwellers and the squatters. All of these result in projects and programs with a strongly punitive flavor strangely out of step with the relatively relaxed and easy pace of the culture.

This book is an attempt to pause for a while and take a second look at urban slums and squatters, especially in the developing countries. It is a close-up view of one community in the Philippines, Barrio Magsaysay, in the district of Tondo. It is hoped that viewing the problem from the heart of the slum, looking out, will give a fresh perspective.

The findings from one year of experience in Barrio Magsaysay sharply contrast with the ideas about slums and squatters described in Western literature. For one, the people in the area don't share the "evil connotations" about slums held by their more sophisticated city cousins. To them, the slum is home, a unified, intimate, and comfortable community. When asked why they chose to stay in Barrio Magsaysay in spite of the government's threat to evict them, many of the residents replied that the place is peaceful; it is close to their relatives; it is near their place of work; and, simply, that they love the place.

This study, therefore, starts with a basic questioning of the current ideas and attitudes toward slums and squatters. Instead of assuming that slums are evil to be wiped out of the city, it starts from the fact of their existence and asks by what means they came about and for what reasons they persist. Surely, their very existence and magnitude are enough reasons for an attempt to understand them, and in so doing, to find out their role in normal urban development. The scope and seriousness of the "slum problem" call for new ideas and solutions. Such ideas and solutions, however, would come about only if the basic attitudes toward slums and squatters are reviewed, understood, and then channeled to new directions.

## The Extent of the Problem

Demographers and urban planners have a way of frightening people with the growth rate of cities. It is estimated, for example, that Metropolitan Manila's population will grow from 2.7 million in 1963 to 5.35 million in 1980, which is a doubling of the population in 17 years.

Of the 2.7 million people in Metropolitan Manila in 1963, 50,427 families (roughly 320,433 persons) were identified as squatters. Another 17,500 families (about 105,000 persons) were living in slum communities. Of the squatters, it was estimated that only 15 per cent of them were living above subsistence levels (an average monthly income from ₱ 120 to ₱ 180); 81 per cent or 40,905 families were living between bare subsistence and destitution; and 1,828 families were registered as destitute.[4]

Table 1 offers further figures on the extent of the problem. The figures have changed somewhat since the survey was made in 1963, though not necessarily for the better. Intramuros and some parts of Tondo (especially the areas near the piers) have been cleared of squatters, who were transferred to Sapang Palay and other relocation areas. However, though slum dwelling has been minimized a bit, the problem of squatting has become more serious.

Since 1946, the urbanized area of Metropolitan Manila has expanded from a six kilometer radius from the center of the

TABLE 1

ESTIMATES OF SQUATTERS AND SLUM DWELLERS
OF METROPOLITAN MANILA

| Location | Area in has. of Slums | No. of Persons in Slums | Squatters outside Slums | Total |
|---|---|---|---|---|
| Tondo | 371 | 152,481 | 18,500 | 170,981 |
| Intramuros | 37 | 4,292 | 1,050 | 5,342 |
| Sta. Cruz | 59 | 19,942 | 3,500 | 23,442 |
| Sampaloc | 88 | 33,088 | 16,000 | 49,088 |
| Malate | 68 | 16,864 | 250 | 17,114 |
| Ermita | | | 2,850 | 2,850 |
| Binondo | 5 | 1,260 | 1,550 | 2,810 |
| Pandacan | 5 | 1,845 | 150 | 1,995 |
| Paco | 31 | 5,704 | 3,700 | 9,404 |
| Sta. Ana | 111 | 24,975 | 1,375 | 26,350 |
| San Miguel | 12 | 1,920 | 1,000 | 2,920 |
| Quiapo | | | 1,750 | 1,750 |
| San Nicolas | 29 | 10,817 | | 10,817 |
| Quezon City | 29 | 8,700 | 19,100 | 27,800 |
| Caloocan City | 47 | 14,100 | 20,500 | 34,600 |
| Pasay City | 50 | 15,000 | 3,000 | 18,000 |
| Metro. Manila | 942 | 310,988 | 94,275 | 405,263 |

SOURCE: United Nations PHHC Housing Research Team, *Metropolitan Manila Sample Survey*, March 1963.

city to about a ten kilometer radius. This means that urban sprawl has set in. Most of the areas on the fringes of the city are highly priced private subdivisions, way above the paying capacity of most urban dwellers. These private subdivisions and the less desirable areas beyond have been affected by squatters. The northern portion of Quezon City (especially the park area) and the southern portions of Parañaque and Las Piñas (especially the railroad tracks and the army reservation) have been invaded by many squatters. Although the squatter problem has not become acutely serious up to now, it will surely become a major headache in the future when city services have to be stretched and extended to meet the demands of people at the city's outskirts.

The problem of squatting and slum dwelling is not confined to Metropolitan Manila alone. Many cities in Luzon, Visayas, and Mindanao also suffer from the same phenomenon. Thus, the UN-PHHC Housing Research Team set the slum and squatter population of Baguio in 1964 at 2,795 families (16,207 persons), which was about 27 per cent of the city's population. The count in other areas is as follows: Davao, 21,000 persons or 8.5 per cent of the city's population; Iligan, 5,600 or 7.5 per cent; Cagayan de Oro, 4,450 or 11.0 per cent; Butuan, 19,800 or 43.5 per cent; Ozamis, 5,250 or 25 per cent; Cotabato, 19,200 or 10 per cent; Marawi, 6,780 or 44.5 per cent; and Surigao, 10,000 or 22 per cent.[5]

These figures are significant in the light of the fact that most migrants to Metropolitan Manila, as shown in migration data from surveys, now come from secondary urban areas. In other words, the difficult life in the rural areas is pushing people to the smaller cities where they become squatters and slum dwellers. When life in those cities becomes also difficult, they take a trip to Manila and continue their old way of life there. The poorer the housing conditions in other cities, therefore, the greater is the possibility that the problems of Metropolitan Manila will become worse.

## Dealing with Slums

The most common ways of dealing with urban slums and squatters are on-site housing and relocation. Both approaches presuppose the razing down of slums and squatter areas and the re-housing of people in better accommodations.

### ON-SITE HOUSING

On-site housing recognizes that certain economic and social factors are responsible for the people's choice of slum or squatter area. It may be near their place of work, they may want to live near relatives, or the place may even possess some sentimental significance. On-site housing, therefore, does not attempt to relocate the people but makes it possible for them to live in the old location under improved conditions. Usually, this is done by high-density housing, such as tenements. Provisions for water, sanitation, and other services are also extended to make life more comfortable for the re-housed urban dweller.

In the Philippines, on-site housing may be seen in the Bagong Barangay Tenement Housing Project in Pandacan and in the Vitas Tenement Housing Project in Tondo. In both projects, the idea was to house the squatters, formerly living around the area, in these tenements or row houses. This way, people would not have to be moved far from their original place of residence—and their environment would be improved.

While the concept of on-site housing in the two projects mentioned above is good, it has suffered in the implementation. Owing to political pressures, allocation of apartments to those living around the area was not really fully achieved. In Bagong Barangay, many apartments went to employees of the Manila city government because the late Mayor Arsenio H. Lacson insisted that they be given preference in the allocation of apartments. In Vitas, some people who were not from the slums of Tondo were allegedly able to get apartments through the intercession of some politicians.

But if apartments are given to squatters in the area, there is no assurance that they will live there. The low rents in these new apartments (from ₱ 13 to ₱20 a month in Bagong Barangay) attract other people who offer to buy the "rights of occupancy" from the original persons who got the apartment. The promise of quick money ("rights" reputedly sell for about ₱ 5,000 in Bagong Barangay) often proves too much for the original lessees who are always hard up for cash. They sell their "rights" and then squat somewhere else again.

Of course, there are legal limits to this practice of transfer of rights. According to the rules prescribed by the People's Homesite and Housing Corporation, which administers the project, rights to an apartment may be transferred only by hereditary succession within the same family (including brothers and sisters). Members of the Central Bank Staff Housing Corporation, the UP Village, Inc., and the Philippine Veterans subdivision also may purchase rights. Despite these limitations, however, many legal loopholes have been found so that anyone who can meet the going price may get an apartment.

Occupancy of an apartment in Bagong Barangay used to be limited to families who earned no more than ₱ 350 a month (later raised to ₱ 500). It is obvious from even cursory inspection, however, that many of the residents in this housing project are earning more than the maximum. The forest of television aerials on the roof, the many cars parked on the narrow alleys at night (since the project was designed for low income families, no parking provisions were made), and the blare of stereo sets and radios are testimonies to this fact. It is too early to tell whether the new Vitas tenement and other recent projects of the government will follow the pattern set by Bagong Barangay. There are no reasons, however, why they should provide the exception.

**RELOCATION**

The other alternative for solving the slum and squatter problem is relocation. In the Philippines, this has found greater favor with officials because of its apparent simplicity. All that a city official does is scare the squatters into submission with a show of force and determination. The police and the fire departments are usually sufficient. All that is needed are a few fire trucks, wrecker crews, and a place to which the squatters or slum dwellers can be transferred. As most simplistic solutions, however, relocation only creates more problems.

In 1951, squatters in Manila were relocated to the North Bago Bantay section of the Diliman estate of the PHHC. About 1,333 families were transferred to the area by the Social Welfare Administration. The trouble, however, was that no provisions for water, light, sanitation, and other amenities were extended to the relocated people. The former squatters and slum dwellers were simply transported to the area on trucks of the Quezon City Engineering Department. They were left there to construct shelters from the debris of their old homes. All that they were given were lots, to be paid for on a long deferred-payment basis. The results of this relocation, of course, were predictable. Ten years after the move, most of the original tenants were not in Bago Bantay anymore. Many of them sold the "rights" to their lots. They simply pocketed the money, went back to Manila, and squatted again, richer by the experience.

Other relocation projects, because of the failure to provide the necessary backstopping, followed the pattern set by Bago Bantay. In 1953, people evicted from the Tatalon Estate in Quezon City were transferred to Bagong Pag-asa, also in Quezon City. Sales contracts were issued by the PHHC to the people who were relocated. Again, the people allotted lots sold their rights and possibly went back to squatting. In 1956, 166 hectares in Kamarin, near Novaliches, were also sold by the PHHC to about 3,542 squatters. When a check was made of these people in 1965, less than 100 of the original grantees remained—the rest had moved back to Manila and the suburbs, though many still continued to pay their installments to the PHHC for speculative purposes. Since one of the conditions in this sale of low-cost lots was actual occupancy, many of the sales contracts were voided by the PHHC. This situation was not unique in Kamarin. In the nearby relocation area of Gabriel Estate, nearly 200 out of 1,220 lot awardees were denied further payments for their lots because they had violated certain provisions of the contract between them and the PHHC.

As late as 1963, the experience with relocation was still extremely unsatisfactory. In December of that year, about 5,975 families from Intramuros, North Harbor, Malate, and Ermita were relocated by the City Government of Manila to Sapang Palay, a hilly place owned by the PHHC located about 37 kilometers outside Manila. As in former relocation projects, there were inadequate provisions for houses, water, roads, electricity, transportation, food, medical services, and other amenities. Many of the able-bodied men and women who were formerly earning something in Manila were transformed into dependents. Children's schoolings were interrupted. Since the area was 37 kilometers outside Manila, those with work in Manila had to spend about 20 per cent of their income for transportation alone. Again, the results were the same. In August 1966, only 2,800 of the original families that had been transferred to Sapang Palay were still living there. The rest had gone back to Manila and the suburbs, though they maintained ghost homes in the relocation area, just in case the government decides to distribute the lands free or in case some speculators wanting to buy "rights" to the lots would be willing to pay.

It is obvious from the cases cited above that the government's efforts to solve the squatters and slum-dwellers problem have been dismal failures. It is rather easy to lay the blame on government officials. In both on-site housing and relocation plans, there were no provisions for administrative and auxiliary support; there was too much haste between planning and implementation; and political pressures played havoc with the well-laid plans (however limited they were) of the administrators. However, to fix the blame does not solve the problem. It may be more worthwhile to find out the reasons for the failures, in the hope that new solutions may be arrived at through an understanding of the factors involved.

### REASONS FOR FAILURE: RELOCATION

Why has the relocation program of the government failed? Several reasons may be given, and they are all highlighted in the many relocation projects from Bago Bantay to Sapang Palay.

In the first place, the administrative procedures for the relocation of squatters, though well conceived, are often not followed. According to the Standard Operating Procedure for relocation, the Social Welfare Administration (or the Department of Social Welfare of the City of Manila) should first conduct a survey or census of the squatter families to be relocated. Such a survey must find out the size of the family, the main source of livelihood, the income, and other factors relevant to the new life that the relocated family will face. The terms of the relocation and all pertinent details about it should be explained to the family by the social worker during this survey.

Before actual relocation is done, the family must already be assigned a specified lot or apartment in the relocation area. In this way, there is minimum confusion in the location of the people. Also, if at all possible, dwellings, must be ready for the people when they arrive. There should be checkers at the relocation site to receive the people, and there should be locators to show them their lot or apartment assignments.

These basic steps in the SOP are more understood than followed. Perhaps, this is due to the heavily charged political climate that usually surrounds a relocation project. The squatters or slum dwellers are understandably in an ugly mood, and there are many policemen and other officers to prevent violence. In almost all instances, lawyers and politicians on the side of the squatters battle with the authorities in the courts up to the last moment. Thus, the rational administration machinery thought out to take care of relocation often breaks down during implementation.

Another frequent cause of failure is the fact that the government planners do not seem to appreciate the fact that relocation is expensive. In the past, cost seems to have been computed primarily from the point of view of transportation. Thus, if trucks of the City Engineers Office could be used to transport people to Bago Bantay or if the dump trucks of the City of Manila could be used to take people to Sapang Palay, costs could be cut and the projects would be successful.

Relocation, to be effective, requires several things. First, the relocation area must be provided with such facilities as houses, water, electricity, medical services, and other necessities. In almost all relocation projects so far, these services were only partly provided, or not at all. In Sapang Palay, only ten bunk-houses were provided for the 5,975 families that eventually moved to the place. Water, electricity, and medical help were given much, much later, after many of the people had gotten fed up and left the place. The planners of the relocation seem to have trusted blindly in the future— that somehow, Fate will provide for the thousands of families uprooted from their homes and dumped in the area.

Another problem involved in relocation is the fact that usually the new area does not possess an economic base rich enough to provide the relocated people a means of livelihood. The people from Intramuros, North Harbor, and other slum and squatter areas, who were relocated to Sapang Palay, were uprooted not only from their old shanties but also from their sources of livelihood as well. When transferred to Sapang Palay, they became unemployed wards of the government. As many of them said, the government turned able-bodied men who had regular means of livelihood into dependents, and then refused them the welfare goods.

If there is no source of income in the new area, it is understood that the relocated individuals will continue to work in the central city. This means that the government should provide good roads and relatively cheap transportation to enable the commuting workers to earn enough. This will mean additional expense for the government. For the relocated person, this will mean that he will have to earn more to make up for the transportation costs and for the fact that he has to eat his lunch in the city as well. Whereas all members of the household hitherto could help in earning extra money (mother washes clothes; children sell things in the market, shine shoes, or engage in the "watch your car" business), the distance from the city now prevents this and hence the income of the family is greatly reduced.

The land where the former squatters and slum dwellers are relocated is not given to them free. They have to pay for it in painful long-term installments. Even if the terms of payment are for fifteen or twenty years and they amount to only ₱ 10 a month, many former squatters are unable or unwilling to meet these payments. Relocation reduces people's income. Having the additional obligation imposed by the installments on the lot, the squatter family finds it extremely difficult to make both ends meet.

The final result of all these difficulties, of course, is speculation. The former squatter will stake out his lot and maybe build a small shanty there to comply with regulations, but he will continue to stay in the city. When buyers of rights and speculators come around and they give him a tempting offer for the "rights" to his land, he willingly sells and returns to the city. There, he will find another place to squat on. Does this mean that the relocated squatter is a heartless racketeer who does not repay the government's efforts to help him? Or can he really be blamed for making the most of a bad situation? The government has relocated him to an area where it would be impossible to live. Would he stick it out there and starve?

It must be remembered, of course, that there are not enough government lands near enough to the city that may be used for relocation sites. With the repeated bungling of relocation projects, most of these lands have fallen into the hands of people who can really afford more expensive housing sites but who would rather buy the rights from hard-pressed relocated persons. Thus far, relocation projects have failed to benefit the poor in the lasting way they should. Rather, they have provided lands on easy terms to speculators.

In July 1966, a new scheme for relocating urban squatters and slum dwellers to rural settlements was proposed. This project envisions the temporary resettlement of urban squatter and slum dwellers to a training area where they will again be introduced to the ways of agriculture. On the assumption that most urban squatters and slum dwellers come from the rural areas anyway, the government trainers hope they will not have a difficult time in teaching farming methods to these people. Once ready, the former squatters and slum dwellers would be transported to rural areas, given homesteads, and then helped by the government until they have become self-supporting. One problem with this scheme (which the government provided for in Republic Act 4852, creating the Central Institute for the Training and Relocation of Urban Squatters or CITRUS) is the assumption that urban squatters and slum dwellers would be willing to return to the rural areas. Fragmentary evidence seems to point to the contrary. For one, the program of the Social Welfare Administration, which extends transportation assistance to squatters and slum dwellers willing to return to the provinces, has been a dismal failure. Many of those who went to the provinces eventually returned to Manila to squat once more. Perhaps, the main reason for this refusal to return to the rural areas is the fact that, although life in the city is harsh, difficult, and dangerous, it is still a little better than life in the barrios. Besides, it takes a major decision to uproot one's family ties to try one's luck in the city. Once the decision is made, it becomes doubly difficult to return because that would be admitting defeat.

Furthermore, the pattern of migration of urban squatters and slum dwellers as revealed in the Barrio Magsaysay and other surveys suggests that many of them did not migrate directly to the metropolitan area from the barrios. Their migration paths usually included the poblacion, a small city near home, and then, Metropolitan Manila. The weaning away from rural life, therefore, was a gradual process that most likely left lasting impressions. The Manila squatter or slum dweller rapidly becomes a very urbanized person. It would be extremely difficult, therefore, to ask him to return willingly to the rural areas.

### REASONS FOR FAILURE: ON-SITE HOUSING

If relocation projects are expensive, on-site housing schemes are even more so. The cheapest estimate for an apartment conforming to the PHHC-adopted minimum standard of 440 sq. ft. for a Filipino family costs approximately ₱ 5,000. The Department of Public Works has produced apartments of only 270 sq. ft., and they cost ₱ 9,000 each to construct. At these rates, if rent were placed at ₱ 5 to ₱ 20 a month, which is the estimated amount a squatter family can afford, on-site housing would entail continued subsidy from the government. On-site housing is also very unsettling for the former squatters or slum dwellers. Their homes would have to be razed down to make way for the new buildings. As present construction methods take months to finish and furnish multi-storey apartments, some provisions would have to be made for families waiting for the new dwellings. The problems involved are obviously tremendous.

On-site housing also invites political interference. Ideally, a census should be taken of the squatter families to be displaced and systems of priorities set up to determine who should get first choice when the buildings are finished. Unfortunately, even if an objective census is obtained of families, those with political connections and pull would most likely get choice dwellings. There may even be non-squatters who would be able to get apartments through the help of politicians.

Many sociologists and psychologists are also worried about the effects of high-rise-tenement dwelling on former urban squatters and slum dwellers. They argue that this is especially true of children, who are exposed to juvenile delinquency and other aspects of life in the "concrete jungle." To people used to living in the slums, life in the tenements brings out their worst habits. Thus, most tenements are dirty, ugly, and dilapidated. Obscene writings cover the walls. Garbage is strewn about. Toilets that run out of order are never repaired. Washings of all shapes, sizes, and colors hang from the windows. The sights, sounds, and smells in tenements, therefore, are not any better than those in the slums. The questions may legitimately be raised then—should the government go to this expense only to perpetuate slum life under different surroundings?

Finally, there is the problem of over-crowding in tenements. When a new family first comes in, there is enough space. However, as soon as the children come, one by one, space becomes less and less. With relatives from the provinces moving in, overcrowding becomes worse. Thus, enterprising tenement dwellers are forced to set up triple-deck beds, mezzanine floors, and "illegal construction." An apartment built for a maximum of six people now accommodates fifteen. Needless to say, life in the tenement becomes very unhealthy because diseases spread rapidly and endanger the lives of people.

At the Bagong Barangay Housing project, for example, the PHHC has set the standard of 8.13 square feet a person as the minimum tolerable density for apartment dwelling. Thus, a one-bedroom unit should normally have only four or five occupants; a two-bedroom unit, five to seven; and a three-bedroom unit, eight to eleven. With the average Filipino family numbering six and relatives or hometown friends moving in, there is overcrowding, which is physically and psychologically unhealthy.

## Why the Apathy?

The government, as provider, is only as good as or as bad as the demands imposed on it by the people. The truth is that, aside from some vocal foreign consultants who risk the displeasure of their host country or some reform politicians who promptly forget their crusade as soon as they get into power, very few people are genuinely concerned about the substandard housing condition in the Philippines. The public attitude seems to pretend that squatters do not exist, that slums are not there to blight the urban scene. In spite of dire threats that "the time-bomb keeps ticking and precious time is running out," [6] the people seem unconcerned.

What are the attitudes (or more aptly, defense mechanisms) that perpetuate the lack of concern for slums and squatters? The following are some of the most obvious ones.

1. *Squatters should not have left their homes in the first place.*

This argument states that the dire condition of squatters and slum dwellers is their own fault. They should not have left their barrio homes in the first place. They came to the city, attracted by the promise of easy living; they found life tough and merciless instead; yet, they don't have the guts and the courage to return where they came from. Instead, they insist on burdening urban property owners, the government, and civic-spirited citizens. Since it is their fault, why should something be done for them? Commonly given by native urbanites, this argument ignores certain things: In the first place, many rural migrants were pushed into the city by natural and political calamities in their rural places of origin. For those who went to the city to try their luck, they had the perfect right to do so—a right specified by the Constitution and guaranteed by the Republic. More practically, how can the exclusivist policy of those who will prevent more rural dwellers from moving to the city be carried out? Shall checkpoints be set up on the city's boundaries, passports issued to *bona fide* city residents only, and those not having the precious documents be turned away? The consequence of such an act, even if it were administratively feasible, are too clear. The city would wither and die. For the essence of urban life is its openness, variety, and heterogeneity. A city walled in is a city under siege. Cut off from the countryside, it dies.

2. *Squatters are violating the law. They should be prosecuted, not pampered.*

Many private property owners who cannot use their lands because squatters refuse to budge and even property owners who are afraid that squatters will some day occupy their properties favor this argument. It is true—there is a statute that metes out a sentence of six months imprisonment or a fine of ₱ 600 or both for "squatting, possession or occupation of any land, or the inhabiting of any building by a person without expressed consent of the owner." The Supreme Court has also ruled that squatting per se is a nuisance.

However, if this law is strictly enforced, all the jails of the government would be filled to capacity. The latest figures estimate the squatter population in Manila alone at 100,000 families or some 600,000 people. It is also estimated that there are 50,000 squatter families in the First District of Rizal; 100,000 families in Samar and Leyte; and 200,000 families in Camarines Sur, Cotabato, Albay, Davao, Negros Oriental, and

Zamboanga del Sur. And in the cities of Baguio, Ozamis, Butuan, and Marawi, squatters comprise about 40 per cent of the population.[7]

If the full letter of the law would be meted out also against squatters, they should be treated equally for justice—justice that will be carried out. However, doing this will destroy the delicate balance of symbiotic relationship between the politicians and squatters. Since some politicians are stronger than others and would therefore be able to get concessions for their bailiwicks, the punitive legal action will only increase inequity and it may even cause bigger trouble.

3. *Helping squatters will only encourage them. If the government does not do anything, life in the slums will become so intolerable that squatters will not be able to stand it and they will leave.*

This argument is usually heard from the pious taxpayer who does not want any of his tax money spent on people who are not willing to be as hard-working and as upright as he is. Life in the slums, it is argued, is harsh and difficult. Government relief programs only serve to make it tolerable. Therefore, the government should not do anything. Then, perhaps, life in the slums will become so hard that the people will leave the place and even return to where they came from.

The fallacy of this argument is rapidly apparent when it is considered that slums thrive on neglect and such leave-them-alone policy. They usually got started because of this, in the first place. The logical consequence of this attitude will be to encourage the growth of more slums, which, eventually, will engulf the whole urban area.

This argument also assumes that slums will be confined to their original areas and that leaving these areas alone will make life there intolerable. Unfortunately, slums are like growing, creeping, living things. Left to themselves, they will annex the other parts of the city. This argument will work if this is possible; however, life there will become so difficult that it will eventually become a major threat to the whole city. Fire, disease, crime, riots, and other urban evils will spread from these neglected areas, and they will not spare the rest of the city.

4. *There are professional squatters who have grown rich by exploiting their condition. Why should squatters be helped?*

There is no doubt that there are indeed some squatters who have lived off their condition and have made this a profitable profession. Many social welfare cases prove this. Some of the more obvious tricks used by squatters are speculating on newly opened government land, squatting on private property and refusing to move out until they are paid off, setting up houses in slum areas and renting them off to other slum dwellers, and so forth. However, this argument will punish the many for the unjust acts of a few.

For every professional squatter, there are hundreds who are there because they cannot afford the high rent that living in a comfortable house entails. They are not evil people, unless being poor is evil. They eke out a meager but honest living, they send their children to school, they obey the laws, and they participate in community activities. Some day, they dream, they will be able to rise out of the slum areas. Some day, their children will be able to live in a decent and comfortable home. Meanwhile, they subsist on what they have. The fatalism of a barrio proverb sustains them—*"habang maiksi ang kumot, mag-aral kang mamaluktot."* * Some day, there will be a longer and larger blanket; then, they will be able to stretch out and live comfortably.

## Slums Are for People

For various reasons, the attitude towards slums is basically negative. However, it has not always been such. There was a time when people, at least in the Philippines, did not think ill of the squatter or slum dweller, when a combination of pity, social responsibility, kinship ties, and charity all combined to create a humane attitude toward squatters and slum

---

* "If your blanket is short, learn to double up to fully cover yourself."

dwellers. There was even an older time when private property was unknown, when grazing lands were communally owned, and when clearing a patch in the jungle was a normal procedure. Because of all this, it is not too farfetched to propose that the Filipino's current readiness to squat on another's land (especially when such land is not being productively used and is obviously just fenced for speculative purposes) may be traced to past social values. The alarmists who point to squatters and slum dwellers as proofs of the breakdown of law and order and the collapse of national discipline among the people may actually be wrong. The trouble is not social disorganization but that old norms have not broken down enough.

The growth of cities, as proposed in an earlier book,[8] is a natural part of nation-building. As such, the movement to urban areas is an inherent part of development. Because cities must depend on migrants from the rural areas for the energy that fuels urban dynamism, there must be natural provisions for the cheap and efficient housing of such migrants. Hence, the growth of slums and squatter areas is only a normal manifestation of urbanization in our time. As Turner puts it:

> Uncontrolled urban settlement is the consequence of normal processes of urban accommodation under the exceptional conditions of contemporary urbanization. By this hypothesis, squatter and other forms of uncontrolled urban settlement are not the 'official aberrations' they so commonly are assumed to be. They are the perfectly natural response to an abnormal situation.[9]

In the Philippines, the abnormal situations that sent the population of Metropolitan Manila shooting from less than two million in 1948 to more than three million in 1967 are many: the Huk rebellion that pushed them away from the rural area, typhoons and calamities, and others. Even after these social, political, and economic upheavals have leveled off, however, the migration to Metropolitan Manila and other urban centers in the Philippines continues. This fact forces us to amend Turner's hypothesis somewhat and pushes us to an even more extreme proposition: that slums and squatters (or uncontrolled urban settlements) are the result not only of "exceptional" or "abnormal" situations but also of the normal course of development.

For the situation in the Philippines, Thailand, Peru, Brazil, and other developing countries is not unique. The population explosion in the primate cities of these countries may have been extraordinary, but it is not the abnormality of the times alone that was responsible for it. The pressure for development in these countries is such that they have to change more rapidly than their more developed counterparts. As the authors of *The Emerging Nations* pointed out, many of the underdeveloped countries of the world today are trying to accomplish within a decade what it took the more developed countries centuries to achieve.[10] One of the symptoms of this faster and hastier growth is "uncontrolled urban development."

The process of development is not only a building up but also a breaking-down process as well. These twin processes become complementary, especially when what has to be built up must first be fragile and transitory in nature. When rural people migrate to the cities in great numbers, it is too much to expect that there will be enough houses, water, electricity, health, and other urban services to meet their needs. Nor can enough temporary homes be provided by city or national government authorities. Since the status quo does not allow resources for this new development, the people take the line of least resistance and troop to the slums and squatter areas.

Researches on the slum or squatter way of life have shown that these areas are uniquely suited for the "shock absorber" role they have to assume to tide over rural migrants from their old ways to the modernity of urban man. As areas in transition themselves, they provide a comfortable abode for the formerly rural migrant finding his way in urban society.

Slums in developing countries tend to make up primary communities in an otherwise anonymous urban society. Intensive studies of slum areas in Metropolitan Manila have shown that they tend to retain many of the traditional characteristics of rural life: a feeling of community solidarity; intensive face-to-face dealings; groupings according to ethnic, kinship, or economic ties; closed communication systems characterized by localized gossip; and a strong "we feeling" felt against the outside world.[11] Although the lives of slum dwellers are often intermingled with the anonymity of the larger urban world, in the slum community they find an oasis of personal warmth and security. As such, slums and squatter communities serve as a base from which the formerly rural man may evolve into a truly urbanized man.

Economically, slums provide the poor rural migrant the chance to exist and, even later on, prosper in the monetized urban world. When a man moves to the city, everything becomes expensive. In the rural areas, because of the bounties of nature and the assistance of friends, relatives, and neighbors, life is not too harsh even in the midst of poverty. In the city, however, the migrant finds that he has to buy everything —from firewood, which he used to take from the forest, to water, which he used to just fetch from the streams and rivers. Considering that the migrant, because of his lack of skills, cannot find a well-paying job, the sudden translation into money terms of all his needs in the light of his low income is a rude shock. In the slums, the expenses of the big city are not so overpowering. Because slums still have rural characteristics, some resource-extending means are present. When he first comes in, the migrant may just stay with relatives, friends, or people from his home town. Soon, he may find a place to squat on, and, with a meager amount, build his own shack. Not paying any rent, often paying a nominal amount for water and light, he is able to subsist (and, perhaps, even save) because he lives in the slums. His children go to the city's schools (where everything is free, as in Manila), and they also help him earn some money by shining shoes, scavenging, watching cars, or selling things in the market. His wife earns additional sums by taking laundry or selling vegetables and other things. For medical services, the family goes to the free hospital or puericulture center. When really faced with a financial crisis, he can always go to relatives, neighbors, politicians, or even to the welfare agencies. With all these opportunities, it is no great wonder that the slum and squatter populations of urban areas are growing by leaps and bounds. In the eyes of the middle-class urbanite, the lot of slum dwellers is really miserable. When objectively considered and compared with the sleepy and lethargic life in the barrios, however, the slum dwellers and squatters may have a better life—and certainly, a much brighter future.

The most important role played by slums and squatter areas in urban centers, finally, is their mediation in the personality transformation of a rural *tao* to an urban man. The process of modernization is rooted in genuine changes in a person's personality structure. If a nation is to progress, there must be revolutionary transformation in the modal personalities of its population. Such personality variables as other-directedness, empathy, universalism, belief in the manipulative nature of reality, secularism, and others have been shown as related to modernization. It has also been proven that they are highly correlated with urbanization and the opening up of people's horizons through expanded communication.

Because slums are related to the process of urbanization, they contribute directly to the modernization of a country. In the first place, it is a very momentous decision to pull up one's roots in the barrios and move to the urban area. There is, therefore, a certain element of self-selection among the inhabitants of slums and squatter areas. If psychological tests would be conducted among them, it would not be surprising to find many slum dwellers showing personality character-istics of innovators and modernizers. It is not only political mythology that makes many candidates for office claim that they have risen from the slums. More and more, it is becoming apparent that there is something in slum life that provides the drive and motive power to achieve social and economic mobility and the will to succeed.

The personality transformation, abetted by self-selection among adventurous people, is hastened in the slum because of the transitional nature of life there. Although there is an initial "culture shock" when a rural migrant first comes to the city, this is softened by the survivals of rural life that still linger in the slums. Thus, what comes about is akin to what Oscar Lewis has called "urbanization without breakdown." [12] The rural person becomes transformed into an urban man slowly and imperceptibly, because in the slums he still has elements of both worlds co-existing harmoniously with one another. When he is already economically and socially able to lift himself out of the slums, he has also been transformed in personality and is now a thoroughly modern and urbanized man.

# CHAPTER 2

# The Barrio Magsaysay Project

In March 1966, a pilot project in urban community development was launched in Barrio Magsaysay, a reclaimed area within the Tondo foreshore lands. The project was initiated by the Office of the Presidential Arm on Community Development and was a joint endeavor of this Office and the City of Manila, Operation Brotherhood International, and the Asia Foundation. The pilot project was an action-research effort, seeking to introduce community development techniques to an urban setting, with the hope that factors related to success or failure of induced social change could be discovered and transformed into concrete change strategies.

More specifically, the project sought answers to the following questions:

1. What social, economic, and political factors affect the entry of Urban Community Development Workers into a slum area?
2. What factors are related to the process of community organization? How may these factors be used to effect social change through organized community efforts?
3. What programs will succeed or fail in a slum community? What roles should the Urban CD workers, the formal community leaders, and the people play? What external and international resources would be needed for Urban CD programs?
4. What problems are involved in inter-agency coopera-

tion? Among government agencies? Among government and civic agencies? What means of coordination may be used to administer a CD program efficiently and effectively?

5. What techniques and methods may be used to evaluate an action program in urban community development?

The action-research orientation was a unique feature of this program. This meant that Urban Community Development Workers would be fielded in Barrio Magsaysay; they would be expected to introduce programs that would help improve life in the community. At the same time, they would be in very close working relationships with trained researchers who would be helping them in the proper analysis and evaluation of their jobs. Also, while the functional distinctions between action and research were clear, a person in the field may be asked to perform dual roles. Thus, the action workers were expected to feed back information to the research staff regarding their work. They were required to submit regular reports on what they planned to do, what they perceived as their main problems, and what they saw as changes in the people. They were also required to write diaries not only to get an account of actual events but also to record their impressions and reactions. The research people, in turn, were expected to conduct surveys and gather all information relevant to the project and to feed back this information to the action people to guide the action program.

Administratively, the pilot project was divided, therefore, into the action and the research phases. In charge of action was Mr. Alberto Virtusio, community development coordinator and head of the Special Project staff, of the PACD. He was assisted by three action teams composed of seven workers from the PACD; three from OBI; three social workers from the Department of Social Welfare of the City of Manila; three teacher coordinators from the Division of City Schools, City of Manila; and two Peace Corps Volunteers. In charge of research was Dr. Aprodicio A. Laquian, deputy director of the Local Government Center, College of Public Administration, University of the Philippines. He was assisted by Mr. Eduardo

Bigornia, a CD analyst with the Operations and Field Training Division, PACD; Miss Belinda Aquino, instructor and research associate at the College of Public Administration; and two research assistants. The Barrio Magsaysay pilot project was completed in one year. At the time of this writing, however, the action phase of the project is still going on. This book is an account of the first year of action-research operations.

## Rural Community Development Precedents

Community development as a philosophy and approach to solving economic and social problems is not new in the Philippines. As early as August 1954, the Philippine Community Development Program had been in existence, first under the Community Development Planning Council (1954–1956) and then under the Presidential Assistant on Community Development (now Presidential Arm on Community Development).

Although community development was a program already formulated when imported to the Philippines, many changes have been made in both its contents and methodology to suit local conditions. As officially understood,

*Community development . . . is a process designed to create conditions of economic and social progress for the whole community with the active participation and largely upon the initiative of the community.* The Philippine Community Development Program aims to induce a long-run, permanent change in community organization and outlook so as to encourage local initiative and self-help, civic consciousness, and democratic community action. The main emphasis of community development work is on the promotion of the organized efforts of the people in the localities —villages, barrios and municipalities—to help themselves in discovering and acting upon their common interests, needs and problems.[1]

The ends of the community development program, therefore, have been seen as: (1) the achievement of a maximum degree of coordination of activities in community development; (2) the strengthening of existing resources for the undertaking; (3) the changing of people's attitudes toward self-help; and (4) the inculcation of civic consciousness into the people.[2] Of these ends, the first two were considered operational while the rest were regarded as long-range prospects. Efforts for social and economic development, prior to the institution of the program, were characterized by confusion and overlapping of functions among the many agencies engaged in the work. The PACD was seen as the coordinating arm to give direction and coordination to these varied efforts.

To achieve the ends of the program, there are three main means that the community development program uses: (1) the training of community development workers, (2) the strengthening of services in community development, and (3) the development of local leadership.[3] The unique work of the CD worker demands thorough training not only in certain operational skills but also in the art of human relations. As a "generalist who can serve as a reliable rural handyman," the CD worker is trained for six months in Los Baños, Laguna before fielded. Services in community development are strengthened not only by the improvement and coordination of existing services but also through the extension of such inducements as the grants-in-aid program, the barrio roads program, and a rural-loans proposal. Local leadership to take over and continue programs started by the PACD is developed through lay-leadership institutes, training grants for local leaders, seminars, and through the use of PACD publications.

Although primarily conceived as a rural program, the community development effort in the Philippines has not lost sight of the rapid urbanization going on in the country. The PACD has City Development workers assigned to chartered cities such as Baguio, Cabanatuan, Cagayan de Oro, Cebu, Dagupan, Legazpi, San Pablo, and others. However, these so-called City Development workers are in actuality Barrio Workers assigned to the more rural sectors of these chartered cities. Their background, training, and preparation are primarily barrio-oriented; and their title is only an accident of the political classification of their places of assignment.

## Urban Community Development

Like its rural counterpart, the theoretical contents of urban community development are largely imported. The main source of the ideas in the program is the Indian experience in urban community development; specifically, the Delhi Pilot Project, conducted by the Delhi Municipal Corporation with the assistance of the Ford Foundation. [4] As evolved in the Delhi Pilot Project, urban community development seeks "to develop community feeling and shared objectives among people." It tries to foster self-help and citizen participation. The project was designed to cope with slum conditions "to prevent further deterioration in the areas as well as to develop a feeling of civic consciousness." More specifically, the objectives of the project were: [5]

1. The social integration of the communities on a local-neighborhood basis through participation in *self-help* and mutual-aid programs.
2. Development of a sense of *civic pride* by stimulating local interest in campaigns for civic betterment.
3. Preparation of the ground for *democratic decentralization* of municipal services through the organization of Vikas Mandals (people's development councils) fostering local leadership.
4. Creation of the necessary climate for undertaking programs of *economic betterment,* based on maximum use of community resources and local initiative.

The similarities between rural community development and its urban counterpart are obvious. To Clinard and Chatterjee, however, there are two basic differences between the two: (1) rural community development seeks economic betterment of the people while the urban program seeks the "amelioration of living conditions and community life"; and (2) rural community development is done "within a traditional framework" of village social structure while urban community development needs "adaptations . . . to new conditions, and urban people must be helped to regain intimacy in their impersonal surroundings." [6]

The differences between the rural and the urban varieties of community development, therefore, rest on the nature of community in these two social settings. Western urban studies have usually noted that while the traditional structure in the rural areas provides unity and cohesiveness, a sense of community may not be too strong in an urban area where people from various backgrounds mingle and where the milieu does not encourage inter-dependence and emotional closeness. More and more, however, studies on urban areas in underdeveloped countries have tended to minimize the truth of this rural-urban dichotomy. The rural-urban distinction was set up by statisticians (mainly demographers) to enable them to classify areas according to the density of population. Sociologists have adopted this distinction and at the same time alluded qualitative differences in the social characteristics, economic variables, and other factors found in rural and urban life. The distinctions became so refined that there is now an urban and rural sociology. Although the tradition of the dichotomous scheme has been useful before, it may not be enough to explain the wide varieties of rural and urban characteristics found in the rapidly urbanizing areas of the world.

It has been noted that most cities in developing areas tend to have pockets of settlements that are extremely cohesive and unified—little societies not too different from the rural villages, where group pressures and common norms tend to exact conformity and a homogeneous way of life. These are the slum and squatter communities that dot the usually ultra-modern urban landscape. In such areas, there is little rootlessness, anomie, or a feeling of being lost. Criminality and juvenile delinquency may be high, but there is no mass social or personal disorganization. The people, in fact, tend to be well organized. Because of political activities, the need for protection and for social and religious observances, and because of the desire to limit violence, urban slum dwellers tend to set up varied and often overlapping organizations of a formal or informal nature.

Clinard and Chatterjee also believe that urban community

development is mainly a stop-gap measure. It does not seek economic betterment but only "creates the necessary climate" for this. A true community development program, however, must have long-range goals if it is to succeed. Within slum and squatter areas, there are many programs that can be initiated that will augment or even provide the main source of income for people. Aside from skills in certain services (waiters, barbers, maids, security guards, etc.) that are easily learned, skills in cottage industries may also be encouraged. An urban community development program may also include such projects as credit unions, employment agencies, and construction teams—which all directly result in the economic betterment of the people.

The urban community development effort described in this book, therefore, has a wider scope than the one described by Clinard and Chatterjee in Delhi. Although it takes off from the medical, sanitation, and social welfare programs familiar in the Delhi Pilot Project, it seeks to introduce projects in economic betterment designed to uplift the lot of people in the slums.

## BASIC URBAN CD APPROACH

Urban community development, as understood in the Barrio Magsaysay pilot project, is basically an on-site program. It attempts to improve the economic, social, and political conditions existing in small urban communities, through the organized efforts of the people themselves as assisted by trained community development workers. Compared to urban redevelopment programs, urban community development gives less emphasis to physical and structural changes in the person's city environment. Like its rural counterpart, it attempts to bring about change in the people's attitudes, values, cognitions, and opinions—that may or may not involve the changing of their physical surroundings.

The government's participation in an urban community development program usually involves: (1) recruitment, selection, training, and remuneration of the Urban Community Development workers; (2) provision of program resources such as grants-in-aid projects involving roads, schoolhouses, health centers, multi-purpose pavements, etc.; and (3) provision of operational resources such as medical facilities, supplies and materials, vocational kits, etc. Items under (2) and (3) may even be obtained from private and civic sources, provided the CD workers have initiative and industry.

The mainstay of an Urban Community Development Program is the Urban CD worker. The program is based essentially on human approach; hence, its success will depend on the organizational abilities, creativity, initiative, industry, and intelligence of the Urban CD worker. If the CD worker knows how to work with people, how to motivate them and harness their energies toward solving community problems, the program will succeed. If he fails to appreciate this human orientation, the program fails.

Basically, the urban CD approach is composed of the following stages: (1) identification of community problems; (2) pinpointing of community resources; (3) analysis of alternative solutions; (4) organization of community efforts; (5) solution of problems; and (6) evaluation of program results. Enumeration of these stages does not mean they neatly fall into the same sequence. Neither does it imply that the boundary of stages may be precisely drawn so that it will be possible to say where one stage ends and another begins.

*Identification of Community Problems.* As much as possible, the perception and identification of community problems must come from the people themselves. Even when the Urban Community Development workers conduct a survey to find out the problems of the community, pains must be taken to view them from the eyes of the people. Usually, CD workers come from a different social background, educational level, and economic status from their clientele. Their perception may be quite different from the people's, and, if this will guide the community development approaches, there is a danger that the program may not achieve desired results.

Many techniques have been developed to get at the people's view of their own problems—what CD technicians call their "felt needs." Usually, a survey question directly asking them: "In your opinion, what are the main problems of people in your community?" yields significant results. When these results are validated through a sample big enough or through the direct observations of trained researchers and field workers —or both—they usually encourage planning of correct programs based on the right information.

*Pinpointing Community Resources.* If at all possible, the problems of the community must be met with resources that are available locally. These will include such resources as leadership skills, economic skills, organized groups, local material resources, positive attitudes, and others. Resources from the outside, such as those from the government or from civic-spirited citizens should be brought in only under certain special circumstances. For example, such external resources may be introduced to gain the people's confidence so that the program may be initially launched; or when there is a willingness on the part of the people to match these external resources with local ones; or when the introduction of the external resources has a pump-priming effect; i.e., when the people will not start a project unless a prior obstacle that can only be solved by outside forces is first removed.

*Analysis of Alternative Solutions.* As in the identification of problems, the search for solutions should be made by the people themselves, with the discreet guidance of the Urban CD worker. In the search for solutions, priority should be given to alternatives that rely on local resources. Alternatives that have a more lasting effect should also be favored to those that promise quick results but fade just as quickly.

The search for solutions and the planning of ways and means by which resources may be made to bear on problems are very important community efforts. The Urban CD worker must be deeply interested in procedures and not only in results. In this way, a definite methodology usually referred to as "the CD way" may be evolved to meet certain problems.

*Organization of Community Efforts.* The CD worker in an urban setting cannot take for granted that the people would possess a "community spirit," more or less organized, which would be the main vehicle for his programs for change. In some urban areas, people may be formally organized, and in some a kindred spirit may be shared. However, there are also certain areas where the main effort of the CD worker would involve creating a community spirit through organized efforts.

Even where a community has indigenous organizations, they may not be the correct ones for the planning and implementation of community development programs. Thus, a CD worker may have to change the structure of such organizations to make them effective. He may also have to take leadership patterns into consideration, instituting changes through democratic means, when necessary.

*Solution of Problems.*  The most important thing a CD worker has to keep in mind is that the problems of a community are solved with the people's efforts, not by his community development skills. The best trained and most motivated CD worker will fail if he does not learn to appreciate this fact. Even if the wants of the community are answered and their most pressing problems solved—if the people were not involved in the process of solving the problems, the CD worker has failed in his job.

Local resources must first be tapped in solving problems. Outside assistance must be availed of only when there are no local resources available. Solving the problem is secondary to the generation of community spirit and to a civic pride that the people themselves solved their problems through their own efforts and with their own resources.

Solving the problem is also less important compared to the manner in which it was solved. Was there community involvement from the start? Were the stages of planning, implementation, and evaluation observed carefully, with the people themselves doing the work? Was full use made of local resources? And finally, did the CD worker motivate rather than lead the people toward solving their own problems? If the answer to each of these questions were yes, the CD worker may be considered successful in his work.

*Evaluation of Program Results.*  In evaluating results of community development efforts, there are several approaches the CD worker may take. One of the most effective of these is building the evaluation procedure right in the planning and implementation processes. This is best done through effective planning by the community leaders assisted by the CD worker.

A detailed work plan is the best way of finding out how successful a CD program is. By comparing actual results and estimated progress as set forth in the plan, the CD worker is able to evaluate his progress. When the plan of work is prepared by the people themselves, then, the variance between their intentions and their actual efforts may serve to spur them into more vigorous action.

A CD worker need not wait until the project is over before an evaluation is made. If a project is effectively phased and properly divided to hit specific targets, evaluation may be done after each phase—and the distance to the final goal estimated. In this way, corrective measures may be carried out, and the success of the project is better assured.

## ADVANTAGES AND DISADVANTAGES OF URBAN COMMUNITY DEVELOPMENT

The main advantage of the urban community development approach lies in the fact that it solves community problems effectively while it provides urban dwellers the chance of using democratic decision-making in the process. One of the main evils of urbanization is its corroding effect on certain social institutions that maintain the smooth functioning of human society. The increasing complexity of urban life and its resultant dehumanization of the individual often brings about social and personal disorganization.

Urban community development, by using the basic human community as the vehicle for decision-making, combats this trend towards atomization. Instead of losing his touch with other human beings and leading a life lacking human warmth, the urban dweller is able to return to this traditional source of comfort, while at the same time improving his own physical environment to cope with urban problems.

Another advantage of urban community development is that it is relatively inexpensive. No matter how rich the city government is, it will never be able to finance all the urban services needed by the people through tax and other proceeds. Urban community development enables the government to rely on personal, family and community efforts to meet part of the cost of solving urban problems. Instead of relying on the police to institute peace and order, the urban community, through its use of volunteer efforts and informal social pressures, may effectively perform this function. Instead of relying on paid street sweepers and garbage collectors, the city can ask the residents of a community to help clean their own surroundings. It is true that urban community development may not entirely replace city services. As a complementary effort, however, it saves the city government a lot of money.

The most important advantage of urban community development lies in its impact on the human side of urban life—the changes in the attitudes, opinions, and motivations of people. The approach brings out the natural leaders in a community and enables them to participate and get involved in worthwhile projects. The real resources of a community—natural, social, and physical—are tapped. In this way, the natural yearning for social well-being, and the viewing of personal success in the light of community service awaken the humanity in people, which the urban environment often stifles.

One main drawback of urban community development, however, is that it takes time to bring about results. Furthermore, results are not readily apparent and not easily discernible. Urban community development takes time because it works on and through people. The process of attitude change is a complex and subtle thing. Even when concrete results are seen (clean surroundings, school buildings, and health centers set up), the work of community development may not have been achieved yet. If the attitudes of the people have not been changed, they would just return to their old habits as soon as the cd worker leaves the place.

Urban community development may also be inapplicable in certain areas where public policy demands that the place be better devoted to more fruitful and economical alternative uses. It will not pay to improve an urban slum area, for example, if the city authorities fully intend to devote the land to uses other than housing (playgrounds and parks, commercial uses, civic uses). Since urban community development is an on-site approach, the people must be assured of land ownership so that their natural pride may be used in improving their own surroundings. In slum and squatter areas where the tenure of the people is indeterminate, urban community development may not be the answer. The urban CD approach, however, may also be used as a short-term stop gap measure. The city may have future plans for an area currently being squatted on but city finances and other factors prevent the use of such lands in the short run (say about ten years). In this case, urban community development may be used to improve the life in the community prior to the land's being used for other purposes. Under these conditions, urban CD may serve to prepare the squatters and slum dwellers for their relocation, both materially and psychologically. It may even be possible that urban CD may bring about their transfer without force and with as little inconvenience as possible.

PROGRAM INITIATION

The nature of urban community development, its main approach, and its advantages and disadvantages cited above are gleaned from the literature on community development (mostly rural), the findings of anthropologists studying urban life, the experience in urban community development in other countries, and, finally, a year's work in Barrio Magsaysay itself. Necessarily, the ideas on urban community development were rather vague and only haphazardly stated at the start. It is the goal of this book to make more precise the findings on urban community development as an approach and as a process.

The idea for conducting a pilot program on urban community development first occurred to this writer in the course of an observation-study trip to India in 1963. While in New Delhi, he was introduced to the pilot project on urban community development in the city, headed by Mr. B. Chatterjee and assisted by Marshall Clinard. The concepts and approaches used in the Delhi Pilot Project greatly influenced the idea of setting up a similar project in the Philippines.

The first concrete proposal for an urban community development pilot project in the Metropolitan Manila area was prepared in early 1966. As originally conceived, however, the project was to be done by researchers of the Asian Social Institute, a private educational institution, with the financial assistance of the Asia Foundation. For some reason or other, this idea was not pushed through although the Asia Foundation signified its interest in the approach.

In January 1966, the office of the Presidential Assistant on Community Development (PACD) decided to expand its urban community development efforts into the Metropolitan Manila area. Barrio Magsaysay was chosen for this project. Because of the close similarity between the original ASI proposal and the work of the PACD, this was brought to the attention of Secretary Ernesto Maceda, and negotiations were started immediately between the Asia Foundation and the PACD for the launching of the Barrio Magsaysay action-research project.

At first, it was proposed that the pilot project be financed by the Asia Foundation and the Community Development Research Council. However, because of certain differences in methodological approaches and techniques, the project did not prosper in the CDRC, and Secretary Maceda agreed to finance part of the project's expenses from the PACD's operational budget.

The Barrio Magsaysay Urban Community Development Pilot Project was officially started on 1 March 1966. At the start, it was an inter-agency effort involving the PACD, Operation Brotherhood International, the City of Manila, and the Asia Foundation. As an action-research project, it sought to introduce urban community development techniques to an urban setting, with the hope that factors related to the success or failure of induced social change could be discovered.

THEORETICAL MOORINGS

Broadly construed, the action-research project was an exercise in induced social change. At the start, it was assumed that there were certain "desirable changes" that needed to be done in Barrio Magsaysay to improve life there and that Urban Community Development as a technique was the approach to be used to bring these about. The area was assumed to have many problems. The precise nature of these problems were to be defined by a community survey, but at the start it was enough that the research group felt that such problems existed and that they had to be solved.

It was readily accepted, even at the start, that a particular bias of the study centered on community efforts—that whatever changes occurred in the community would have to be generated by the people themselves, although the Urban cd workers may initiate such changes. Thus, the emphasis on community organization faced the fact that lasting changes in the community would be effected only if the people themselves brought them about, that involvement in the achievement of such changes is necessary for them to be meaningful.

It was also understood that a large-scale urban community development project would have to be an inter-agency effort because of the complexity of the task and the presence of many agencies in an urban setting. Thus, the difficulties and techniques of facilitating inter-agency cooperation and coordination were sought to be covered in the study.

**ACTION-RESEARCH ORIENTATION**

At the outset, the intimate relationship between action and research programs in the study was questioned by people who were worried about the methodological implications of such a relationship. Traditionally, because of the influence of the experimental school in social science, the roles of research and action have always been kept distinct. Thus, research came into play before the launching of an action program to assess the situation. It also had a role after the completion of the action program in the form of evaluation. During the course of an action program, however, the role of research is believed to be confined to that of a silent observer. Research findings, if revealed to those in charge of the action program, may unduly influence future actions. Once this happens, the success or failure of the action program would be very difficult to assess. It would be impossible to find out whether such success or failure is due to the nature of the action program, the warning signals given by research, or both. From the point of view of the researcher, also, it is argued that involvement in the action program tends to "contaminate" research findings—making the researcher biased, which may force him to justify his actions. Where the researcher had a hand in the formulation of the plans of activities and in the action program, it is feared that his evaluation would be invalidated by his partisan interests and prejudices.

The Barrio Magsaysay project, with its intimate link of action and research, was based on the faith that the social sciences have achieved enough sophistication and maturity to avoid the bias that those schooled in the experimental method were so afraid of. It is a common adage in research methodology that it is not the presence of bias that counts in a research undertaking—it is rather the researcher's awareness and perception of the extent of his own bias that are important because such awareness then enables him to compensate for it. Thus, a social scientist advocating a program of action may be all for it, but this does not mean that, if he is trained enough, he would not be able to objectively assess whether such a program of action is succeeding or failing. Advocacy does not preclude awareness of the factors that are contributing to this success or failure.

Rather than action and research contaminating each other, the Barrio Magsaysay pilot project hoped that they would complement and assist each other. In the experimental framework, the researcher has to wait until an action program is finished. Even if the program is already miserably failing before his eyes, a misguided value for complete objectivity may prevent him from suggesting ways and means of averting the disaster. Evaluation researches, therefore, are valuable in the sense that post mortems done on cadavers are valuable. The Barrio Magsaysay researchers believed that while post mortems have value in social science, the feedback of information from research group to action group may actually yield more information—and better action results to boot.

As shown in the diagram on page 56, the tie-up between action and research in the Barrio Magsaysay project was a rather close one. The roles of the research group were the following:

1. To conduct a survey of the area and its population, to gather information that would assist the action group in planning its program of activities;
2. To make special studies, independently or upon the request of the action group, on specific problem areas that need further investigation;
3. To make a continuing evaluation of the action group's efforts, their impact on the community, the people's reactions, and other factors relevant to the success or failure of specific programs;
4. To provide continuous "feed-back information" to the action group, based on their studies, surveys, and other researches.

The action group, of course, was primarily charged with the planning and implementation of the urban community development program. They helped in the research, conducting the initial community-wide survey and writing a running account of their activities in the field in diaries. They also submitted to the research group all their written plans and programs, which helped greatly in pinpointing desired attitude changes and in evaluating the extent of progress of such programs. Because they were mostly in the field and knew the people at close range, they introduced the research staff in their field forays and helped them with special projects.

As a precaution against too much danger of research group involvement also, the action and research groups were administratively separated. As already mentioned, both groups were led by separate chiefs. Maximum chances for close relationships were encouraged, however. Thus, both research and action groups took a common training program, and they attended group meetings together. Although there were instances of friction between action and research personnel at some points, the tie-up seemed to have been successful. The danger of bias was not acutely encountered, and the joint work proceeded smoothly.

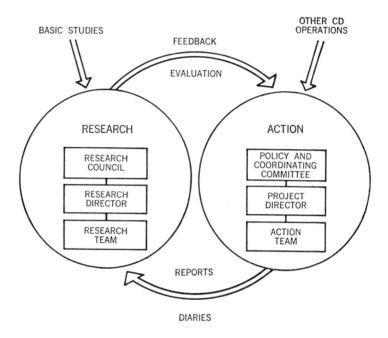

FIGURE 1
RELATIONSHIP BETWEEN ACTION AND RESEARCH:
BARRIO MAGSAYSAY PILOT PROJECT

## TRAINING THE URBAN CD WORKERS

It was realized early in this study that the Urban Community Development workers to be used in Barrio Magsaysay needed further training to be more effective. In the training program prepared for these workers, it was stated that "Since urban community development is a new endeavor, it cannot be ascertained at this point which problems, processes and techniques will be involved in the work to be done. It is therefore suggested that training of the field workers will be a continuous process.... However, an initial training period is necessary before fielding the action teams." [7]

The whole Barrio Magsaysay project, aside from being an action-research venture, was also an on-the-job training program for future Urban CD workers. Up to that time, what the PACD called urban community development was no different from rural community development. Urban CD workers were so only by technicality—they were assigned to barrios that are within chartered cities. These barrios, however, were no different from other rural barrios. They became urban areas only because of legal definition.

The initial training program was considered necessary because of various factors. In the first place, most of the PACD personnel assigned to the Barrio Magsaysay project were rural CD workers. Other personnel from various agencies were also assigned to the job (aside from the nine PACD personnel assigned to the project, there were five from the City of Manila government, three from the Peace Corps, and four from Operation Brotherhood International). Finally, the workers came from various occupational and educational backgrounds, and there was need to imbue them with the importance of their own task—urban community development.

### PREVIOUS PACD TRAINING

Of the nine persons from the PACD, who were assigned to the project, two were members of the headquarters staff, one was a Municipal Development officer, and the remaining six were all Barrio Development workers. All of them had gone through the basic training program in Los Baños and were all fully conversant with their roles as community development workers.

More than any other training program in the Philippines, the one given by the PACD is the most elaborate and consciously constructed to bring about the "right" community development worker. During the six months that a worker is training in Los Baños, Laguna, he is expected to learn the following: [8]

1. Some basic technical skills the worker can use to carry out his role as a multi-purpose worker;

2. Some social skills he may need in dealing with local people and groups;
3. Certain operational values consistent with the national program and philosophy of community development;
4. Understanding of the difficulties of introducing and getting the program accepted through his exposure to the idiosyncracies of Philippine rural culture and government structure;
5. Some pertinent administrative information about PACD operations;
6. Some program planning skills; and
7. Other types of information considered germane to field operations.

Aside from these consciously inculcated program contents, the PACD training program is also guided by certain assumptions. Villanueva has stated these assumptions as: [9]

1. The possession of a high degree of rural bias is indispensable to the success of a community development worker;
2. The content of the training program must reflect the job description which the trainee will eventually carry out;
3. Community development is a *holistic* and integrated activity . . . it requires the pooling together of all locally available resources and the coordination of the same for maximum development;
4. A thorough understanding of the purposes and philosophy of the government's program of community development is necessary for a proper implementation of the same; and
5. Community development must be based fundamentally on self-help and local determination . . . responsibility for it must be institutionalized in purely local organizations that are truly representative of local citizens and local sentiments.

The most important things to remember about the training program given to community development workers are the emphasis on self-help and the presence of a rural bias. Each CD worker ought to identify local needs and resources, not because he is to use them personally, but because he has to point them out to local leaders and members of local institutions that the latter may solve their own problems. In other words, the whole approach is based on the assumption that "community spirit" would be available and that it could be used to achieve development goals. In official community development philosophy, the barrio council was regarded as the institution through which all efforts at development should be coursed and achieved. In Barrio Magsaysay, where no barrio council existed, certain modifications in approaches were therefore called for.

Because the Philippine community development program was meant for rural areas, there was the assumption of rural bias. This was explained as "indicative of a healthy regard and respect for rural propensities and ways of life" and was considered indispensable for the success of the field worker.[10] Again, this particular emphasis in the training of CD workers had to be revised to meet the new conditions in Barrio Magsaysay.

In the design of the initial training program, the rural orientation of the CD workers was the primary consideration. Therefore, the program contents were geared to work in an urban setting. Thus, the similarities and differences between rural and urban community development were emphasized. Lectures on the nature of the urban community, urban social institutions, demographic characteristics of urban populations, rural-urban migratory patterns, and community organization in urban cultures were given. At the same time, approaches to the solving of urban problems such as city planning, land use, zoning, and relocation were also discussed by experts.

A great deal of attention was placed on the nature of the urban community because it was felt that the success or failure of the workers depended on their full appreciation of the urban way of life. Unlike the rural barrio, which is characterized by primary social relationship, the urban community tends to be structured by secondary relationships that tend to be more formally initiated and imposed. Preliminary surveys

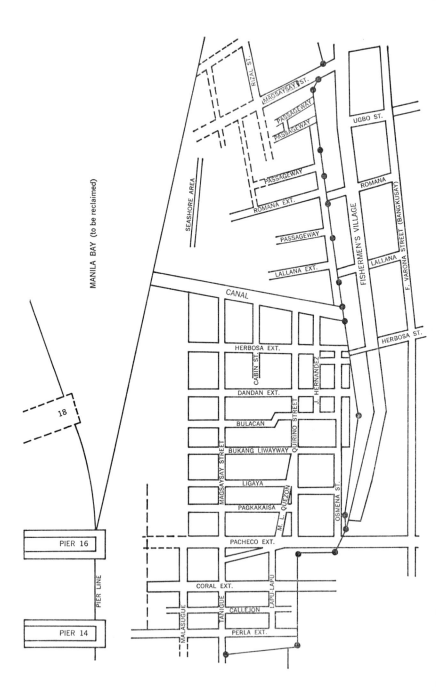

of Barrio Magsaysay conducted before the training program indicated the presence of six formal organizations, loosely federated into one community-wide association. Instead of the barrio council, there were many neighborhood associations and organizations based on geographical, sex, age, and other functional factors. The nature of these organizations and the roles they played in the life of the community received close attention in the training program.

FIGURE 2: (*opposite page*)
MAP OF BARRIO MAGSAYSAY, 1967

# CHAPTER 3

# Barrio Magsaysay

The choice of Barrio Magsaysay as the site for the first pilot project in urban community development in the Philippines was made by PACD Secretary Ernesto Maceda. There were certain misgivings about the site, raised especially by social science researchers interested in methodology. Some of the objections raised were:

1. Barrio Magsaysay is not really an urban area. Its population is primarily composed of migrants from the rural areas. Because it was a newly opened land reclaimed from the sea, about 40.8 per cent of the population had been residing in the area for less than one year, while 36.8 per cent had been living there for about four to six years. In fact, although 66.7 per cent of the population had just moved into Barrio Magsaysay from adjoining parts of Tondo, a full 14.8 per cent of the area's population came directly from the provinces.

   Some researchers, therefore, questioned the use of an area predominantly occupied by former rural dwellers as the site of a pilot project in urban community development. The findings from the project, it was feared, would not be useful in the formulation of programs designed to solve urban ills of squatting and slum dwelling. Urban community development is an instrument for meeting urban problems. Why will it be tested in a semi-rural area?

2. Barrio Magsaysay suffers from instability because of the uncertain tenure of the people on the land. The whole

of Barrio Magsaysay is reclaimed land belonging to the national government and administered by the Land Authority. The people just squatted on the land as soon as it was reclaimed from Manila Bay. Although legislative enactments have been passed providing for the survey, subdivision, and distribution of the land to the *bona fide* occupants for residential purposes, there were other plans to use the area as part of a general ports-improvement plan. Many urban planners, in fact, objected to the setting aside of Barrio Magsaysay for residential purposes. They considered the land too valuable to be devoted to such an uneconomical use. They believed that the land should be devoted to port facilities, warehousing, and heavy industrial use. If these proposals were followed, the residents of Barrio Magsaysay would have to be relocated. Introducing urban community development, therefore, with its emphasis on on-site improvements, would only be wasted effort.

In spite of these objections, however, the pilot project was launched in Barrio Magsaysay. To those who participated in the project, the choice of site had to be taken as given.

## Physical Characteristics

The author's first physical contact with Barrio Magsaysay is especially noteworthy because it gives a fresh impression of the physical character of the place. At the time, his perceptions were guided by the methodology devised by Kevin Lynch in *The Image of the City*.[1] A description of this first visit and the impressions gathered then may give the reader some idea of the physical elements of the Barrio.

The methodology used by Lynch, was as follows:

A systematic field reconnaisance of the area was made on foot by a trained observer, who mapped the presence of various elements, their visibility, their image strength or weakness, and their connections, disconnections and other inter-relations, and who noted any special success or difficulties in the potential image structure.

These were subjective judgments based on the immediate appearance of these elements in the field.[2]

Lynch divides the cityscape into paths, edges, districts, and nodes. Paths are channels through which people move; edges are boundaries; districts are sections of the city that one enters; and nodes are points of entrance or junctions, concentrations of elements or activities.[3]

Entry into Barrio Magsaysay is best done at Coral Extension, which is in Area III. (See map). Coming from the south along Sta. Clara Street, one enters Area III through a node where Sta. Clara bisects Coral. To most residents of the place, this is the normal break in the transportation point. If they are taking the jeepney from North Harbor or Divisoria, they get off at this corner. The place is well marked by a basketball court, right in the middle of the street.

Coral Street is the path into the area. It becomes Coral Extension, past the intersection with Bangkusay. The point where one enters Barrio Magsaysay is clearly defined by a landmark —a tall electric post with a big transformer, which stands out from the flimsy houses made of wood, with galvanized iron roofings. Electric posts, in fact, are the most prominent features of the street scene. With their many lines parallel to the main path and with many more lines flowing from the posts to the houses lining the streets, they make up the main feature of the skyline.

Where Coral is bisected by Tanigue Street, there is a cemented area, flanked on both sides by two public wooden structures. This is the center of the neighborhood, the headquarters of the Kapisanan ng mga Taga-Dalampasigan, Inc. The small "plaza" is definitely a node in the community: it is dominated by the headquarters of the association, which also doubles as a nursery school building. The other public structure on the right side of the concreted portion serves as an occasional chapel. The real social center in the plaza, however, is a *sari-sari* store that has a very loud jukebox and benches and that sells hard drinks. Many people congregate around this store. Although the two public structures are much bigger, they are usually untenanted and are used only for

rare public occasions. The small store that has the loud jukebox is almost always crowded with people. Late afternoons,
members of the youth groups and clubs gather around the
store, drinking and joshing each other, and, often, dancing
the latest steps on the pavement. Weekends, older folks take
over the store who have heavy drinking bouts and story-
telling sessions.

The end of Coral Street is well marked by an edge made
up to the fence erected by the Ports and Harbors Division, of
the Bureau of Public Works, to serve as the boundary of their
new reclamation project. Malasugue Street, which runs parallel to the fence, forms a secondary path that bisects Coral.
Following Malasugue toward the south, one can readily see
the edge of the community. A clear landmark is the roof of
the Bureau of Public Works shed, which is prominently etched
in the horizon. Small paths, some of them made of plank catwalks, run perpendicular to Perla Extension. Walking on one
of these, one finds suddenly a small open square dominated
by a public wooden structure: the headquarters of the Kapisanang taga-Baybay Dagat, Inc., a definite node in the community, which is also a core.

More so than the "plaza" on Coral Extension, the cemented
square of the Kapisanang taga-Baybay Dagat serves as the core
of the community. Perhaps, this is due to the fact that this
place is within the interior of the community and is not along
a well-traveled path like Coral Street. Around the square are
no less than seven *sari-sari* stores, three of which have blaring
jukeboxes. A basketball court stands on one side of the square.
There is also a small fish and vegetable stand, which really
makes the square the commercial and social center of the
community. As in Coral Street, however, the headquarters of
the organization, though it was the most prominent structure
in the place, was closed and unoccupied. The stores, especially
those that have jukeboxes, had young males seated on benches,
strumming guitars, drinking, and generally, just talking and
watching. The headquarters, billed as a community center,
was not being used, and its tables and benches were thick
with dust. Its lack of occupancy might be related to the big
sign tacked on to it: *Bawal Magsugal Dito* ("No gambling in

this place"). Children and young adults used to play coin games (*tanching* and *cara y cruz*) on the cemented square, but the community association officers have prohibited this. The physical characteristics of Area III clearly revealed that it was composed of two definite and distinct communities. This is shown in the two nodes in the area, which may be considered as community cores. As the public, commercial, and social centers of the community, the squares or plazas served as a means of identity to the neighborhoods. Although the public community centers did not really perform their functions (being unused by the people), the stores that cluster around the square, with their jukeboxes and hard drinks, serve the social purpose.

## The Project Site

The area known as Barrio Magsaysay forms part of the Tondo Foreshore Lands, reclaimed by the Bureau of Public Works as part of a massive plan to expand international and domestic port facilities in the City of Manila.[4] In this plan, facilities for international shipping would be expanded and shifted to the northern side of the Pasig River. Huge parts of the bay will be reclaimed and devoted to port facilities, warehousing, industrial sites, and commercial uses. Only a small part of the reclaimed area would be devoted to low-cost housing to accommodate laborers, whom any port needs. Some sections of the reclaimed land would also be used for parks, playgrounds, and other civic purposes. A super-highway, extending Roxas Boulevard northward to Navotas, was designed to cut through the area, dividing the port zone from the rest of the city.

As in most big projects, however, it took plenty of time before stages in the phased programs could be carried out. Thus while the government was able to reclaim some land, the loans, equipment, and men necessary for pushing the project through did not readily materialize. Meanwhile, the city's housing needs became so acute that people started building their shacks on the reclaimed land. In less than four years, more than 3,000 families had squatted on the Tondo Foreshore

Lands, and more were coming in as the news spread that the government would give the lands to squatters if they just fought hard enough.

The indeterminate tenure of the people over the land has made it difficult for the tenants. Because the land is newly reclaimed, it is still subject to inundation—especially when heavy rains coincide with the high tide. The land is technically still public domain, and the city government hesitates to extend services and utilities to the people in Barrio Magsaysay. Because the land has not been surveyed, there are no official street layouts; hence, the thoroughfares were marked only by the people—and were, of course, not maintained by the government. In fact, some people have even set up their shanties right in the middle of streets, because nobody knew that those sites would be used for streets at the time they set up the houses.

Barrio Magsaysay, aside from having no officially recognized roads, is also not entitled to water, electricity, health, and other facilities. Because residences are not supposed to be there, the government corporations providing these services cannot extend water and electricity. What water and electricity is available in the place is provided by "special arrangements" that are often extra-legal in nature.

The settlement pattern, as it developed, was mainly an extension of the sprawl of Tondo. First, those reclaimed areas adjacent to the privately owned residential lands in Tondo were occupied by squatters. This encroachment steadily grew until it reached the Estero de Vitas. Makeshift bridges were soon set up by the people, however, and relatively high grounds across the *estero* became settled first. The people just extended footpaths through the reclaimed land—and pretty soon, even marginal land that could still be had was occupied by stilt houses, joined together by plank bridges.

The Bureau of Public Works, alarmed at the encroachment by the squatters, set up a barbed wire fence. Soon, houses reached the fence also—and people started moving the fence at night to occupy more land. Meanwhile, the undesirable land beside the *estero* was still being occupied. The presence of a high-rise tenement housing project in Vitas did not help much because it could accommodate only a hundred or so families. At the time of the project, there were more than 3,000 families in Barrio Magsaysay and people were still coming in. Squatters had even occupied the seawalls and the breakwater, up to what was known as Islang Puting Bato and Pulong Diablo. As the people settled down, natural neighborhoods started growing. Usually, these neighborhoods centered around certain strong leaders and respected or feared families. The need for self-protection forced the people to organize, a process that was enhanced by the hostility of adjoining neighborhoods, usually reflected in gang wars, teenage rumbles, and political rivalries. Soon, boundaries of neighborhood "territories" were mutually set up and respected—and the jurisdictions of the now formalized organizations mapped out.

At the time of the survey, researchers covering Barrio Magsaysay found through interviews that about six definite "areas" were recognized by the people. The extent of these areas was rather definite and recognized by the residents in the community. Because these areas did not have definite names, the research team arbitrarily gave them designations, which were used by the action team members as well. The people, of course, using their own means of identifying areas— preferred to use "blocks" as designation—but the CD teams used their own designations.

As divided by the CD teams, Barrio Magsaysay was composed of the following areas and neighborhoods:

AREA I

Physically, this was bounded by a canal on the south, another canal on the east, by Bonifacio Street on the north, and the fence set up by the Bureau of Public Works to mark their new reclamation work in the west. The people referred to this area as Magsaysay Village and considered it distinctly separate from Barrio Magsaysay proper. The canal on the south provided a natural boundary. Although there were suggestions to set up a big bridge across the canal, most residents of Magsaysay Village did not favor this because they were afraid that the troubles of the barrio would reach them. Area I had many organizations but the most dominant one was the Sangguniang Nayon, Inc. Some of the residents were rather well off, because they worked at the Philippine Manufacturing Company (PMC), whose plant and compound was in the area. The character of the place is also influenced by the presence of the City Slaughterhouse in the area, which contributes to the peace and order problem because many toughies were employed at the *matadero*.

### AREA II

This is the central part of Barrio Magsaysay and is bounded by Pacheco Extension on the south, Fisherman's Village on the east, the canal on the north, and the reclamation fence on the west. Because it was a big area, three distinct neighborhoods existed, each one dominated by an association. These three were:

1. Magsaysay Neighborhood Association, Inc. This neighborhood clusters around Herbosa Extension, especially where that street intersects with Cabili, Quirino, and J. Hernandez Streets. The president of the neighborhood association was also the president of the federation of neighborhood associations for the whole Barrio Magsaysay.

2. Damayan ng Nayon, Inc. This organization exists mainly around Bukang Liwayway Street, especially where it intersects with Osmeña and Bulacan Streets. Many of its members reside along the canal, which is sometimes called Fisherman's Harbor.

3. Kapisanang Tanglaw ng Mahihirap, Inc. This association, also on Bukang Liwayway Street, occupies the western end of that thoroughfare, especially where it intersects with Magsaysay Street and Quirino Street. Some members also reside along M. L. Quezon, Ligaya, and Pagkakaisa Streets, though many are along Bukang Liwayway.

Of all the areas in Barrio Magsaysay, Area II feels the most threatened by the outside world mainly because the area has been proposed to be the site of the Andres Bonifacio

Memorial Stadium and also because the proposed Roxas Boulevard extension would neatly cut the community in half, requiring the eviction of many homeowners.

## AREA III

This is the southernmost portion of Barrio Magsaysay and is bounded by Pacheco Extension on the north, the boundary of the Tondo Foreshore Land on the east, the Bureau of Public Works site on the south, and the fence of the reclamation site on the west. This is the most crowded portion of Barrio Magsaysay. Two organizations dominate the lives of the people here, namely:

1. Samahang Taga-Dalampasigan, Inc. This occupies the area north of Coral Extension, and members mostly reside around Malasugue, Tanigue, and Lapulapu Streets. This place is not only crowded but troubled as well, with many riots occurring on Coral Street.
2. Kapisanang Taga-Baybay Dagat, Inc. This area lies south of Coral Street and extends down to Perla Extension. A small alley (*callejon*) cuts across its center, which is bisected by three streets (Malasugue, Tanigue, and Lapulapu).

## Legislative History

The Tondo Foreshore Lands were reclaimed by the national government as part of a plan to expand and improve the port facilities in the City of Manila. However, squatters occupied the area, making it difficult for the Bureau of Public Works to push its plan through. The bureau's difficulties, however, were compounded when the squatters agitated to own the lands they were occupying and, through political pressures, appealed to the legislative and executive officials for this.

The first victory of the squatters in their fight to get the land they were occupying was in the issuance of Proclamation No. 187, signed by President Elpidio Quirino on 17 June 1950. This proclamation rather vaguely declared that the "tract of land located in the district of Tondo, City of Manila, and bounded on the north by the Tondo Tenement House of Government and the Estero de Vitas, on the east, by private properties, on the south of Azcarraga Street, and on the west by the Dewey Boulevard Extension" was "reserve [d] as a site for low-cost housing projects under the administration of the People's Homesite and Housing Corporation . . . ." The proclamation did not declare the land open for low-cost housing. It was just *reserved* by the President for this purpose.

The Federation of Tondo Foreshore Land Tenants Association, which was behind the enactment of Proclamation No. 187, succeeded in 1956 in getting a law through Congress, making their claims stronger. Instead of just reserving the site for low-cost housing, Republic Act No. 1597 (16 June 1956) directed the Director of Lands "to survey and subdivide immediately" the land in question. The Director of Lands was given one year within which to finish this job, after which, he was instructed to turn over all records or papers to the Land Tenure Administration, which was "Authorized and directed to sell without delay and without the necessity of public bidding the lots as subdivided to their respective lessees and *bona fide* occupants."

Terms of payment were rather easy for the occupants— ₱5 a square meter, no down payment, fifteen years to pay in 180 equal installments, and with an annual interest rate of only 4 per cent on all installments due and payable. The size of lots for each buyer was not specified in the law. The piece of land actually leased or occupied by the present tenant was to be the one actually sold to him, as is gleaned from the provision that "every lessee of any lot in said land or *bona fide* occupant of any parcel thereof will not be deprived of any part of the same, should he decide to buy it under this Act."

Actual occupany was respected by the law. In fact, it was provided that "all streets and alleys existing on the date of the approval of this Act within the Tondo Foreshore Lands shall not be changed either by the city Government of Manila or by the National Government, unless the public interests demand that they be changed." In the eventuality that the public interest demands the opening or widening of streets, people who are displaced are given preference in the award and sale of vacant lots.

The strength of the tenants federation may be seen in the fact that the area to be subdivided was extended from the old Dewey Boulevard extension line to 300 meters from the pier line. The sum of ₱ 400,000 was also appropriated for the survey and subdivision work, and, finally, the Land Tenure Administration was instructed to consult with the federation in the implementation of the act.

The one year given to the Director of Lands to effect the survey and subdivision of the Tondo Foreshore Land passed, however, and still nothing came out of the legislative directive. Three years elapsed, and more people settled in Barrio Magsaysay. In June 1959, House Bill No. 1630 was passed by the Fourth Congress, and, though it was not signed by the President, it was allowed to lapse into law, as Republic Act No. 2439. This law amended RA 1597 and provided not only that the land now subject to survey and subdivision was that part of the reclaimed land 300 meters from the pier line to the East but also that the line had been moved 100 meters from the pier line. This amendment enlarged the land to be subdivided from 130.5 hectares to 185.75 hectares and reduced greatly the amount of land available for port improvements and facilities.

During this time, however, there were already moves from the City Government of Manila to get some land away from the squatters and devote it to civic uses. On 22 September 1961, the squatters were rudely shocked by a Presidential Proclamation that reserved nine hectares of the Tondo Foreshore Land for the Bonifacio Memorial Stadium. Presidential Proclamation No. 788 withdrew from sale or settlement this parcel of land and reserved it, under the administration of the City of Manila, for the site of the stadium. The site was properly surveyed and planned for from 8 to 15 December 1960.

Realizing now that they had to act fast if their claims to the land would be realized, the officers of the tenants federation labored mightily for the passage of Republic Act No. 3794. When this was signed into law on 22 June 1963, the tenants federation officials were overjoyed because it appropriated an additional ₱ 300,000 for the implementation of RA 1597. The momentary setback of the squatters in Proclamation No. 788 was also remedied when President Diosdado Macapagal, in one of his twilight acts, issued Proclamation No. 515, on 26 December 1965, which revoked Proclamation No. 788 and declared the land formerly reserved for the Bonifacio Memorial Stadium "open to disposition to actual occupants and qualified landless persons . . . ."

At the time the project in Barrio Magsaysay started in March 1966, therefore, the people had all the legal rights over the land they had been squatting on. The original intentions of RA 1597 had all been restored—all 185.75 hectares of the Tondo Foreshore Land was open for disposition, ready to be surveyed, subdivided, and sold to lessees and *bona fide* occupants. Money had been appropriated for this job to be done. Mayor Villegas, in spite of his attempts to evict the squatters from Barrio Magsaysay and in spite of his triumph in evicting many others from Intramuros and other parts of Tondo, had failed in the former. The political strength of the squatters, arising from their unity and organization, had given them the legal right to stay where they were.

Finally, because of the triumph of the squatters within Barrio Magsaysay, many other squatters ejected from their former places flocked to it. At the time of the survey, there were some people within the barrio who had come from as far away as Sapang Palay, the relocation area some 37 kilometers outside Manila, where the squatters of Intramuros, North Harbor, and other places had been transferred when they were ejected in 1963 and 1964. The added numbers made more formidable the political strength of the tenants' federation. At the same time, internal political squabbles also resulted from the influx of new people into the area.

## Conclusion

Barrio Magsaysay is typical of slum areas that grew up in Manila immediately after the war. While it is of relatively recent vintage, the same physical and social characteristics found in other areas apply to it. The homes in Barrio Magsaysay are often of the *barong barong* type, built of flimsy materials, with little or no plans and with little attention to boundary lines and other niceties. The lack of roads and a physical plan for the area contributed to this lack of order. In sharp contrast to the physical disorganization is the social order that prevails among the people. The people in Barrio Magsaysay are organized according to neighborhood ties. They have their own associations, and the physical elements of the place, in fact, follow this social order. The headquarters of the community association is invariably the center of the community. The leadership of organization officers is recognized. People participate actively in community affairs, and there is a feeling of unity within communities.

To a great extent, the internal problems of the community and the external threat from the government may be responsible for the people's unity. It is remarkable, however, how this unity has been revealed in the "lobbying" activities of the Barrio Magsaysay dwellers. From the internal elements of the community, therefore, as revealed in the physical layout of the environment and the leadership network, and the external elements, as seen in the reaction to the legislative process and political activities, it can be concluded with little fear of contradiction that Barrio Magsaysay is indeed a functioning community.

# CHAPTER 4

# The People

Statistics on population has a way of dulling the human insights, but it is necessary for the setting up of objective programs. Early in the project, therefore, it was decided that a survey of the people of Barrio Magsaysay would be made. Prior to the survey, team members already met with some of the people casually. Often, such meetings were held with the community leaders and officers of the various organizations in the place. These early impressions, however, were deemed insufficient for program-planning purposes.

Initial surveys of Barrio Magsaysay were made by the Operations and Field Training Division of the PACD. From 7 to 12 January 1966, some eight researchers from this division and twenty-one social workers from the City of Manila interviewed people in the area, using a two-page questionnaire. A partial report on 513 family heads interviewed was soon released. Based on this initial work, a full survey was planned.

When finally concluded, the full survey covering 2,625 family heads was made by the combined teams from the PACD, Operation Brotherhood, City of Manila, and the College of Public Administration. For further analysis, the data from this survey were punched on IBM cards at the Bureau of the Census and Statistics. A set of cards was sent to the University of Hawaii for cross tabulations and for other analyses, and the final results became available about the middle of 1966. Initial findings through hand tabulations were used, however, for the planning of various programs during the course of the project.

## General Profile

Heads of families in Barrio Magsaysay tended to be young. Of the 2,625 people interviewed, about 68.2 per cent were below 42 years old. Of these young community members, 33.0 per cent were between ages 25 to 30. There were, in fact, seven family heads below 18 years old.

One surprising finding in the area (surprising because the poverty-stricken surroundings did not prepare one for it) was the fact that the income of the people was not too low. Thus, 43.6 per cent of the people earned from ₱ 100 to ₱ 149, while a full 3.9 per cent of the people interviewed earned more than ₱ 300 a month.

Closely related to the income of the people was the relatively good education that some of those interviewed had. Thus, only 4.0 per cent of those interviewed had no education at all. About 26.7 per cent reached primary school; 34.7 per cent reached intermediate school; 28.2 per cent got to high school; and 4.5 per cent had college education. A few people obtained vocational schooling.

The people in Barrio Magsaysay were predominantly Catholic (92.7 per cent). Other religions were also represented. Some 4.5 per cent of the respondents were members of the Iglesia ni Kristo, and 2.4 per cent were Protestants. The fiesta of the Barrio was widely celebrated, and religious activities, especially during Holy Week, were closely observed.

Most of the residents in Barrio Magsaysay have lived in the surrounding areas of Tondo before moving to the barrio. Some 66.7 per cent of those interviewed said they had lived in and around Tondo previously. About 14.8 per cent of the sample came directly from the provinces, while the rest came from other parts of Manila and the suburbs. The youth of the area was revealed in the fact that about 36.8 per cent of the population had been residing in the area for about four to six years; another 40.8 per cent had been there for less than a year, and only 6.4 per cent had been living in Barrio Magsaysay for more than six years. These old timers were mostly residents around the present fringes of Barrio Magsaysay, lands first to be reclaimed from the sea.

Family life was quite close for most people of Barrio Magsaysay. About 71.0 per cent of those interviewed lived in single-family homes, but about 16.6 per cent had two families living under the same roof. Some 4.6 per cent had three families living together and 6.9 per cent had more than three. Of the families, 84.0 per cent were nuclear, while 15.5 per cent had other members of the extended family living with them.

Like in other parts of the Philippines, sizes of families were quite large, averaging about six members. About 61.9 per cent of those interviewed had families of more than five members while 38.1 per cent had less than four members. The great extent of dependency may be seen in the fact that 70.6 per cent of all family members listed were below 18 years old. Of the dependent members (persons 18 and below), about 32 per cent were still below school age, while 11.9 per cent were already of school age but were out of school.

One noteworthy fact about the Barrio Magsaysay families was the extent to which other members also earned some money. An estimated 11.7 per cent of family members other than the main breadwinner had extra sources of income. Although many of these had incomes that were not fixed and steady, they still contributed to the family coffers.

All in all, life in Barrio Magsaysay seemed to belie the misery and poverty that one assumes upon seeing the place. A full 67 per cent of the families interviewed owned the houses they were living in. The 26.6 per cent who were renting paid only small amounts (70.3 per cent paid less than ₱ 15 a month), while some people did not even pay any rent at all. Most households had good lighting facilities; 65.1 per cent used electric lights. Some 42.8 per cent of those studied owned radios. The main things that people complained about were the lack of water, roads, and toilet facilities.

With conditions being what they were, a full 72.5 per cent of the people studied in Barrio Magsaysay were unwilling to move out of the place. Only 17.7 per cent were willing to move out, and many of these expected the government to

assist them in such an effort. In fact, many of those interviewed were willing to pay for the lands they were squatting
on. Some 63.7 per cent said they would be able to afford less
than ₱ 10 a month for payments, and 30 per cent said they
would be able to pay less than ₱ 20 a month.

Reasons for staying in the place and refusing to move out
were many, but 19.2 per cent said they had no other place to
go; 17.3 per cent, because it was near their place of work;
16.3 per cent, because the place was nice and peaceful; and
11.9 per cent, because it was cheap to live in Barrio Magsaysay. It was obvious from these answers that most of the people
in Barrio Magsaysay were happy where they were and unwilling to move to other places. Thus, an urban community development program was deemed necessary in the place.

## Age

As mentioned above, the population of Barrio Magsaysay
was relatively young. This could be gleaned from the information that the modal age of heads of families interviewed
was between 25–30. Only 31.73 per cent of the family heads
were 43 years old and above.

This finding was especially meaningful because the research
and action teams detailed to Barrio Magsaysay were composed
of relatively young people. Many of them were young college
graduates who had been working with their agencies for less
than five years. Easier rapport between the teams and the
family heads in the community was anticipated because of this
similarity in age structures.

Another significant finding in the survey was the high correlation found between youth and education. It was found
that a full 38.24 per cent of all family heads who were 24 years
old and below had gone through high school. The percentage
of secondary-school graduates declined as age increased, as
shown in Table 2. Conversely, the percentage of people with
no education increased with age. The relationship between
youth and education was held significant because having a
certain amount of education is necesary for the individual's

TABLE 2
AGE AND EDUCATION

| Age | Per Cent Finished High School | Per Cent with No Education |
|---|---|---|
| 24 and below | 38.24 | 1.47 |
| 25–26 | 33.93 | 1.50 |
| 37–48 | 24.69 | 4.11 |
| 49–60 | 18.83 | 10.88 |

involvement in community projects that form the main activity of urban community development.

Although educated young people were expected, by the urban community development teams, to be the main supporters of their activities, the research also revealed that leadership in the community was held by relatively older people. At least, in the perception of the researchers, the community was still quite traditional, and age was a requisite for leadership. Thus, this was revealed in the interviewers' evaluation of their interviewees. Asked to rate interviewees as "leader types" or "follower types," interviewers in the research survey ranked only 18.88 per cent of those below 24 as leader types, as against 19.17 per cent for those between 25–36; 19.39 per cent for those between 37–48; 20.54 per cent for those between 49–60 and 29.70 per cent for those 60 and above.

Here, then, were the potentials for conflict. Leadership qualities, as in most traditional communities, were associated with age (at least in the perception of interviewers). However, more of the younger people tended to be educated, which made them ideal participants in community projects. Urban community development workers, being young themselves, tended to find it easier to work with younger people. The age structure of the community, therefore, greatly affected the type of projects introduced by the CD workers, the ease or difficulty with which such projects were launched, and the success or failure achieved therein.

## Education

Using education as an independent variable, correlations using the chi square test found it significantly related to a host of other variables important in urban community development. Although the correlations do not necessarily reveal that causation exists, they are important enough in guiding interpretation of survey findings.

Table 3 shows the educational levels of Barrio Magsaysay family heads.

An important fact revealed by the survey is the close relationship between education, income, and the type of occupation of the family head. Thus, of people who have had no education at all, 96.1 per cent were earning less than ₱ 200 a month. The percentage of those earning less than ₱ 200 among primary-school individuals was 95.3; that for intermediate-school individuals was 90.7. On the other hand, 81.4 per cent of high-school persons were earning less than ₱ 200, and only 52.7 per cent of those who have reached college were earning this amount.

The income of a family head, of course, depends on the occupation he pursues. Again, education was found to be

TABLE 3

EDUCATIONAL LEVELS OF FAMILY HEADS

| Education | Number | Per Cent |
|---|---|---|
| No education at all | 118 | 4.5 |
| Caton * | 6 | .2 |
| Primary (grades 1 to 4) | 688 | 26.2 |
| Intermediate (grades 5 to 6) | 918 | 35.0 |
| High School | 730 | 27.8 |
| Vocational School | 14 | .5 |
| College | 122 | 4.7 |
| No response | 29 | 1.1 |
| Total | 2,625 | 100.0 |

* Spanish-style education where a person learns the alphabet and how to read and write.

closely related to the type of occupation. Many people in Barrio Magsaysay "engage in private business," which means that they are sidewalk vendors, itinerant peddlers, sellers of goods and sweets, and the like. Of the 398 persons who said they were engaged in this occupation, 139 had a fixed place of business (a small stall, a street corner, or a *sari-sari* store), while 259 were mobile. When these "private businessmen" were analyzed, it was found that those with little or no education predominated among them. Thus, 16.4 per cent of those without any education belonged to this group. The percentage for others was 15.2 per cent for elementary school, 11.5 per cent for high school, and 10.6 per cent for college.

This type of business, however, does not pay too well. Thus, 50.0 per cent of those engaged in it earn less than ₱ 100. Only 2.6 per cent of them were found to earn more than ₱ 400 a month.

The possibility of landing a white-collar job (becoming an *empleado*) is, of course, affected by education. Thus, only 1.8 per cent of those who have had no education at all regard themselves as employees. The other percentages are 2.6 for primary school, 11.4 for high school, and 31.7 for college. This is significant because it was found that 92.2 per cent of unskilled laborers earned less than ₱ 200 a month, while 70.5 per cent of employees and skilled laborers earned from ₱ 100 to ₱ 300 a month. Furthermore, unemployment is also influenced by lack of education. Thus, 22.7 per cent of those without any education were found to be unemployed; 9.5 per cent of elementary and high-school graduates were unemployed; and only 7.3 per cent of those who had been to college were unemployed.

Aside from affecting occupation and income, education also influenced the style of the life of Barrio Magsaysay residents. In such things as toilet habits, radio ownership, health practices, and maintenance of clean surroundings, those with relatively higher education tend to have different styles of living from those with lower education. If these are reflective of willingness to do something for their environment, then the more educated persons are assets in the pursuit of urban community development.

In Barrio Magsaysay, a total of 1,834 family heads interviewed admitted that they had no toilets at all. This made up about 70.2 per cent of the total population. When asked how they disposed of their wastes, 21.0 per cent of these family heads said they wrapped their wastes in newspaper and threw it either in the canal, the sea, vacant lots, or garbage heaps. About 8.2 per cent of those interviewed even admitted that they just squatted on the sea wall when the call of nature visited them.

Among people with no education at all, it was found that 43.0 per cent used the "wrap and throw" method, 22.1 per cent used the sea wall, 6.25 per cent have pit toilets, and only 1.2 per cent used flush or water-sealed toilets. The remaining 27.45 per cent of people with no education were rather vague about how they disposed of their waste—though it can be assumed that they also have no toilet facilities.

The percentage distribution for college graduates is relatively better as far as waste disposal is concerned, especially when the conditions in Barrio Magsaysay are considered. Thus, of the 122 heads of families who have reached college, 27.1 per cent used pit toilets; 11.5 used water-sealed or flush toilets; 29.2 per cent used the "wrap and throw" system; and 9.4 per cent used the sea wall. The remaining 22.8 per cent were vague about their means of waste disposal, but it can also be assumed that they have no toilet facilities.

The survey also revealed that residents who have had some education are more health conscious. They tend to go to private doctors rather than to government-run health centers when there is sickness in the family. Maybe, this is also related to their income. Because they can afford to pay the fees of private doctors, they do not go too frequently to government hospitals, clinics, and health centers.

This difference in health awareness may be reflected in the way families maintain cleanliness in their environments. To test this, interviewers were instructed to observe around the house while conducting their interviews and to rank the surroundings on a nine-point scale ranging from "neat environs" to "dirty environs." When the data from these rankings were

TABLE 4
RELATIONSHIP BETWEEN EDUCATION AND SANITATION

| Educational Level | Per Cent Rated with Clean Environment |
|---|---|
| No education at all | 12.1 |
| Primary education | 19.3 |
| Intermediate education | 19.5 |
| High-school education | 25.2 |
| College education | 34.5 |

correlated with education, a positive relationship between clean environs and educational attainment was shown.

The importance of an educated citizenry in the launching of urban community development projects is highlighted when we consider that the choice of leaders among slum dwellers is also influenced greatly by education. Thus, in the survey of leaders (Chapter 5), people with high-school education were seen as the leader types. The correlation between education and leadership choice was not complete, however. People with college education were not always ranked as good leaders—perhaps, because they tend to be overeducated for the type of followers they have.

All the factors analyzed above showed the importance of education in the life styles of squatters and slum dwellers. Since education is crucial in the choice of an occupation, income, leadership, and community position, it is easy to conclude that projects with an educational slant would most likely gain the support of squatters. In view of this, the earliest projects of the urban CD teams revolved around the opening of nursery and kindergarten classes, of adult education through lay leadership institutes, and of vocational education (tailoring, dressmaking, beauty culture, etc.). A project to start a regular primary school in the area was also pushed. In this way, the thirst for education of the people became the vehicle for the introduction of social-change projects.

## Income

Squatter and slum areas are poor. Life is so difficult there that we can anticipate the income of a person to influence such things as his ability to leave the area, his leadership role, the type of services and facilities he has, and other aspects of his everyday life. Thus, in spite of the difficulties of getting accurate income data, the survey of Barrio Magsaysay residents focused on this important factor. Table 5 shows how income is distributed among Barrio Magsaysay residents.

One of the hopes for solving the squatting and slum-dwelling problems is that, as people living in such areas earn more income, they would be able to move to better areas and vacate the slums they formerly lived in.[1] This hope, however, is complicated by several factors, some of which are: (1) the more income a slum dweller or squatter has, the greater is the likelihood that he would own his home and would, therefore, be

TABLE 5
INCOME OF BARRIO MAGSAYSAY RESIDENTS

| Monthly Income | Number | Per Cent |
|---|---|---|
| No regular income reported | 221 | 8.42 |
| Income variable, not definite | 163 | 6.21 |
| Less than ₱ 50 | 207 | 7.89 |
| ₱ 50–99 | 580 | 22.10 |
| 100–149 | 610 | 23.24 |
| 150–199 | 560 | 21.33 |
| 200–249 | 153 | 5.83 |
| 250–299 | 48 | 1.83 |
| 300–349 | 50 | 1.90 |
| 350–399 | 11 | .42 |
| 400–449 | 10 | .38 |
| 450–499 | 1 | .03 |
| 500 and above | 11 | .42 |
| Total | 2,625 | 100.00 |

unwilling to leave it; (2) the higher the income of a person, the better are his chances of paying amortization rates for the land he is squatting on, and, therefore, he would be unwilling to move out. These propositions, however, are relevant to people who are still within slum and squatter areas. As the income of a person reaches such a proportion that the advantages of slum and squatter living cease to be attractive, he may go to other more convenient places.

The income of a person, it was found by the survey, is greatly correlated with home ownership and renting. Of course, considering the materials and labor required for building a house in the slum and squatter areas, it can be anticipated that many people living there would own their homes. Still, a relatively higher income is needed for being able to afford a house. Table 6 shows a direct correlation between home ownership and income, while it also shows an inverse relationship between income and renting. These may imply that one of the strongest motivations for living in slums and squatter areas is the security of knowing that one has his own roof over his head. Renting a home, in the slums, is one of the indexes of poverty. Thus, many squatters are motivated to earn more to be able to set up their own homes, no matter how humble and poor these may be.

The relationship between home ownership and willingness to move out is revealed in the finding that a full 84.20 per cent of people who owned their homes were not willing to leave Barrio Magsaysay. Of those renting, 68.64 per cent said

TABLE 6

RELATIONSHIP BETWEEN INCOME, HOME OWNERSHIP, AND HOME-RENTING

| Income Level | Per Cent Owning Homes | Per Cent Renting Homes |
|---|---|---|
| Less than ₱ 100 | 60.41 | 31.42 |
| ₱ 100–200 | 66.98 | 27.33 |
| ₱ 200–300 | 71.59 | 16.59 |
| Over 300 | 76.07 | 14.08 |

they would be willing to leave the place. Furthermore, all those interviewed who had enough income to say they would be willing to pay any amortization rates set by the government were not willing to move out. Of those who said they had no money to pay for amortization, 19 per cent were willing to move out.

If higher income tends to make people less inclined to leave Barrio Magsaysay, it, however, gives them a better chance of being good cooperators in community improvement projects. We have just seen how income is related to education and how higher education tends to make people more receptive to cooperative community efforts. Like those with higher education, those with higher income tend to lead a style of life different from those with low income.

The survey showed that people with higher income tend to own their homes. As such, they have a bigger stake in the improvement of the community. They also tend to be leaders in organizations: while only 2.6 per cent of family heads with incomes less than ₱ 100 a month were officers of community organizations, 69.1 per cent of those with incomes above ₱ 300 were officers. Even the rankings of interviewers regarding whether respondents are the leader or the follower type are related to income. Of people earning less than ₱ 100 a month, only 14.8 per cent were rated as leader types by interviewers. Of those with incomes above ₱ 300 a month, however, 32.8 were rated as follower types, compared to only 20.9 per cent for those earning above ₱ 300 a month. People with higher income tend to have wider interests and have more access to the mass media. While only 27.4 per cent of people with income less than ₱ 50 own radios, 75.9 per cent of those with income of more than ₱ 300 own radios. Because of this and other factors, many high-income people were rated as "interested" in community affairs by interviewers, while relatively more low-income people were rated as apathetic. While 56.14 per cent of those earning below ₱ 100 a month were classified as interested, 67.65 per cent of those earning ₱ 300 and above were classified as interested.

With higher income, of course, people are able to pay for the basic things in life. Thus, 25.35 per cent of those with income above ₱ 300 a month have pipe water connections, while only 8.82 per cent of those earning less than ₱ 100 have this. A total of 72.76 per cent of the latter people have to buy their water from peddlers, while 52.11 per cent of the former have to do the same. The use of electric lighting is also related to income—only 61.1 per cent of those earning less than ₱ 100 use electric lighting, while 86.0 per cent of those earning above ₱ 300 use electric lighting facilities. For cooking, the use of wood and charcoal for fuel is related to low income. About 54.74 per cent of those with income less than ₱ 100 use this type of fuel for cooking, while only 25.26 of those with income above ₱ 300 use it. Those with higher income tend to use kerosene (75.36 per cent of those with high income use it as against 42.56 per cent of those with low income). Electric cooking facilities are used by 10 per cent of those with high income, while only .5 per cent of those with low income use them.

As previously stated, those with higher income tend to go to private doctors for their medical needs, while those with lower income tend to patronize public health centers. The breakdown is as follows: only 16.4 per cent of those with incomes less than ₱ 100 go to doctors and hospitals for their health needs, while 25.7 per cent of those with income between ₱ 100 to ₱ 200 do so; 28.4 per cent of those earning between ₱ 200 and ₱ 300 and 37.5 per cent of those earning more than ₱ 300 go to hospitals and private doctors. The capacity to pay, of course, is a big factor in the choice of medical services, although prestige and community status values cannot be ignored.

A most interesting finding is the correlation between the perception of the community's problems and income. For those with higher income, roads improvement, food, and employment were seen as main problems, while those with lower income see water and toilet facilities as main problems. These findings seem to indicate that, for people with low income, the most basic necessities of life (drinking water and waste disposal) were perceived as the most important community problems, while, for those who could already afford these, roads and income were seen as problems. As people tend to have a higher income, they are motivated to earn more—and thus see employment as the problem. Those who are pressed by poverty have not even seen their incapacity to earn more as a problem; they have not, therefore, started their emancipation from a poor life.

## Length of Stay in Barrio Magsaysay

Barrio Magsaysay is a relatively young community. Reclaimed no more than seven years ago, it has only recently begun to be occupied by people. From the survey, it was found that the modal length of stay was from one to three years, which means that real migration to the community peaked around 1963, when the anti-squatting campaign in the City of Manila was also higher.

The first people who moved into Barrio Magsaysay considered themselves the pioneers in the place. In the interviews, they talked of clearing the tall *talahib* grass and of battling snakes and goons, during the early days of settlement. It was mainly for self-protection that they set up community organizations—protection both from outside and from more unruly members within the community. It was not strange, therefore, that many of those who had stayed long in the community were also the main backbone of the organizations.

A direct relationship was found between length of stay and membership in an organization. Among people who had

TABLE 7
LENGTH OF STAY IN BARRIO MAGSAYSAY

| Length of Stay | Number | Per Cent |
|---|---|---|
| Less than one year | 430 | 16.4 |
| One to three years | 982 | 37.4 |
| Four to six years | 1,035 | 39.4 |
| More than six years | 172 | 6.6 |
| No response | 6 | .2 |
| Total | 2,625 | 100.0 |

been in the area less than a year, only 41.09 per cent were members in any organization. The percentage increases as the length of stay increases: 70.40 per cent for those with a tenure of 1–3 years; 84.27 per cent for those living in the area for 4–6 years; and 85.83 per cent for those who have lived in Barrio Magsaysay for more than 6 years. Needless to say, people who are not members of any organization tend to be those who are recent arrivals.

The stake of family heads in the community's future is also related to length of stay because people tend to develop roots in a community with the passing of years. People also tend to own their homes as they stay longer in Barrio Magsaysay. While only 37.62 per cent of those who have lived in the area for less than a year own their homes, 84.09 per cent of those who have been there for more than six years own their homes. Since we have also found that 84.2 per cent of those who own their homes are not willing to leave the cummunity, the roots developing with years of stay is amply proven.

In some ways, having lived in the area a longer time seemed to have improved the living conditions of the people. Thus, the percentage of people with pipe connections for drinking water was found higher for those who have lived in the community longer. While only 11.15 per cent of those who have been in the area for less than a year have pipe connections, 15.42 per cent of those who have been there for more than six years have pipe connections.

As people stay longer in a community, they tend to become more involved and more interested in community affairs. They also tend to be more cooperative in the pursuit of community projects, a function, most probably of their familiarity with other members of the community. Thus, in the rankings made by interviewers, 66.10 per cent of those who have been in the community for more than six years were rated as interested, while only 52.77 per cent of those who have been in the community for less than a year were rated as such. The percentage of people ranked as cooperative also increased with length of stay. The corresponding percentages were 73.76 for those who have been there less than a year; 80.18 for those residents from 1–3 years; 80.15 per cent for residents from 4–6 years; and 87.14 per cent for those who have lived in Barrio Magsaysay for more than 6 years.

One very important finding was an incomplete correlation between being selected as a leader type and length of stay in the community. Although the relationship was positive, there was a point where it diminished. The survey found that 16.11 per cent of those who have stayed in Barrio Magsaysay for less than a year were chosen as leader types; 17.31 per cent of those residing there from 1–3 years were chosen; 23.75 per cent of those living there from 4–6 years were also chosen; but only 20.9 per cent of those who have lived in the area for more than 6 years were chosen as leader types. This finding seems to suggest that, although length of stay in the community was related to leadership, some other factors are also at play that influence the relationship.

One possible reason why some people living in the area for more than six years tended to be passed up as leader types may be the mobility from the squatter and slum area of people who have better means and better leadership qualities. Possibly, the more aggressive people tend to leave the slum area after a while, leaving behind those who are not as able to fend for themselves. Hence, there may be found less of the leader types among those left behind. Although the youth of Barrio Magsaysay community as a whole may make it a poor area for testing this hypothesis, the correlation between length of stay and leadership abilities suggests this.

## Conclusion

From the various factors studied and analyzed in the survey, the four variables of age, education, income, and length of stay were found to be the key factors that correlated with life in a squatter and slum community. Urban Community Development workers, therefore, would do well to keep these factors in mind for they greatly influence the success or failure of projects that they will introduce.

We found that, although family heads in Barrio Magsaysay tended to be young as a whole, there was a relationship between age and traditional leadership. Thus, while established leaders may tend to be the older people, potential and future leaders would most likely come from the younger people.

The fact that Urban CD workers would most likely be drawn from younger people gives the age structure of slum communities great importance. Initially, as in Barrio Magsaysay, entry may be made rather difficult by the age difference between established leaders and the CD workers. As younger, more educated, and higher-income people become involved in community development projects, however, the age structure would tend to work positively.

The survey also revealed that there is a close correlation between education, income, and length of stay. In other words, the elite of a community of squatters and slum dwellers may tend to be composed of people who have relatively higher education and income and who have stayed longer in the community. The close link between these three factors and such dependent variables as health habits, home ownership, interest in community affairs, cooperation, and other factors related to community improvement was shown in this section. As such, knowing these links is of utmost importance in the planning of projects and programs to be introduced by the Urban CD worker.

CHAPTER 5

# Community Leadership

An advice commonly given to a Community Development worker entering an area for the first time is "work through the leaders." Usually, this means the "formal" leaders, such as officers of organizations, heads of institutions, or political leaders. As the CD worker stays longer in the area, he is advised to work with the "informal" leaders as well, the influentials, "functional," or "natural" leaders. With these two groups on his side, he is told, the CD worker cannot fail.

This advice, simple as it is, assumes several things. First, that there is an easy way of finding out who the formal and informal leaders are. Second, it is assumed that these leaders have common goals, or, if they don't, it will be possible to find common areas of activities where they would be, at least, able to work with each other. Finally, it is assumed that the prestige, status, and standing of the leaders will be enhanced by their cooperating with the CD workers. All these assumptions presuppose prior knowledge about the leadership structure in the community and the functional areas in which leadership is divided.

## The Survey

Before fielding the CD workers into Barrio Magsaysay, a complete survey of households in the community was first conducted. This survey revealed the existence of about twenty community organizations in the area. Defined as formal leaders of the community were the officers of these organizations, which numbered 219. For economy and other reasons, only 80 of these officers were actually interviewed for this survey.

Interviewing of the leaders chosen for the survey was done from 7 to 8 March 1966, or barely a week after the formal inauguration of the pilot project. It was done by the personnel of the PACD and the Department of Social Welfare of the City

TABLE 8
DISTRIBUTION OF SAMPLE OFFICERS
AMONG ORGANIZATIONS

| Organization | Number |
|---|---|
| Incorporated associations | |
| Kapisanan ng Taga-Baybay Dagat, Inc. | 8 |
| Sangguniang Nayon, Inc. | 7 |
| Kapisanang Tanglaw ng Mahihirap, Inc. | 6 |
| Samahan ng mga Taga-Dalampasigan, Inc. | 3 |
| Kapisanang Damayan ng Nayon, Inc. | 3 |
| Barrio Magsaysay Neighborhood Assn., Inc. | 2 |
| Other adult associations | |
| Barrio Magsaysay Tenants' Association | 4 |
| Kapisanang Lakas na Pinag-isa | 4 |
| Samahang Busilak | 4 |
| Women's associations | |
| Pagkakaisa ng Kababaihan sa Dalampasigan | 7 |
| Women's Club of Barrio Magsaysay | 4 |
| Kapisanang Tanglaw ng Kababaihan | 5 |
| Samahan ng Kababaihan ng Baybay Dagat | 4 |
| Youth associations | |
| Magsaysay Village Club (Mag-ville) | 4 |
| Ramon Magsaysay Youth Club | 4 |
| D'Youngsters' Club | 4 |
| Blue Star Youth Club | 3 |
| Tanikala ng Pagkakaisa | 2 |
| Seaside Youth Club | 1 |
| Brotherhood Association | 1 |
| Total | 80 |

of Manila. The interview guide used went into the social backgrounds of the leaders, the objectives and functions of the organizations, organizational activities, formal organizational procedures, and perceived problems in the area.

Of the 80 formal leaders actually interviewed, 19 were presidents; 8 vice presidents; 10 secretaries; 1 assistant secretary; 6 treasurers; 2 assistant treasurers; 9 auditors; 4 business managers; 5 sergeants-at-arms; 1 councilor; 9 board members; 1 general collector; and 5 public relations officers. It must be noticed that many of those interviewed belonged to the top leaders of the organizations.

## The Organizations

One of the common clichés about slum life that has its roots in urban studies conducted in Western cities is that slum people are disorganized, alienated, rootless, and suffering from *anomie*. In Barrio Magsaysay, the Urban CD Team found exactly the opposite—a community of about 2,625 families tightly knit together through more than twenty organizations set up to achieve various purposes.

Probe questions in the survey and casual conversations with local leaders revealed that the primary objective in setting up and joining organizations was protection and safety. Some of the older leaders remembered that when the community was first starting, it was not considered prudent to be alone. The locality had the widespread reputation for trouble. Many criminal elements found it convenient to hide in the area. Not far from the community, in fact, is the place known as *Pulong Diablo* ("Devil's Island"), and it lives up to its name.

The first organizations in Barrio Magsaysay were community protection systems known as *rondas*. They had the twin function of maintaining peace and order and acting as fire brigade. The *rondas* have been maintained. While many of the leaders interviewed were grateful for the protection they gave, there were some grumblings, also, about the monetary dues that the *rondas* demanded, especially from families with no able-bodied men to perform *ronda* service.

Barrio Magsaysay is divided into six distinct geographical

communities, with each community having an association, formally incorporated and registered with the Securities and Exchange Commission. With the growth of the communities has come a new type of threat—eviction from the place by the city authorities. The formal incorporation of the associations was considered a necessary step in the legal battles that the people waged to legalize their tenure.

Traditionally, each community had its own "territorial limits." This was especially true with the youth associations, whose members often engaged in open conflict. Even the older leaders freely admitted that there was a time when a member of one community could not enter another place for his own safety. One leader said:

> Noong araw, hindi kami nakakapasyal diyan, lalo na kung ang isa sa aming mga bata ay may naka-away sa kanila. Kani-kaniya noon. Pag may nakagawa ng kasalanan sa bata nila sa aming lugar, kahit mali pinaninindigan nila.*

There was prevalent sectionalism. Community brawls and riots were frequent. As a result, many criminal elements and escaped convicts found their place in the community, with the tacit blessings of the associations. Things were so bad that, according to some informants, the police did not dare enter the community and left the people to settle their own troubles.

It was a bigger threat from the outside that finally forced the warring communities in Barrio Magsaysay to unite. City authorities, from the very start, had wanted to evict the squatters. In late 1963, for example, Mayor Antonio J. Villegas of Manila started mass eviction of squatters from the city, relying on the powers granted to him by the city charter to "abate nuisances." Although the land occupied by the squatters of Barrio Magsaysay is owned by the national government, the mayor still had jurisdiction over it because it was within the city limits. As the pressures from city hall grew, the six major organizations in Barrio Magsaysay decided to band to-

---

* In those days, we could not even pass there, especially when one of our boys had a fight with one of theirs. Each one kept to his own. If one of their boys created trouble in our place, even if he was in the wrong, they stood by him.

gether into a federation to enable them to fight eviction effectively. Together, they solicited the help of a certain congressman and other local politicians. Up to the present, this united strategy has paid off because the mayor has failed to evict the Barrio Magsaysay squatters, although he has been successful with many squatters in the city.

As seen in Chapter 3, the lobbyist activities of the leaders and people of Barrio Magsaysay reveal their unity in the face of the outside world. Because of the insecurity involved in squatting on government land, the people have been forced to set up and join existing associations. What started out as associations meant to protect the people and communities against each other were transformed into larger associations to protect Barrio Magsaysay against an outside threat.

Interviews with many leaders, however, showed that in lobbying they did not see themselves fighting against something but rather as maintaining unity to achieve something. They want the land. By their long stay on the land, they feel that they have already earned the right to own it. The many legislative and presidentials acts abetting their claims have made their determination stronger. This more positive viewpoint is doubtless a strong factor in the unity of Barrio Magsaysay squatters and their belief in their leaders.

## Goals and Activities

The goals of the squatter associations, as perceived by the leaders themselves, were primarily aimed at internal community life rather than the outside world. In fact, when the leaders were asked to freely respond to the question "What are the main goals or purposes of your organization?" a negligible 2.2 per cent of the responses were tabulated under "To acquire land for immediate subdivision." The primary concern of the organization was peace and order, as revealed in Table 9.

The perceived goals of the associations greatly influenced the type of leaders who would succeed in a community like Barrio Magsaysay. The need to maintain peace and order demands strength and courage from would-be leaders. Leaders

TABLE 9

GOALS OR PURPOSES OF ORGANIZATIONS

| Goals or Purposes | Number of Responses * |
|---|---|
| Maintenance of peace and order (prevent crime and juvenile delinquency) | 46 |
| Community improvement, beautification, construction | 37 |
| Mutual aid, cooperation, assistance during deaths | 22 |
| Health and sanitation, medical service, health center | 15 |
| Education and recreation, schools and playgrounds | 6 |
| Religious and social, chapel, the fiesta | 6 |
| Land acquisition for immediate subdivision | 3 |
| Don't know | 3 |
| Total | 138 |

* Free responses, more than one answer allowed.

have to be tough and must be able to fight when necessary. As one leader puts it:

*Kailangang paluin mo na ang isang kriminal kung ayaw na niyang tumanggap ng katuwiran.**

In assessing the leadership qualities of another leader, a critical respondent said:

*Mahina iyang si Juan, hindi niya kayang suwetohin ang kanyang mga batang malilikot.†*

The potentialities for violence in Barrio Magsaysay arise from many reasons. Being close to the piers and the city slaughterhouse, the place is the home of many persons who take pride in being brave and courageous. Because the police rarely enter the place (the roads are not wide or firm enough for police cars; foot patrols consider the place too dangerous), criminal elements gravitate toward the Barrio. The presence of gangs in the area is one frequent source of riots. Mention

---

* You have to beat up a criminal when he doesn't listen to reason anymore.

† Juan is weak, he cannot control his naughty boys.

has been made of the territorial limits and claims of the gangs—trespass on alien territories brings about instant retaliation. Finally, the leaders of Barrio Magsaysay are involved in political and personal intrigues, which often result in violent struggles for power.

The second most important preoccupation of associations in Barrio Magsaysay is the improvement of the community. As an area considered "unoccupied" by city authorities because of the indeterminate character of the people's tenure and because of the fact that the land belongs to the national government, city services are available in the area only through informal arrangements. Technically, the city government cannot build roads or extend city services to Barrio Magsaysay until the land question is settled. No permits for the construction of school houses, health centers, and even plank bridges can be issued until the tenure of the people is clarified. Because of these technical difficulties, the people have had to provide for the services they need. Thus, the person who could pull strings to make water and electricity available in the place naturally becomes the leader. One who could organize and mobilize people for community improvement projects also becomes a leader.

For all its urbanizing character, Barrio Magsaysay still retains many traditional characteristics that typify life in the rural communities of the Philippines. Thus, there are associations for mutual aid, cooperation, neighborliness, and reciprocal assistance during times of trouble such as deaths in the family, illness, acute poverty, and the like. Leaders chosen to head organizations set up for this purpose are usually members of the local elite who are relatively more educated, older, and more respectable. They maintain community harmony through paternalistic styles rather than through the use of violence. Most of the time, they are also traditional political leaders providing the broker role between politicians and the people. By interceding between the people and the politicians, services get distributed through them, and they maintain their leadership positions this way.

To find out the actual roles of organizations in Barrio Magsaysay, leaders were asked what types of activities their

organizations had engaged in. As shown in Table 10, the most
frequently mentioned activity was community improvement
through the construction, maintenance, and setting up of
needed services. Activities mentioned under this category included construction of the Barrio chapel and hall, setting up
of a basketball court, construction of the association headquarters, building of plank bridges and catwalks, and the in-
stallation of electrical and water facilities.

The second most frequently mentioned activity that people
engaged in relates to the community's social life. Thus, the
organizations help with the community fiesta; sponsor dances,
excursions, and athletics; and engage in traditional social
observances such as the *pabasa* * during the Holy Week. In
most instances, these activities are not ends in themselves.
They are introduced to raise funds for the organizations or to
honor visiting politicians and officials who may help the
people.

Because of the peculiar conditions in the place (lack of
water, no drainage, distance from hospital), people are pre-
occupied with health and sanitation activities. Some of these
activities include cleanliness campaigns, filling up of low
places, distribution of free medicine, garbage-collection cam-

TABLE 10
ACTIVITIES OF ORGANIZATIONS

| Activities | Number of Responses |
|---|---|
| Community improvement projects | 64 |
| Social activities and benefits | 38 |
| Health and sanitation projects | 34 |
| Maintain peace and order | 21 |
| Mutual aid and assistance | 17 |
| Total | 174 |

* Literally, the reading, but actually the singing of the story of the life
and death of Jesus Christ. This is a community affair, often held in a
makeshift chapel, with loudspeakers used to broadcast the singing and
food (usually coffee and biscuits) served to those who sing or kibitz at
the chapel.

paigns, arrangements for home-nursing classes, and the temporary construction of a health center. This great interest of the people in health and sanitation made it easier for the action teams to enter the place because they were preceded by doctors and nurses who answered this need of the people. (See Chapter 6.)

It is interesting that, although many leaders perceived their organizational goals to be involving mainly the maintaining of peace and order, activities in this category came in only fourth. Those mentioned by the leaders frequently were maintaining the *ronda* system, fire brigade, pacification of warring groups, minimizing juvenile delinquency, and keeping people peaceful generally. The main reason why peace and order activities came in only fourth may be the fact that, although activities in this area are infrequent, they have much weight and meaning to the community.

Mutual aid and assistance was also a frequent activity of formal organizations in Barrio Magsaysay. Some of the activities often mentioned included collection of money when a member of the community dies, asking for assistance from government agencies during calamities, and, generally, coming to each other's aid.

All in all, the picture given by the formal organizations in Barrio Magsaysay revealed that the communities in the place were functioning smoothly through the mutual cooperation and protective activities of the people. Although public services were lacking and could not be extended by the authorities, the people had banded together to make these available to themselves through organized efforts.

The problems faced by the people came from external and internal sources. From the outside was the threat of eviction, which resulted in the setting up of formal associations that even went as far as incorporating under the laws of the country. This problem was also met externally by appealing to politicians, who championed the cause of Barrio Magsaysay residents in dealing with the President, Congress, and City Hall.

Internal problems provided the main preoccupation of many organizational activities. The factionalism and territorial viewpoint of the people made it necessary for organizations and strong leaders to intervene in community affairs. Peace and order became the main goal of many organizations. Another internal problem arose from the failure of the outside authorities to provide services and amenities of urban life to the people of the area. Thus, organized effort was required to arrange for these services and amenities, even though such efforts often resulted in informal arrangements, and, sometimes, corrupt practices.

One final proof that Barrio Magsaysay was a well functioning set of communities was the existence of mutual aid and assistance patterns that are survivals from the rural life of most of the residents. Deaths, religious festivals, and other important occasions elicited cooperation and mutual aid. In this sense, the communities in Magsaysay do not show the disintegration and disorganization generally associated with squatter and slum areas in the city.

## The Leaders

Providing leadership to the twenty or so organizations found in Barrio Magsaysay at the time of the survey were 219 formally selected leaders typified by the 80 surveyed for this study. These 80 leaders were generally young, 32 being the modal age. Fifty or 62.5 per cent of them were males, and 30 were females. The modal income ranged from ₱ 150 to ₱ 199 a month; education was at high-school level. More than half of the leaders had lived in Barrio Magsaysay from four to six years.

Statistics, however, has the disadvantage of blurring the image of the men who make up the Barrio Magsaysay leadership. A "leader's profile" assembled from modal characteristics may provide a clearer picture.

The typical leader of Barrio Magsaysay is a male, 30 to 35 years of age, who has lived in the place from four to six years. He is a "white collar" person who is regularly employed and earns an income that fluctuates between ₱ 150 to ₱ 199 a month. His education is relatively higher than most members of the community because he has graduated from high school.

He was elected by secret ballot to his position of leadership, primarily through his ability to make people follow him by the show of his courage, strength, and persuasive abilities. He is a Roman Catholic, a migrant from the rural areas, and a father of six. He runs his organization tightly, consulting frequently with his fellow leaders and the politicians that support him. He dispenses favors freely, accompanies residents of the place when they want to seek favors from politicians, and shows people around when they visit the area. He is generally recognized as the leader and is regarded with a mixed feeling of respect, cynicism, and fear.

The average Barrio Magsaysay leader is set off from the rest of the community by four main factors: education, income, occupation, and length of stay in the place. The survey of leaders and statistical analysis of the larger survey revealed these important characteristics of the leaders.

*Education.* As mentioned above, the modal Barrio Magsaysay leader finished high school. When a chi square test was made, correlating leadership position in an organization with education, a positive correlation was found. Thus, in the analysis of data from the larger survey, it was found that the percentage of officers holding positions in organizations increased with the level of education of the respondents.

The larger survey revealed that there were no officers in community organizations among family heads who have had no education at all. There were only 2.4 per cent among those who have finished primary grades; 3.1 per cent among intermediate graduates; 6.2 per cent among high-school graduates; 6.7 per cent among vocational-school graduates; and 14.6 per cent among those who have finished college. Thus, although only 4.5 per cent of all Barrio Magsaysay family heads had finished college, almost 15 per cent of these were assuming leadership positions.

To serve as a check on the survey of leaders and the larger survey of 2,625 family heads, all interviewers in the Barrio Magsaysay study were asked to rate their interviewees as to whether they were "leader" or "follower" types. Although this was a subjective way of gauging leadership abilities, it was believed important as a check on the purely statistical data.

The ratings of the interviewers substantiated the hypothesis that education was correlated with leadership, although it also hinted at certain qualifications. About 83.4 per cent of all family heads who have finished high school were rated by the interviewers as leader types. However, only 2.97 per cent of college graduates were so rated. These findings hint at the fact that high education alone was not a very good determinant of one's leadership abilities. The nature of the Barrio Magsaysay population (a full 89.6 per cent of all family heads had obtained high-school education or less, and 4 per cent have had no education at all) seemed to exercise a "democratizing effect" on the quality of leaders considered acceptable, at least in the perception of the interviewer-raters.

*Income.*    The modal income of leaders in Barrio Magsaysay was in the range ₱ 150 to ₱ 199, which is slightly higher than the modal income of all family heads in general which ranged from ₱ 100 to ₱ 149.

When cross tabulating income with leadership position, this tendency of leaders to have higher income was shown. Thus, only 2.6 per cent of family heads receiving income less than ₱ 100 held positions in organizations. A slight 2.77 per cent of those receiving income from ₱ 100 to ₱ 200 were officers. On the other hand, 7.74 per cent of family heads receiving from ₱ 200 to ₱ 300 were officers, while 69.1 per cent of people with income above ₱ 300 were officers of organizations.

These figures hint that leadership in Barrio Magsaysay carries with it certain economic responsibilities. Because of the poverty in the place, people tend to choose their leaders from those with means. In this way, leadership falls on the shoulders of those who can afford to carry it.

*Occupation.*    The sources of income of the eighty leaders surveyed for this study are revealed in Table 11.

As readily shown in Table 11, employees in private or government firms, clerks, and other "white collar" workers predominated among the leaders. Skilled persons and self-employed persons, however, were also greatly represented.

The larger study confirmed the predominance of employees among the leader groups. Thus, about 30 per cent of all employees were holders of positions in the organizations, as com-

TABLE 11
OCCUPATION OF LEADERS

| Occupation | Number | Per Cent |
|---|---|---|
| Employees in private or public firms; clerks, retired employees, etc. | 20 | 25.0 |
| Skilled persons such as mechanics, radio technicians, tailors, etc. | 15 | 18.8 |
| Unskilled persons such as laborers, housekeepers, fishermen, etc. | 14 | 17.5 |
| Self-employed persons such as *sari-sari* store owners, vendors, etc. | 13 | 16.2 |
| Students | 5 | 6.3 |
| No fixed occupation | 13 | 16.2 |
| Total | 80 | 100.0 |

pared to 8.7 per cent among unskilled workers, 4.3 per cent among skilled workers, and 4.3 per cent among people who are self-employed. Since the statistical analysis revealed a very close association among education, income, and occupation and since the two former variables have been found associated with leadership, the correlation of occupation with leadership is not at all surprising.

*Length of stay.* The modal length of stay of the typical Barrio Magsaysay leader was from four to six years. Normally, a person must have stayed long enough in the place to be known by the others before he can ascend to a leadership position.

Among all heads of families surveyed in Barrio Magsaysay, however, 59.6 per cent have been in the area for three years or less. Thus, people who came into the area early seem to have taken the leadership positions.

One clue to the requirement of length of stay for leadership may be seen in the rankings made by the interviewers in this study in their rating of leader and follower types. Their rankings showed that among interviewees who have resided in Barrio Magsaysay from 4–6 years, 23.7 per cent were rated as leader types. The corresponding ranking for others were:

16.1 per cent of those who have stayed in the place less than
1 year; 17.3 per cent of those who have stayed 1-3 years; and
20.1 per cent for those who have stayed more than 6 years.
These correlation show that the bulk of leaders were taken
from those who have stayed longer in the community, especially those in the 4–6 years bracket.

## Uses of the Data

The analyses done in the previous pages took a great deal
of time to crystallize because of many reasons. The survey of
eighty leaders, while done during the second week after operations in Barrio Magsaysay formally started, was only tabulated
much later and the results were not known to the action teams
except in informal discussions and team conferences. The results of the larger survey of 2,625 heads of families were made
available to the action teams in mimeographed form. However, only the frequency distributions and percentages were
done. Certain "highlights" of the survey findings were given,
though no clear guidelines were provided on how the findings
were to be of use in field operations. The statistical analysis
came much later, after the data were punched on IBM cards,
sent to the East-West Center at the University of Hawaii for
tabulation and printing of cross tabulations, and then analyzed
through standard chi square tests. Because of these long and
time-consuming processes, the analytical information came too
late for actual guidance of field work.

Even with incomplete information, however, some knowledge about the leaders gained by the action teams from the
research team and from their own field experiences guided
the programs introduced in Barrio Magsaysay. The ways in
which action was influenced by such knowledge may be seen
in the following patterns.

*Entry through established leaders.* From the very start, the
research and action teams in Barrio Magsaysay worked
through the established or formal leaders. According to the
team members, this was a normal procedure for CD workers
when entering a rural area, and they did not see anything
wrong in using the same approach.

By and large, the names of the leaders were obtained from the survey results of the research team and through interviews and conversations with residents. The leaders' assistance was sought for two main reasons: the place was not considered safe by the CD workers, and the people were very suspicious about the presence of the workers in the area.

When the purpose of the project was explained to the community leaders, they readily agreed to cooperate. The action team members saw this as not entirely voluntary—the leaders might have thought that the CD workers would be able to help them get the land from the government and, perhaps, strengthen their leadership positions in the place. This belief was further buttressed by the visit of Secretary Ernesto Maceda to Barrio Magsaysay and his promise that everything would be done to help the residents.

From the start, the "work through the leaders" strategy was considered successful. During the evaluation conference at the end of the project, the teams listed the following as benefits arising from the technique:

1. The workers can walk around the area freely after having been introduced to the leaders and the people.
2. They are greeted by the people wherever they go.
3. They are invited to snacks and lunches by the leaders of the place.
4. They are able to get commitment of most of the leaders of the place.

The above factors were considered as the gauge of the extent to which the team workers were accepted in the community. Acceptance was the first step in the introduction of programs of change.

As admitted by the CD workers themselves, however, working through established leaders also had its pitfalls. For example, when the research teams first entered the area, they asked around for the known leader in the community and were introduced to Mr. Alvaro * by one of the interviewees. Mr. Alvaro was initially suspicious, but, as the researchers explained their purpose, he very willingly escorted them

* Names disguised for obvious reasons.

around and introduced them to other people in the community. He also showed the researchers a list of his alleged members and several documents pertinent to the land question in Barrio Magsaysay. Happy with this relationship, the research teams always sought Mr. Alvaro out for advice and were very happy when he volunteered to help them with what they were doing.

After about two weeks of this fruitful relationship, one of the research teams accidentally interviewed a family head who was curious about the team's connections with Mr. Alvaro. Upon being informed that they were working through Mr. Alvaro because he was the leader in the place, the interviewee quickly told the researcher that Mr. Alvaro was already *laos,* a has-been, that he was not the real leader in the place anymore. He pointed to Mr. Beltran as the real leader, duly elected by the people of the community as president of their association.

When this information was relayed to other researchers, it was considered advisable to interview people not recommended by Mr. Alvaro. As more and more persons in the community were interviewed, it became apparent that the chance interviewee was correct. Mr. Alvaro was a former president of the association, but he had been defeated in a previous election. The teams now faced a dilemma—how to shift their attention and work through the real leader of the community without openly antagonizing Mr. Alvaro.

Things became very difficult when the action team members started operating in the place. With the advice of the research teams, they approached and got the cooperation of Mr. Beltran. Being new workers, they were not tied to the original working relationships that had been established with Mr. Alvaro. When Mr. Alvaro heard about this new relationship, however, he became angry. He demanded that all persons entering the place should clear their visits through him. He claimed that the research team had promised him this—that he would be consulted regarding any development in the place. When the action teams reasoned that they did not know of the agreement, Mr. Alvaro became very uncooperative and even threatened the team with reprisals. These threats brought about a minor crisis in the team's operations. Finally, the difficulties were relayed to Mr. Beltran, who became quite angry. It was decided that the teams would lie low for a while and wait until the leaders resolve the conflict. Much later, the team received word from Mr. Beltran that everything was all right. Still, it took them a long time to go back to the area known to be dominated by Mr. Alvaro.

In another instance, the research team that entered one area of Barrio Magsaysay easily located the house of the leader. As was customary, they were invited and asked to partake of some snacks. Repeated visits were made, and each time, the CD workers were asked to eat, drink, or even have lunch or dinner at the leader's house. The CD workers felt rather uneasy about the relationship, but they had no choice because they had to work through the leader.

In their interviewing, however, the CD workers soon learned that everything was not sweet hospitality on the part of the leader. People they interviewed revealed that the leader had taken to collecting ₱2 a household, giving the reason that he had to entertain and feed the CD workers, who always dropped in at his place. He allegedly said that the workers were government people who were working for the early release of the lots to the people in Barrio Magsaysay and that it was the people's duty to at least show their gratitude with occasional snacks and meals. Upon learning this, the CD workers were really put on the spot. In the first place, the leader was spreading false information about their real objectives in the place. It was also quite obvious that he was profiting from the collections because the meals and snacks he was serving certainly did not equal the money he was getting.

With this revelation, the CD workers slowly stopped visiting the original leader. Luckily enough, they found other leaders in the community who really understood their aims and who worked with them without demanding private gain. The CD workers also took to bringing their own lunch kits with them, and they learned to say "No" politely to invitations extended by leaders.

*Working through willing leaders.* As already mentioned, the CD workers in Barrio Magsaysay found the people already organized, and working through the established leadership became a given of the situation. However, as shown in the examples cited above, the formal leaders did not always turn out to be the desirable persons for program implementation. The teams, therefore, had to devise strategies of finding out other leaders and establishing working relationships with them without bringing about open conflict.

In one area of Barrio Magsaysay, the CD workers found the adult leaders lukewarm to their programs. They had been there almost a month, and the best they could do was get people to attend a couple of meetings and listen politely to their proposals. Intensive interviews and probings revealed two main sources of trouble: the adult leaders were divided, and the two camps were warily eyeing each other; and the leaders, in general, were skeptical about the possibility of the CD workers truly helping them with their main goal—possession of the land.

Faced with this situation and unwilling to wait until a true change of attitude among the adult leaders took place, the CD workers decided to use a substitute maneuver. They concentrated their attention on the youth organizations, which up to that time had mainly focused their activities on social and entertainment functions.

After establishing personal contacts with the youth leaders, the team decided to call an informal meeting at the team headquarters. Some eighteen of the youth leaders attended. In this meeting, the workers explained the reasons for their presence in the area and spoke frankly of their problems with the adult leaders. In no time at all, they struck a sympathetic chord with the youngsters, and a bigger meeting was arranged —with the youth leaders promising to invite others.

In the larger meeting, the youth leaders decided to formally organize into a more unified association. Represented in the meeting were four youth clubs in the community, which, up to that time, had not met with each other and just warily went each other's way. They decided to form a federation and elected a new set of officers.

In subsequent meetings, programs were discussed. The CD workers, however, afraid that they might push the enthusiasm of the youngsters too far, proposed social occasions and festivities that would double as fund-raising events. They worked on programs that would make the group more cohesive—a drama group, a glee club, dance groups, and the like. By working, playing, and just being together, the youth groups found a new solidarity.

When the CD workers saw that the youngsters were already prepared for more substantive work, they introduced new projects. A house-numbering project was started. With the help of the youngsters, tables, benches, and chairs were made for a new kindergarten class. A health and sanitation campaign was launched, with garbage compost pits being introduced to the community for the first time. Low-cost toilets were also introduced.

All these activities, conducted by noisy, enthusiastic, and very jolly young people attracted the attention of the adult leaders who had been unwilling to cooperate with the CD workers in the beginning. Slowly, some adult leaders approached the CD workers and shyly inquired how they could be of help. They also saw that the re-channeling of their children's energies was bringing about good results, and they encouraged their children to join the youth clubs. Soon, the different adult groups or *juntas* also became active, and they initiated their own projects. Thus, by working through another group, the CD workers were able to motivate their original targets—the adult groups.

In retrospect, the CD workers analyzed the reasons behind their success. In the evaluation conference that closed the project, one of the workers said that since they themselves were young, they found few barriers between themselves and the youth leaders. The youth leaders also tended to be above the ordinary run of youngsters in the place—they were going to college and belonged to families with relatively higher income.

Another reason given was the fact that the youth leaders were less obsessed with the land problem. It was an adult problem as far as they were concerned. It was also a problem that was thoroughly mixed up in politics, and the youngsters did not particularly like that part of life in Barrio Magsaysay. Finally, the rapport with the youngsters might just be traced to the enthusiasm and lack of inhibitions of youth. Since they found the CD workers receptive to their ideas, they gave them their utmost cooperation.

*Revising leadership structures.* Lest the example cited above is seen as coming about too easily, it must be mentioned that the CD workers also had a hard time reviving the youth organizations because this required a restructuring of the leadership patterns among the youngsters. As already mentioned, four youth organizations existed in the area where the CD workers operated. These organizations, though not exactly in open conflict with each other, were not in the habit of cooperating together. It was strictly "leave each other alone" among the youth clubs.

The CD workers had two alternatives: they could feed on the latent competitive instincts of the clubs, or they could try to bring about a cooperative attitude. Because one of their main objectives was to bring about a closer community-wide identity, they chose the latter course. They decided to try and make the four clubs work together.

The first move of the CD workers was to approach the youth club officers individually. They explained their objectives in the place and slowly brought up the idea of cooperating with other youth clubs and the advantages that could arise from such an arrangement. The first meeting arranged by the CD workers was strictly a social occasion—to enable the different club officers to meet and know each other. After the meeting, the CD workers followed up the idea of a cooperative effort, and the club officers seemed to be receptive.

In effect, the second conference was the most difficult one because the election of officers for the new organizational structure took place. The CD workers proposed that it be called a Youth Coordinating Council (YCC) and that it should be composed of all the officers of the four youth clubs. The council, in turn, would elect its own set of officers to preside over the federation.

In the election, the youth clubs very wisely parceled out the various positions among the presidents and other officers of the four youth clubs. Thus, they elected a president; a first, second, and third vice-president; a secretary; and, again, a board of secretaries. In effect, the officers of the YCC were also the top officers of the four youth clubs. It was also interesting that the newly created positions were neatly parceled out among the male and female officers. While the positions of president, vice-president, and secretary were filled by males, the board of secretaries composed of six people was occupied by females.

Even with the setting up of this new organizational structure, things did not still come easy for the youth federation. For one thing, activities always had to be balanced and parceled out to avoid jealousies among the top officers. A maximum of personal contact and social exchanges was also encouraged by the CD workers to unite the new set of officers into a new group. Thus, during the first days of the YCC, activities were primarily confined to socials and entertainment functions. It was only later when the bonds were stronger that more difficult and substantive projects were introduced, luckily, with much success.

*Working through specialized leaders.* The emphasis on finding the typical leader of Barrio Magsaysay, using modal characteristics found in the survey data, yields results useful for operations. However, the research and action teams also found out that there was leadership based on narrow and specialized functions in Barrio Magsaysay and that this was also good to know to achieve results.

The first common division of leaders was between those who were useful for matters involving relations with the outside world and those who played a leading role in purely community functions. To the former group belonged political leaders who had very close ties with leading city or national politicians—councilors, mayors, congressmen, senators, and even the president. These leaders owed their positions to the fact that they mediated between some people in Barrio Magsaysay who needed favors and the politicians who could dispense such favors. Some of the more common items achieved in this way were: temporary jobs; fixing licenses confiscated by traffic cops; contributions for death in the family; prizes and awards during community celebrations; admission to the city schools; preferential treatment at the hospitals or other public offices; and the like. The leader, once approached by a resident, accompanied the latter to the politician or his top leaders. Sometimes, he does not even have to go through the politicians because, through the years, he has developed his own sphere of influence.

There are several leaders who primarily play a role within the community only. The most conspicuous among these is the person who controls violence, the person people run to when there is trouble. He is usually a person known for his toughness and strength who can fight troublemakers when needed. People respect him because they are afraid of him. Even troublemakers know him and quit their antics when he arrives.

Another type of internal leader is the person who is highly respected because of some highly traditional characteristics. He tends to be older, religious, educated, and sober. People know him as a good man. He is the one picked to lead the fiesta activities, the one people go to during Lent or other religious seasons for him to take the leadership position. He is known and highly respected in the community.

To get these specialized leaders, a question was included in the interview guide, asking respondents to name the person they go to when there are disturbances in the community, when they need certain services (medical, educational, welfare), or when they have to borrow money. The question yielded a number of names that consistently appeared in the answers of many people. Except for the question on borrowing money, where majority of the people cited their relatives rather than leaders (or moneylenders), the rest of the questions gave the CD teams the names of persons who could help them in projects related to the leadership specializations of those named. These leaders willingly and ably cooperated with the teams in their lines of specialized leadership.

## Conclusion

Knowing the leadership of the community is the first task of an Urban Community Development team that wants to operate in an area. The leadership survey is an important and useful tool. It need not be a complete survey of the leaders (assuming that an effective device for the identification of all the leaders is possible). What is important is knowing the bases for leadership (physical courage, political influence, age, affluence, etc.) and how leadership is exercised over the people.

A leadership survey not only serves to identify the leaders but also enables the CD team to get a profile of their characteristics. From this knowledge of the leaders, possible patterns of cooperation and possible types of projects that may become successful may be drawn up. Knowing the leaders also facilitates entry into the community.

Working through the established community leaders, however, may have its pitfalls. In the first place, the traditional leaders, because they stand for the status quo, may not be too eager to accept the changes introduced by the team. Because some of them profit from the way things are, they may actually use the team to further their ends. Working through the established leaders may also inhibit the development of other persons with leadership potentials. Because cooperating with the CD teams bolsters the leadership position of the old leaders, they become more firmly entrenched, and this may make the development of new ones more difficult.

Knowing the community leadership, however, is the first stage in the entry phase. Working through specialized leaders, willing leaders, and the development of new leaders would depend on how well the leadership profile of the community is delineated. In Barrio Magsaysay, the ease of entry was largely due to this knowledge. There is no reason why this approach will not work in other communities.

# CHAPTER 6

# Entry

In previous chapters, we discussed how the urban community development project in Barrio Magsaysay was started by using the leadership in the community as the entry wedge. It was mentioned that the community survey made up the people's first knowledge of the project, that the head of the PACD, Secretary Ernesto Maceda, paid the community a special visit and thereby made the project official, and that working relationships were first established with formal leaders. In this chapter, other approaches that facilitated the entry of the community development teams are more fully discussed. These approaches are: (1) research survey; (2) service impact; (3) use of political officials; (4) use of traditional government workers; (5) social activities; (6) economic appeals; and (7) appeal to main community interests.

## RESEARCH SURVEY

Rational administrative decision-making depends on the information it is based on. One of the first steps in any action program, therefore, is knowing about the situation, which is best done in community projects through a survey. Aside from the fact that research provides important information, it also performs a most important task as an entry wedge into a community.

In most cases, the entry of CD teams into a community is met with suspicion. When the workers state that they are merely making a survey or study of the area, however, the suspicion is usually lessened. In Barrio Magsaysay, people were used to what they called community "census." A young man or woman asking questions and writing answers on a questionnaire is a familiar sight. When the person making the survey mentions that the information gathered would be used in planning projects for the community, he is accepted all the more.

Another advantage of the survey is that the CD team members are given a change to explain the project in the community. Before conducting interviews or even during lulls in the question and answer sessions, the objectives and procedures of the program may be explained. In this way, the people are gently introduced to the program and are prepared for the actual action projects.

Finally, the results of the survey provide the best data on which the planning of the program may be based. It is very useful, for example, to ask the community's residents about what they see as the most pressing problems and how they believe such problems can be solved. Usually, because CD workers are more highly educated or because they come from different backgrounds, they tend to see problems and resources of the community differently. Getting the information itself from the people through surveys assures that valid data are gathered. This would mean better information on which planning could be based.

### SERVICE IMPACT

Most slum and squatter communities are so hard up that many of their inhabitants are frequently assisted by welfare agencies. The sight of social workers and other government personnel offering relief is not new to them. It then becomes rather easy to enter a community, when it is known the workers are there to help the people.

In Barrio Magsaysay, the entry of the CD teams was made much easier by the fielding of doctors and nurses in the area. It was not difficult to conclude that health and sanitation were major problems in the community. The place was not readily accessible to government health teams, there was no puericulture center in the area, and the hospitals were quite a distance. If people got sick, they usually had to go as far as Mary

Johnston Hospital, or even to the Philippine General Hospital across the Pasig. It was decided, therefore, that doctors from Operation Brotherhood and volunteer doctors who were friends of Secretary Maceda would be sent to the community to provide medical service.

Sending doctors and nurses into a community is helpful not only because the other members of the team also get readily accepted but also because, when properly trained, medical personnel are able to get most important information that may be used in planning community projects. The medical consultation atmosphere is natural for data gathering. The doctor, aside from asking questions related to the ailments, may also probe into community problems, health and sanitation habits, community leadership and resources, and other factors relevant to the success of the project.

One useful method is to include a social worker with the medical team. Professional social workers are carefully trained to conduct interviews. They can be used for noting down intake data before a patient is actually diagnosed or treated by the doctor. Since it is usual to ask patients some preliminary questions before they see the doctor, the social worker can naturally probe for other data while conducting the interviews. The social worker may also get additional information through casual conversation while patients are awaiting their turn. Provided the project staff has given her a list of questions, cues, and possible problem areas, the social worker would be able to get information unobstrusively.

The effectiveness of medical service as an entry device is shown in the diary entries of a CD worker:

20 April 1966

The group went to the house of Mr. Sevilla in order to gather some information regarding the sickness that is spreading in his block. Mr. Sevilla was not feeling well at the time. He told us that he had a stroke last Monday. In spite of his illness, he entertained the group. He told us that there were two brothers who died of ascariasis and bronchitis; two, of gastro-enteritis. One family was a victim of ascariasis.

According to Mr. Sevilla, the occupants were already disgusted the moment they see somebody going around from house to house asking for "dead aid."

## 22 April 1966

The team went to the area of Mr. Sevilla to see if the medical team requested for arrived, since it was their scheduled date. The group inquired about the conditions of the two children. He said they were both in fair condition.

Mr. Sevilla then offered the group the ground floor of his house for training site in dressmaking, in case we will put one in their block.

It is seen from the diary that sickness and death are not strangers in the community. In fact, the entry for 20 April indicates that the member of the community "were already disgusted" because people go around asking for "dead aid." While it is a common traditional practice to solicit contributions when somebody in the community dies, the poverty of the people makes them resentful of this when too many deaths occur.

The presence of medical service, therefore, was warmly welcomed by the people. As seen in the diary entry for 22 April, the presence of the medical team elicited an offer of a community leader for the team to use his home as a training site. The entry through medical service had opened up new doors.

### POLITICAL OFFICIALS

One possible means of entering a community is to do it through the known political officials who have a following in the place. If the official is in power or holding a strong position, then the entry is facilitated. One main danger in this approach, however, is that the team may be identified with the political ambitions of the official—and the initial welcome may wane when the political official disappoints the demands of the people.

In Barrio Magsaysay, entry through a political official was not consciously used, although there were plenty of opportunities to do so. As mentioned above, a councilor and a congressman were known as the supporters of the Barrio Magsaysay dwellers in their fight for the land they were squatting on. It could have been easy to have these politicians "sponsor" the CD teams. Entry, at least initially, could have been achieved, and, once accepted, the teams could have weaned themselves from the politicians' influence. The attitude of the teams is summed up in one diary:

22 March 1966

Rene, Elsa, Andy, and I met with Mr. Soriano, the councilor. First thing he asked was whether we were eligible for our position and advised us not to let others use it. We briefed him about our activity and role in the village. He said *bahala na siya sa lahat!* * —if we need something, just tell him. We knew this was a lot of baloney. But we intended to use this promise one of these days.

It is revealed in this entry that the CD teams, aware that they were government workers who were qualified for their positions, resented the question of the politician regarding their eligibility for the job. The team was also aware that the councilor could only be feeding them "a lot of baloney." But still, the team was not blind to the fact that the politician could be of some use.

The councilor, in time, came in handy when the team called the people to a meeting. With the councilor making the summons, many of the leaders came. The team was then given a chance to explain their project, and entry was achieved. Still, this was only done once because the team feared that they would be identified with the politician too much, and this may prejudice their work.

### TRADITIONAL GOVERNMENT WORKERS

The CD teams assigned to Barrio Magsaysay were mostly young workers fresh from college. While this was advantageous in dealing with younger community members, it was something of a disadvantage when working with older people. Luckily, however, there were three members of the team who were school teachers working as "Teacher Coordinators," and they were very useful in introducing the project in the area.

---

* He will take care of everything.

The Philippine educational system, some time ago, tried an experiment in the community-school movement. The idea behind this was to make the school the center of the community, especially in bringing about desirable social change. Thus, the school teacher not only stayed in the classroom but also brought the gospel of change to the community. Sometimes, the school teacher actually acted as the coordinator of activities which were not only school-oriented but also community-oriented.

Two of the teacher community coordinators were relatively older than the other CD team members. They were also familiar with the place because the schools they taught in (on the elementary grade levels) were in the vicinity. As teacher coordinators, they had launched several projects in the community, and they knew many of the leaders. They took the young CD workers in tow, and the entry was hastened in this way.

Because urban community development is a new idea, there is no reason why traditional government workers cannot find place in it. As seen in this project, because of their familiarity with the place and the people, the traditional workers had a built-in advantage. They could enter the community faster and get projects started earlier, with the support of the community's leaders.

### SOCIAL ACTIVITIES

In the Philippines, one of the strongest bonds that keep a community together is social activity. In fact, the traditional fiesta is less a religious observance than a chance for the community to maintain its social bonds. Holy Week, elections, death in the community, weddings, baptisms, and other occasions—these are fully celebrated to keep the community socially unified. Because of this fondness of the people for social activities, entry may be achieved through this avenue.

In Barrio Magsaysay, the CD teams used traditional social activities and helped in setting up new ones. The summer months usually herald the coming of Holy Week, which is celebrated by the people through the *pabasa*. In this singing of the passion and death of Jesus Christ, the community participates actively. In the Summer of 1966, therefore, CD teams also joined in the celebration and thus endeared themselves to the people of the community.

Other social occasions were the inauguration of new organizations or the community dances sponsored by youth clubs. The CD teams were well aware that, as soon as an organization gets set up, its first activity involves an induction and inauguration ball. They, therefore, encouraged this, knowing full well that the enthusiasm generated and the organizational experience of observing this social occasion could be used later on for community projects.[1]

Social activities need not be formalized. Sometimes, just joining people while they chatted, drank, or merrily gossiped at the corner store was good enough. These social occasions could even lead to more formal projects, as revealed in the following diary entry:

15 April 1966

At Mang Dolfo's, there was an ongoing *concierto* * as usual—beer, San Miguel gin, with crabs. We were invited, so we sat down with them. Some *calderetang aso* † was also served . . . .

Mr. Cruz came later with his guitar. Together with Berto, they played; both of them, they said, are already *laos.*‡ Mr. Cruz gave an exhibition on his guitar—La Cumparsita, marches, and "Hernando's Hide Away." We invited them, and they all agreed to join a choral group we were organizing. We left them singing their hearts out.

It must be mentioned here that the choral group held several practice sessions, which served to unite the singers and made them more cooperative. The group was able to present a few numbers during the formal induction and dance of a community club, so the social activities paid off.

**ECONOMIC APPEALS**

Although they drown their troubles in social activities, people in slum and squatter areas are rarely able to forget their

---

* *Concierto* is literally a concert, a euphemism for "drinking bout."
† *Calderetang aso* is a heavily peppered dish of dog meat.
‡ *Laos* means a "has been."

main problem—the fact that they are poor. Therefore, one of the most effective means of getting them interested enough to join in community activities is to show that they can learn something that can help them improve their means of livelihood.

In Barrio Magsaysay, there were several appeals in this direction. Early in the project, such training classes as dressmaking, beauty culture, tailoring, and instruction for waiters were initiated. It was quite difficult at the start to make the people realize how they would benefit from these classes, but, after a while, they were convinced; and they thanked the CD workers for trying to help them.

One factor that makes this training so easy is the fact that instructors can easily be located in the community itself. There is always somebody who knows a trade and who would be willing to teach others for nothing. There are also business firms that would be only too eager to make arrangements for their services. In Barrio Magsaysay, it was easy to teach dressmaking and tailoring because the Singer Sewing Machine Company readily agreed to lend some sewing machines for the training classes. They have a program of lending, which they would be willing to do, provided security of the machines is assured. It is one of their promotional campaigns. So, the interest of the business firm, the community, and the CD workers all coincided; thus, entry was facilitated.

### APPEAL TO MAIN COMMUNITY INTEREST

Finally, of course, the easiest way of entering a community is to try and solve the main problems in the area. In Barrio Magsaysay, this was not too viable because the main interest of the people was to own the lands they were squatting on, which was beyond the capacity of the CD teams to provide. In fact, a decision was made early in the project to avoid all talk about what came to be known as "the land question."

While this one interest could not be used for entry, there were other problems that were within the means of the CD teams. The roads were the most pressing problems of the people when the teams first came into Barrio Magsaysay. They were so muddy during the rainy season that they became impassable. Drainage was another problem; hence, the digging of canals also became a project. The problem of health and sanitation, of course, was answered with the fielding of the medical teams.

All in all, it is best for the cd teams to study the main problems of the community and to help or at least sympathize with the people in this respect. Knowing that the cd teams are with the people, in their effort to solve pressing problems, is one of the best ways of gaining entry into the community.

## Actual Entry into the Community

After enumerating and discussing the various means of entering a community, it is interesting to find out how the three teams actually made their way into Barrio Magsaysay. As already stated, the whole cd staff, supplemented by graduate students in research, first conducted a complete survey of the area. This served to make the people aware that something was going on in their community. Even before preliminary analysis of the survey results were in, the cd workers were divided into teams and assigned to definite areas.

ENTRY THROUGH TRAINING (TEAM I)

Final briefing of the action teams was held on 14 March 1966 at the pacd office in Port Area. After this, Team I was brought by car to Area I. They immediately went to the house of Mr. Pedro Nobledo, president of the main organization in the area. Mr. Nobledo was out, so they talked with his brother. One diary written about this visit goes as follows:

The group met the brother, Mr. Roman Nobledo, who recognized the social worker member of the team as his interviewer when the Dept. of Social Welfare had coordinated with the Social Welfare Administration in the survey of squatters in the reclaimed area in Sunog Apog, Balut.

We started the conversation by introducing ourselves as team members and the agency that we were representing. Mr. Nobledo told the group that he also owned a house in the area and was trying to sell his house in Balut. He also told us that there were so many new houses that were built in the area; and, up to the present, the construction is still going on.

The team was introduced to Tony Viado, who guided us in going around the area. We met so many people, the old folks, as well as the youngsters. While going around, the group met a woman who lived outside the community but owned a newly built house in the area. She asked the group if the lots will be awarded to them. Another woman asked the group if we were going to buy lots.

That was the first day of the team in the field. It must be noticed that they went to the formal leaders and got their information from their family. They also used an intermediary (Tony Viado) before roaming around the place. They definitely saw the main concern of the people (land ownership) and observed the main problem (buying and selling of lots even without any legal rights to the land).

The technique of entry through organized clubs was pursued in subsequent days. Thus, on 15 March, the team went to the officers of the various organizations in the community. Furthermore, they also got in touch with the political ward *liders* of a councilor, who were quite influential in the place. They were invited to a meeting of club officers at the place of the councilor where they met more important leaders in the community.

On 22 March, some leaders of one of the clubs requested that something be done for the drainage of their area. They were expecting that in May the rains would come and that the place would most likely be flooded. Initial discussions were conducted—with the people promising to provide their free labor if the CD teams would look after materials and equipment. It was obvious that the entry of the CD teams was now assured. They only had to do something about this community problem, and they could now launch other projects; and the people would follow.

Realizing, however, that plenty of resources were needed for the drainage problem, the CD teams decided to introduce more manageable projects. Thus, they initiated the idea of setting up a dressmaking class and talked this over with the officials of the five or so organizations with which they were cooperating. There were immediate volunteers to help in this project.

On 11 April, the team went to the Singer Sewing Machine Company to find out how they could be helped. They met with the sales and the advertising managers, who asked them to prepare a formal letter stating their request for the loan of sewing machines. They were also asked to request the people in the community to prepare a resolution requesting the loan of the machines and the reasons for the project.

Meanwhile, knowing that the people were more interested in the drainage project, the team went to the National Waterworks and Sewerage Authority to ask them about the water table in the area and about how deep a drainage ditch would be needed. They also requested the people to draw up a list of volunteers and asked when these people could actually work.

An instructress for the dressmaking class was recruited through the Department of Social Welfare on 12 April. To make the project official, however, the number of people to be trained and benefitted was needed, and the social worker had to interview them using regular intake forms. On 14 April, a sewing machine repairer volunteered his free services to the team. Other volunteer instructors were also located—one who could teach how to make polo shirts and another who knew how to sew polo *barong*. Mr. Nobledo, the leader of the community, also started preparing the ground floor of his house to be the site of the dressmaking class

When the first class was actually held on 19 April, only nine trainees out of a possible seventy applicants listed showed up. The team members were disappointed, but they decided to redouble their efforts. Subsequent interviews showed that the people thought the site of the classes was too far from their place. They were mostly housewives who could not be away from their homes for long, and they were not properly notified when the class would actually start. Learning from these interviews, the team now campaigned actively for attendance to the dress-making class and by 21 April, eighteen trainees showed up. More attended the classes when the Singer sewing machines were delivered. In fact, a second class was opened in another part of the community later on to accommodate the people who complained that the original site was too far from their place. The sewing classes even competed with a bingo session regularly held in the community so that this pastime lost more and more participants.

By the end of April, although the drainage project was still being planned, the CD team in Area I thought that they had gained proper entry into the community.

### A CENTER FOR UNITY (TEAM II)

The first day for the action phase in Area II came on 14 March. Previously, the team members had done some interviewing in the area and had talked to some leaders. The diary notes of a team member, clearly marked "Entry" are reproduced here:

14 March 1966

After having been briefed on "rules of the road," so to say, during our entry into Barrio Magsaysay, Tondo, we left on a PACD Volkswagen for what will be our area of operation for the coming months, Barrio Magsaysay. We left with the enthusiasm that comes naturally during a take-off, but not without the apprehension that comes from not knowing what lurks beyond the hours before us. Terry re-introduced us to Mr. Abcede, president of the area's association, who received us with routine hospitality but with the unenthusiasm that comes from meeting a group; he was, in the first place, not bound to by any favor received or granted. Mr. Abcede, a resigned schoolteacher, served us each a bottle of Pepsi Cola, which we did not drink even halfway because of the swarming flies and also because we tried to suggest to them not to bother at all about feeding us since we will be coming to their house very often.

The seeming lack of enthusiasm, it turned out, was due to the feeling of the area's leader that the team was not acting fast enough. During the survey period, the leader had suggested to the team members that cottage industries be started in his area. He had been impatiently waiting for something to be done, and it took some time before the team was even fielded for action. Besides, he was also being bothered by the increasing competition being put up by another leader in the place, who was only too anxious to take over and get the team on his side.

The usual visits to leaders of the area came next. Some officers of neighborhood associations, women's clubs, and youth clubs were contacted by the team. They found that the leadership rift in the community was rather serious. Most of the people had already taken sides—and it would be a problem to unify the community and make the people cooperate.

After several meetings, the team decided that what the community needed was a center for activities—so they proposed the construction of a community center. Even here, however, it turned out that the fight for community leadership had been one step ahead of them. Mr. Abcede informed them that they had specific plans for such a center already. He was thinking of using the barrio fiesta to get some money for the center.

Calling on their backgrounds and special skills, the team members hastily drew up plans for their activities in the community. They decided that they would undertake the training of girls and women in dressmaking; the training of young boys and out-of-school youth for being waiters; the setting up of a credit union; and the recruitment of youngsters for junior apprenticeship work. Unfortunately, these plans were set up before the needs of the community were actually intensively surveyed and understood. The projects reflected more the fields where the teams thought they could do something (in other words, their personal proficiencies, aptitudes, and skills) rather than the actual needs of the people in the community.

The idea of setting up a credit union was met with some criticism and hostility from the start. The diary of the team member who presented the idea follows:

After these preliminary plans were formalized on paper, we discussed their feasibility with the project and research directors. . . . The credit union was looked upon with more apprehension because of the greater complexity of starting it and getting it smoothly going once it is started. I was advised to proceed with great care . . . .

I went to the Cooperative Administration Office to inquire about the details of organizing a credit union. I met Mr. Nebrida, the executive officer, and I asked from him a bunch of brochures on credit unions.

I talked with Mr. Bernabe about the prospect of organizing a credit union in Barrio Magsaysay, and his first reaction was one of apprehension. He recounted his own knowledge about similar undertakings—that they have been good only as far as power work was concerned.

In actual operation, he told me, the members actually tended to be [so] selfish that they borrow money without any desire to pay it back. "I wouldn't want to put in money if only other people will benefit from it," he said. "I need the money myself." However, he said that, if ever the plan is pushed through, "you can count me in—but only as a member."

Because of the negative reactions to the proposal to set up a credit union, it was abandoned by the team. However, the incident shows the dangers lurking in the difference in perception between more educated CD workers and their clientele. If the project had been pushed through, the likelihood of failure would have been great.

Heeding the views of the community leaders, the team now decided to support Mr. Abcede's idea that a community center was what the place needed. Mr. Abcede said that the team could use the community center for all their activities. He also had just the idea to finance the construction of the center—to collect for the barrio fiesta and then use some of the excess money for the center.

Setting up the center, however, proved to be a more difficult job than the team thought at first. There was the land question to worry about. To construct the center, a building permit was needed from the government. Since the land did not belong to the association, they had no legal rights to build a center there.

The team went to the Bureau of Lands and inquired about procedures. An official there told them that presidential authority was needed and advised them to write a letter to the President through the director of the Bureau of Lands. This letter would be studied by "different agencies," and a decision would be made. The team, wanting to get through the procedural difficulties, said that the community center would be used as a schoolhouse because one was needed in the place. The official said that was a valid reason. The team said it would not even cost the government a single cent, since the barrio association would pay for the materials and the construction. In fact, the schoolhouse would be turned over to the barrio organization after the project was over. To this, however, the Bureau of Lands official objected. He said, if the permit to construct would be for a school, then the building must be used as a school. If this were the case, it should be turned over to the Bureau of Public Schools, not the association. Stalemated again.

At this point, the community leaders decided to take matters into their own hands. Mr. Abcede, with the backing of a councilor who even went to the extent of donating lumber and other materials, just went ahead with the construction of the schoolhouse *cum* community center. After all, the people of the community had constructed hundreds of houses without getting building permits or presidential authorizations. They just continued with their squatting activities and inclinations and built the center. As a kind of personal touch, the leader of the community also decided that, if the building would be used as a schoolhouse, then the city government should pay rent for it since it was now the private property of the association, and the association needed funds very badly.

Even before the construction of the community center, however, the team tried other means of making their acceptance into the community faster. Two specific projects were thought of: a course for waiters and another course for the making of bags. The team believed that, since poverty was the main problem in the area, such skills would be helpful in augmenting the income of the people. Getting these projects launched, however, proved to be very difficult. After initial contacts with a private university that offers training of waiters in its vocational curriculum, the team met a dead end. The bag-making class was held up because of the difficulty of finding an instructor who had to come from another slum redevelopment project of Operation Brotherhood, located outside the city proper. While the initial contacts made to plan these projects served to keep the team members busy and in close touch with community leaders, the fact that the projects were not pushed through limited their importance as entry projects. The entry of Team II in Barrio Magsaysay was characterized by an attempt to interpret the main problems of the community and to launch projects that would meet these problems. Unfortunately, the team's perception of the real problems differed somewhat from what the people were really interested in. Thus, while in the opinion of one of the team members, a credit union was the thing needed in the place, the initial difficulty encountered in the execution of the idea doomed the project from the start. While launching a waiter's course and another one on bag-making was, in the opinion of the team members, a good way of augmenting the income of the people, the failure to launch these projects because of the difficulties encountered might have been due to the misperception of the real problems of the people again.

One very serious difficulty that the team in Area II had to be saddled with was the serious personal rift between the two main leaders in the area. Faced with two groups that distrusted each other and caught in the cross fire of intrigue and invectives, the team found it very difficult to make a dent into the community easily. Thus, compared to the other teams, those in Area II took a longer time before they could really say that they had been accepted by the community.

### THE DOCTORS OPEN THE WAY (TEAM III)

The entry of Team III into their area was greatly helped by the medical service given by the doctors and nurses that preceded them. On their first operational day in the field, they were greatly heartened by the reception of the people.

14 March 1966

Team III, conveyed to the area in a PACD vehicle, found the volunteer medic team in operation in block no. 2, the block hall chockfull of citizens and many of the local leaders in attendance. It is easy to see that officers and members of the organizations in the place and the local citizens were happy about our being there. About what we could do in the area, they must foresee something I can't.

Area III on the PACD map was composed of six blocks, with three organizations dominant in the place. With the formal organizations very active, the team decided to hold meetings or community assemblies on weekends. The same diarist who chronicled their first day described a typical meeting or community assembly:

19 March 1967

We attended a community assembly in block 1, which lasted about five-and-a-half hours and the principal speakers of which were the team's three members and Mr. Terry Vitug, of the volunteer medical team (PACD). We emphasized our project as divorced from the lot-awarding function of the Land Authority. We wooed the crowd with the promise to sit with their leaders in the planning of self-help projects and activities.

A song program put the lid on the meeting. The male officers of the block came in ties. The vital thing is that there was a general atmosphere of success to the affair. The leaders pledged to cooperate with and support the program.

In the meetings and casual conversations, the team started learning of the community's problems. As one team member noted in his diary, "I got the opportunity to talk with (felt more like being talked to) some 'natives.' I could have made a list of problems a yard long in small prints." When the team members compared notes, the main problems at the top of the list were floods and health. The people were worried that as soon as the steady rains came, they would all be swimming in dirty water again. In March, all that they complained of were the dust and the flies. In May, they knew they would complain about the floods.

The team's solution to this problem was to get some help from the city government for the filling up of the main roads in the area. With a big delegation of people from the squatter area ("to increase our bargaining power"), the team went to Mayor Antonio Villegas for assistance. The Mayor received them cordially, told them about his ambitious plan to have all city streets cemented, and then referred them to the Department of Public Works. Here, they were able to get the officials to promise that they would haul some soil to Barrio Magsaysay, provided able-bodied workers helped them in loading, unloading, and spreading the soil. This was agreed upon, and on the following day truckloads of filling materials started arriving.

In subsequent meetings, other ideas also came up. The people realized that, even with the filling, the roads would still be flooded if it rains really hard and this coincides with high tide. So, to meet this problem, the people suggested that donations of lumber should be requested from private citizens. These planks would be turned into catwalks by the people, constructed on the side of the roads, so that even when the streets are flooded, people would still be able to walk about.

As mentioned above, the medical service was quite a hit with the people. With the prompting of the CD teams, it was decided that the doctors would extend their work from a merely curative to a preventive aspect. The first campaign thought of was a de-worming project. It was aptly reasoned out that, as it is, slum dwellers don't get enough to eat to begin with. With intestinal worms still sharing in their little food, malnutrition was the obvious result.

A de-worming campaign, however, is effective only if the people have the proper way of disposing of their waste. The sad thing about Barrio Magsaysay, however, is that people have no toilets. So, it was decided that a toilet-construction campaign be conducted at the same time. Unfortunately, because of the condition of the land (always threatened with floods) and the people's lack of money, only a few toilets were built. Still, the de-worming campaign was pushed through, with medicine being donated by a local drug company.

Like the two other teams, the one in Area III also thought of introducing projects that would help augment the income of the people. Some of the projects mentioned were dressmaking; the accepting of small assembling jobs from big factories, to be done at home by residents of the area; and hair science. Unlike the other teams, however, Team III went slow in these projects and concentrated on only a few. In this way, they did not raise the expectations of the people too much. The few projects they did launch, however, they pursued to finish.

Another activity the team used to gain entry into the community was the introduction of training programs, one for leaders and another for people who wanted to learn first aid. The first training program was managed by the team, using the standard procedures for lay leadership institutes already known by PACD workers. The other was jointly sponsored with the Philippine National Red Cross, which kindly gave the team their instructors in first aid and in child care.

Finally, the team gained acceptance in the community primarily by just being there. They frequented the place, talked with the people (especially the leaders), and just mingled with the residents freely. A diary entry, for example, just said: "Informal chats in block 3 and block 2 with residents and more, like walking a bit, smiling here, and nodding there, and creating conversations at the slightest opportunity." Another diary entry for 22 March read:

We were just like taking a walk in block 1. We, however, hoped to accomplish a very important task. We are sure they will notice us going there all the time, passing their way now and then, and we hoped to arouse in them a bit of curiosity. That will, in one way, help us in being known in the area and later helping them know why we are there, without us individually approaching them.

## Conclusion

People go by first impressions, and slum dwellers and squatters are no exceptions. The entry of urban community development workers into an area, therefore, is a very important part of the CD operations because future success or failure would depend on this a great deal. Initial mistakes in dealing with the people will cost the team many hours of trying to make amends in the future. Big promises given at the start and later unfulfilled reflect on the sincerity of the team and affect outcomes negatively.

The experience of the CD teams in Barrio Magsaysay showed that there are many ways of gaining entry into a community. These approaches, however, are also dictated by the particular circumstances the teams find themselves in. A great deal of flexibility, therefore, is a must for the effective entry of CD teams.

It seems safe to conclude that the service impact is one of the surest ways of gaining entry into a community. However, even this relatively simple approach is full of pitfalls. For example, what services are really needed by the people, as the people perceive them and not according to the viewpoint of the CD workers? What should be the balance between service and self-help? In too many instances, because the Urban CD worker is anxious to get started and achieve results, he tends to do everything for the people. If the CD agencies are in a position to backstop the service projects he has, the more he is encouraged to give and help. However, providing help and welfare aid may not actually be the best way of gaining entry. Instead of assuring community development, the CD worker may just be developing dependence and a dole-out mentality. This would make his real community development goals difficult to achieve later on.

# CHAPTER 7

# Inter-Agency Cooperation

Urban community development, if it is to succeed, must involve the joint efforts of different agencies engaged in making urban life as pleasant and productive as possible. This, in fact, is the source of strength of urban programs. The urban environment is characterized by the diversity of groups and the variety of resources available for development. An urban CD program must tap these groups and resources for the accomplishment of its goals.

The number and diversity of groups that may be involved in an urban CD program, however, pose a big administrative problem. Agencies have a way of preserving their own identities, developing their own loyalties, and evolving their own methodologies. Coordinating the effort of these agencies, therefore, is a most difficult task. While the urban CD program may benefit from the specialized skills and approaches of agencies involved, it must have enough coordinative devices to make sure that individualist efforts fall within a program of concerted action.

## Agencies Involved in Barrio Magsaysay

The Barrio Magsaysay Pilot Project in Urban Community Development involved the Presidential Arm on Community Development, the Department of Social Welfare of the City of Manila, the Division of City Schools of the City of Manila, Operation Brotherhood International, the Asia Foundation, the Peace Corps, and the College of Public Administration of the University of the Philippines. The organizations, therefore, included a national government agency, two local government units, a private civic organization, two foreign entities, and a public educational institution. Other agencies and institutions were involved in the project from time to time, but the agencies mentioned above were the ones that fielded personnel or disbursed funds specifically for this project.

### PRESIDENTIAL ARM ON COMMUNITY DEVELOPMENT (PACD)

The PACD was founded as the office of the Presidential Assistant on Community Development in 1956 "to plan and implement the President's community development program in barrios, municipalities and chartered cities, and coordinate offices of the Government engaged in community development in order to increase their effectiveness, achieve maximum benefits and avoid duplication and overlapping of activities." [1] Coordination was the key function of the agency. While it has a grants-in-aid program of its own, its personnel are meant to be multi-purpose workers at home in both the technical and organizational phases of CD work.

Barrio Magsaysay was the first involvement of the PACD in real urban community development. Commitment to this project was spearheaded by Secretary Ernesto Maceda. The secretary's interest is no accident: his roots are in Manila, he grew up and was educated in the city, and he was a former councilor in the Manila Municipal Board. Although there were some political suspicions regarding his motives for wanting redevelopment of slums and squatter areas, his actions in the project were ample proof of his genuine interest.

As a PACD-coordinated project, the Barrio Magsaysay effort was under the direction of Mr. Alberto Virtusio, director of Special Projects, PACD, and coordinator of the PACD-Peace Corps project. Mr. Virtusio had been with the PACD for ten years, starting as an administrative officer at the Community Development Training Center in Los Baños. He holds a Bachelor of Science in education and a Master of Science in rural sociology.

The other PACD personnel involved in the pilot project were:

Eduardo Bigornia, Community Development analyst; Head, Research and Evaluation Section, PACD. Mr. Bigornia holds an AB in anthropology.

Belinda A. Aquino, Community Development instructor, PACD. Miss Aquino has a Bachelor of Arts in English from the University of the Philippines and a Master of Arts in political science from the University of Hawaii on an East-West Center scholarship. Before the end of the project, she transferred to the College of Public Administration, University of the Philippines, as a research associate and instructor.

Andres Burgos, Barrio Development worker. Graduated with a Bachelor of Arts in public administration from the University of the Philippines. Was a Barrio Development worker in Bustos, Bulacan, prior to the Barrio Magsaysay project.

Margo R. Viray, Barrio Development worker. Graduated with a Bachelor of Science in business administration from the University of the East. Was a BDW in Bustos, Bulacan, before being recruited for the pilot project.

Renato Casaclang, Barrio Development worker and Municipal Development officer. Holds a Bachelor of Arts and was formerly assigned to San Pablo City, Laguna.

Eustaquio Joven, Barrio Development worker. Holds a Bachelor of Science in agriculture.

Ruperto Ilaya, Barrio Development worker. Holds a certificate in vocational education.

Nelia Liwag, Barrio Development worker. Holds a Bachelor of Science in elementary education.

Gaspar Nepomuceno, Barrio Development worker. Is a junior civil engineering student.

Of the ten PACD people detailed to the Barrio Magsaysay project, six were Barrio Development workers who had been working in the rural areas prior to their recruitment to the pilot project. All but one were college graduates. Their educational backgrounds were varied, ranging from agriculture to engineering. All of them had in common the basic training given to all CD workers and were conversant with the concepts and methodologies of the Philippine community development program. Of all the agencies cooperating in the project, therefore, the PACD had the most homogeneous group. In addition to conceptual and methodological unity, the PACD personnel also knew that this was mainly a PACD program. The program initiation was by the PACD. Resources for the action projects to be introduced would have to come from the agency. Auxiliary services, such as supplies, materials, transportation, and others were to be provided by the PACD. Finally, the program was a PACD program, and official commitment was centered on PACD officials. All of these factors were to affect inter-agency cooperation.

### OPERATION BROTHERHOOD INTERNATIONAL (OBI)

OBI is a private civic organization established in 1954 in response to the sad plight of Vietnamese refugees in the Indo-China War, especially after the fall of Dienbienphu. It was first set up as a project of the Philippine Jaycees, with the goal of sending medical and social welfare personnel to Vietnam to help refugees and other displaced persons. The project was soon sponsored by Jaycee Asia, Jaycee International, and, finally, the Agency for International Development of the U.S. Government. OBI transferred its operations to Laos in 1956 and has been there ever since. They maintain a hospital, field clinics, and roving teams of doctors and nurses to help people in the villages and the cities.

In addition to its overseas operations, OBI also has the Operation Brotherhood (Philippines), financed primarily from local grants and contributions, and earnings from overseas operations. OBI (Philippines) has both rural and urban programs. Under the former, the agency maintains an experimental farm in Los Baños, Laguna, a community improvement project in Nasugbu, Batangas and other similar projects in other parts of the country. Under the latter, OBI sent a complete team to Sapang Palay, a squatter relocation center 37 kilometers out of Manila, to provide medical, social work, vocational training, and other services to persons uprooted from their urban homes.

Because of its experiences in Vietnam, Laos, and the Philippines, OBI has evolved its own methodology in improving community conditions. The OBI approach is characterized by definite stages: entry, establishment of headquarters-operating group, expansion, coordination, and, finally, withdrawal. OBI efforts are also typified by the "balanced team" concept, where each OBI team sent to the field is expected to have all the necessary skills needed for the project.

The manner of entry of an OBI team into an area usually depends on the most serious community problem. Thus, if health and sanitation were considered to be the most important problems, medical personnel are the first ones to enter the area. If infra-structure projects were needed, an engineer and construction crews may be sent first. The important thing is that the team would perform a most needed service, and, in so doing, attract the attention and the cooperation of the people.

As other problems are defined, other members of the team who can help are introduced. The OBI approach is a "total" one. Complementarities in projects and services are usually taken advantage of. Each OBI worker is trained to look at a problem from various angles. Although he is a specialist, he is encouraged to find out how other skills would fit into the whole program.

When the community has already accepted the main team, a headquarters group is maintained in the area. From this center, specialist teams radiate to other areas pinpointing problems and offering solutions. With the people's acceptance of the team in the adjoining areas, field clinics or centers are set up, serviced by mobile teams. Other headquarters units may be set up in these field centers if the magnitude of the problems warrant it.

With the expansion of the operations, both in functional scope and geographical area, the problem of coordination comes up. OBI solves this by decentralizing authority to the field teams as much as possible. A continuous system of reporting is also considered an integral part of operations.

As the activities of OBI progress, the team members look for local people to serve as counterparts. These people are attracted as volunteer trainees and encouraged to help around the OBI center. As they become trained, the OBI team members gradually transfer duties and responsibilities to them. When the community becomes self-reliant, therefore, assistance of OBI is gradually withdrawn until the time comes when the team can totally pull out and transfer operations to another place, with services being continued by the now thoroughly trained local people.

This approach, learned and taken to heart by every OBI trainee, is the ideal to which they all aspire. When OBI agreed to participate in the Barrio Magsaysay pilot project, the organization requested that a certain area be set aside for the OBI team. During the organizational phase, it was considered desirable to field three teams in Barrio Magsaysay, with each team composed of representatives from the various cooperating agencies. However, this approach would have interfered with the basic OBI methodology. As a compromise, therefore, all OBI workers were assigned to only one area, although other workers from other agencies were also fielded with them. It was reasoned out that the "balanced team" approach would still hold, for although other members of the team were from other agencies, the skills they represented were complementary to those of the other team members.

The OBI workers who participated in the pilot project were:

Truman Cainglet, team leader, Bachelor of Science in mathematics.

Teofista de los Reyes, home technologist. Bachelor of Science in home technology. Had worked as a home technologist with OBI in Laos.

Rodolfo Combalecer, Doctor of Medicine. Finished his M.D. and was being trained for duty in Laos.

Ma. Aucema Romero, registered nurse, training for Laos duty.

### DIVISION OF CITY SCHOOLS

The City of Manila, under the provisions of its charter (Republic Act No. 409), is charged with proper implementation of the constitutional provisions on education. The Division of City Schools carries out this task. It has jurisdiction over 94 public schools, 32 day and night classes, 5 evening vocational schools, and 57 elementary schools. Since 1961, complete free education has been provided by the city government to *bona fide* city residents.

One of the services offered by the Division of City Schools includes adult and community education. A special section was set up on 1 July 1963 to take care of this program. The unit is charged with the job of educating children, youth, and adults more effectively through active participation in the study and solution of community problems. In what is known as the community-school movement, the City of Manila decided to involve members of the community in the function of education.

The Adult and Community Education Services promotes functional literacy, develops occupational skills and competencies, inculcates healthful living, fosters civic consciousness, helps improve the cultural and social life in the community, and promotes education of out-of-school youth and adults.

On the community level, this program is represented by the teacher-coordinator, who is usually assisted by teachers and *pook* advisers. The teacher-coordinator is supervised by the chief of the Adult and Community Education Services. He usually performs his jobs through demonstrations, community assemblies and forums, study sessions, literacy classes, opportunity classes in dressmaking and handicrafts, mass education through audiovisual aids and television broadcasts, library and museum facilities, field trips, inter-community visitations, and other means.

In the Barrio Magsaysay pilot project, the Division of City Schools was represented by three teacher-coordinators:

Francisco Nerecina, Bachelor of Science in elementary education.

Matilde Rodriguez, holder of an elementary teacher's certificate.

Maria Sugay, holder of an elementary teacher's certificate.

## DEPARTMENT OF SOCIAL WELFARE

The Department of Social Welfare in the City of Manila was created on 18 June 1964 to "establish and operate a comprehensive social service program for the City of Manila, consisting of basic services and assistance to families and children, service for groups, and community service." [2] Prior to the creation of the department, social services had been provided by the various offices in the city government such as the Division of Recreation under the Department of Engineering and Public Works, the Social Service Section of the Manila Health Department, the Youth Welfare Council under the Office of the Mayor, and the Youth Reception Center under the Manila Police Department. The newly created department was an attempt to coordinate all these services and place them under one unit.

As set up in 1967, the Department of Social Welfare had 382 officials and personnel, working in four operating divisions—the Division of Child and Family Welfare, Community Welfare Division, Division of Institutions, and the Division of Recreation. The department had a budget of ₱2,038,475 in 1966, 60 per cent of which went to salaries and wages, 38 per cent for operation and maintenance, and 2 per cent for general assistance.

The DSW unit that participated in Barrio Magsaysay was the Community Welfare Division, which handles such services as disaster relief, service for slum dwellers and squatters, introduction of self-help projects, and organization of neighborhood associations and community and day-care centers. This unit also makes surveys of squatters, takes charge of relocation, and initiates self-help projects to augment the income of poor people.

The personnel from the DSW who participated in the Barrio Magsaysay pilot project were:

Lolita Garcia, social worker. She holds a Bachelor of Science in education.

Carmelita Urquico, social worker. Holds a Bachelor of Science in education; major in social work.

Elsa Clemente, social worker. Holds a Bachelor of Science in social work.

## PEACE CORPS-PACD PROGRAM

The Peace Corps was one of the new programs started with a great deal of enthusiasm during the Kennedy Administration in the United States. In 1964, an agreement was reached between the Peace Corps office and the Presidential Assistant on Community Development to launch a joint program. One main complaint against the Peace Corps program in the Philippines and elsewhere was the lack of experience of the volunteers sent by the U.S. government. The Peace Corps-PACD program tried to remedy this, by specifying that people with some definite experience in a specialized skill would be recruited for this joint program.

Most of the volunteers who arrived in the Philippines in 1965 were indeed experienced and skilled in some particular lines. Many of them, however, were suitable skills for urban work. The industrial United States produces not quite enough people with specialization in agriculture. Hence, many of the PCV's were assigned to urban areas, where their skills would be more useful.

At first three PCV's were assigned to the Barrio Magsaysay project. However, only two of them remained. They were:

John Haley, Bachelor of Science in psychology; a graduate who had done some research work in urban sociology.

Walter R. Turner, Bachelor of Arts in history; a graduate who had some experience in urban community organization work.

John Haley was attached to the research team and Walter Turner was assigned to Team I, where he concentrated on organizing youth clubs, seeking assistance for medical aid to the community, and organizing residents of Barrio Magsaysay for community self-help projects.

## U. P. COLLEGE OF PUBLIC ADMINISTRATION

The College of Public Administration of the University of the Philippines was established as a teaching, research, and extension agency in the field of public administration. It was founded in 1952, under a joint program between the University of Michigan and the University of the Philippines, with the financial assistance of the U.S. Agency for International Development and a number of private foundations in the United States.

Aside from its teaching functions (offered are a Bachelor of Arts in public administration and a Master of Arts in public administration), the CPA faculty engages in researches, ranging from technical assistance to urban governments. The CPA provides extension service as well (training, organization and management audits, personnel, fiscal matters, etc.).

The Barrio Magsaysay study was one of the special projects under the CPA's Local Government Center. As deputy director of the center, I was directly in charge of the research function. (I have a Ph.D. in political science from the Massachusetts Institute of Technology and have written a book on Metropolitan Manila politics, *The City in Nation-Building.* I am especially interested in the social and economic factors that influence voting behavior in urban slums.)

Other personnel of the CPA who worked with the Barrio Magsaysay project were:

Mila Abad, Bachelor of Science in foreign service; a graduate of the University of the Philippines, who was then working toward her Master of Arts in public administration at the UP.

Nilda H. Lopez, Bachelor of Science in foreign service; a graduate, also working toward her Master of Arts in public administration at the UP.

Roberto C. San Juan, Bachelor of Arts in political science; a graduate of the University of the Philippines, who was also working toward his Bachelor of Laws from the UP.

All of the persons mentioned above were with the research team.

## Cooperation and Coordination

The team approach to urban community development is based on the assumption that varied factors account for community problems. While it is often tempting to readily provide simple solutions to problems, a healthy respect for their complexity is often necessary for a thorough and complete solution. To meet complex problems, we need varied skills. Hence, a team of technicians trained to take a composite view and made up of varied and complementary skills will most likely solve a problem more effectively than just one person. Several heads are better than one.

Team cooperation is based on the willingness of people to participate in a certain activity. Hence, it assumes agreement with the main goals of the activity, or, at least lack of antagonism to it. Some administrative writers have theorized that a person will cooperate in an activity if it falls within his "zone of acceptance"; that is, if it does not run counter to his values.[3]

The usual concept of cooperation connotes concerted action among equals. The superior-subordinate relationships of people, especially in organizations, however, are not barriers to cooperation. The most important ingredient of cooperation is willingness to take part in the activity. It requires assuming the role expected of the member and "doing one's share of the work."

Coordination, like cooperation, has for its goal the accomplishment of the job with each necessary action occurring at the proper time and with desired results. The main difference between the two concepts, however, is the role played by authority in coordination. Cooperation mainly relies on voluntary actions and informal sanctions. Coordination is enforced authoritatively.

In the Philippine setting, this authoritative character of coordination tends to be overemphasized. If there are people being coordinated, then there must be coordinators. In the hierarchical way of thinking of most Filipinos, superior-subordinate relationships are the most important aspects of coordination.

It is true that according to administrative management, the specialized work of organizational units may be tied up together by hierarchical specialization that helps coordination. However, the arrangement of jobs in superior-subordinate levels is only one of the means by which coordination may be achieved. Coordination, after all, is mainly goal-oriented. One author has even given a simple definition of it as "letting the left hand know what the right hand is doing with respect to matters of mutual interest so that courses of action subsequently taken by both hands either jointly or separately may be so enlightened as to have a relevant bearing on whatever problem is at hand." [4] Meeting the problem is the primary goal of coordination. Information exchange, planning, fiscal controls, and dominance of an idea, and even cooperation itself, therefore, may be used as coordinative devices.

One of the main blocks to agency coordination in the Philippines is the idea that the coordinator has higher power and prestige than the one being coordinated. This is especially true, as it was in Barrio Magsaysay, where several agencies with no official superior-subordinate relationships are involved in performing a job. Thus, in inter-agency cooperation, the lines of authority as the source of coordinative power cannot be availed of. Instead, such approaches as teamwork, democratic leadership, open consultation, committees, planning, and communication devices have to be used.

To achieve coordination, one need not always resort to authority and the use or threat of formal sanctions. This other form of coordination may be called "cooperative coordination." Through this method, coordination may be exercised through communication, persuasion, open consultation, teamwork, and other non-coercive means.

### GUIDES TO COOPERATIVE COORDINATION

Based on the experience in Barrio Magsaysay, certain generalizations may be made regarding ways and means of making cooperative coordination work. With allowances, these may be also revelant to other projects requiring inter-agency efforts.

1. *Cooperative coordination is enhanced by emphasis on the main task to be done.*

If the cooperative efforts of participating agencies are to accomplish their aims, emphasis must be placed on the importance of such aims. Lacking the specific statement of goals set by formal authority, cooperating persons must first agree on the importance and dominance of what they set up as their main goals. This must be done to the extent of each participant subordinating his agency loyalty or personal preferences to the goal commonly agreed upon. Only when the "dominance of the goal" is clearly seen may one expect a willing cooperative attitude.

Agreement on goals is usually helped by the sharing of common frames of reference. The idea of community development, for example, must be clearly understood by all participating individuals if CD projects are to succeed. In a paper, Castillo posed the question: "Does it mean that a deeper understanding of the community development program would solve the problem of lack of coordination?"[5] The answer to this, of course, is a qualified yes. By itself, a deeper understanding of the community development program is not sufficient to solve the coordination problem. However, it does help enhance the chances for coordination. If cooperating individuals share the same goals, the same concepts, and similar terminologies, it is easier for them to work together effectively.

2. *The roles of each participant in a community development program must be clearly defined to prevent friction.*

The action and research officials of the Barrio Magsaysay pilot project tried to define clearly the various functions involved in the undertaking. Since new approaches and techniques were being used, however, it was not possible to anticipate all activities. Many of the decisions made during the project, moreover, were the results of "brainstorming sessions" and formal meetings, where each participant was thoroughly involved. As such, it was sometimes difficult to arrive at common understandings of definite roles because most decisions were the products of bargaining and compromise.

The Barrio Magsaysay experience showed that where individual roles of CD workers were not clearly defined, friction was likely to arise. The most common sources of misunderstanding was the functional distinction between action and research. Another frequent source of friction was the area of personal responsibility. The CD teams usually parceled out responsibilities according to function (fund raising, organizing, evaluation) or by geographical areas (blocks 1 to 3 would be the responsibility of Worker A; 4 to 6, of Worker B; etc.). Where such distinctions were not observed, the misunderstandings were frequent.

The distinctions between action and research were functionally differentiated in the research design. There were some grey areas, however, where the distinction was not clear. For example, interviewing of persons in the community could be done both by research or action personnel. Though functionally this could be assigned to research, action team members would also benefit from it.

Since both action and research teams were working in the field, it was inevitable that they helped each other in their functions. Thus, action team members helped locate research subjects for the research team. The researchers, in turn, fed back information to the action teams to help plan and improve their programs. In this exchange of favors, however, frictions sometimes arose. Thus, when a researcher helped with the conducting of a nursery class, some action team members considered this as "meddling." When an action team member tried to give some comment on the design of a particular specialized study, it was also resented by some research team members.

Not only functional roles but also vertical or hierarchical roles were subject to misinterpretation. A person given responsibilities without the knowledge of other team members was likely to be teased or reprimanded by the others for "usurpation of powers." Thus, when one team member was asked to look into such details as reminding the others about submitting their reports or clearing their requests to the project director through him, this was taken by team members as undue assumption of prerogatives by this person. This matter was raised in one discussion meeting, and it was clarified. But before this, some friction arose between the person and other members of the team.

3. *Coordination among participating agencies must be conducted at all levels.*

The team members in the Barrio Magsaysay project were individuals with aptitudes, skills, and their own ideas. They were also members of organizations to which they owed loyalty, their status, and their pay. As such, they were subject to the policies, rules, and regulations of their own agencies, even as they subordinated themselves to the points agreed upon in the team discussions and to the directives of the project staff.

In the memorandum of understanding among the various agencies involved, it was made clear that all persons detailed to the project would be subject to the project administration but would be paid from their own agency funds. Although this was clear enough, there were certain problems during the operations that could not be avoided. For example, though the team members reported to the project staff (their time records were signed by the project director), they knew that this was only a temporary assignment and that, at the end of the project, they would have to go back to their old jobs. In the meantime, certain developments would be going on in their offices, events that would affect their long range careers and plans. Thus, the team members had their attention keenly attuned to things going on in their agencies. This prevented them from devoting full attention to the project itself.

Even with the agency's formal commitment to the pilot project, there were times when developments in the participating agencies required the immediate withdrawal or transfer of some of the personnel involved in it. When this occurred, the progress of the project was affected. For example, Operation Brotherhood participants in the project were primarily trainees being prepared for overseas work. Thus, as vacancies in Laos occurred, or when they were already considered trained enough for overseas assignment, they had to be pulled out of the pilot project.

The team member's identification and allegiance to two

types of bureaucratic structures inevitably brought about conflicts of orders—because they were still technically subject to orders from their own units that conflicted with those issued by the project management staff. This only showed the importance of coordination at all levels among the agencies concerned. If this is achieved, through open communication or frequent consultation among the officials of the participating agencies, these misunderstandings could be avoided.

4. *Cooperative coordination is achieved through joint planning.*

Inter-agency cooperation is most needed in planning, which may be conceptually defined as the laying out of future courses of action. Through frequent meetings and discussions, the cooperating team members must agree on the action to be taken to achieve their goals. They must come up with suggestions on alternative means, participate in estimating the relative costs and benefits of such alternatives, and then have a hand in the choice of such means. In this way, all the skills and experience of team members are brought out, and the best lines of action achieved.

Another benefit of joint planning arises from the sense of participation that comes from it. Participation means involvement, and this in turn brings commitment. Because a team member had participated in the formulation of a certain plan, he develops a stake in it. This motivates him to do his best for the effective implementation of that plan, which, needless to say, improves the chances for success.

Finally, a plan is one of the best ways of assuring coordination. A good plan is frozen action. If it is properly phased and regulated and if it is flexible enough to allow for changes arising from effective "feed-back" communication, it maximizes the chances for success. The plan, if it provides for the specific roles of the team members in the implementation phase, provides them with clear lines of action. Thus, even with minimum intervention from persons holding superior positions of authority, action will flow smoothly if it is performed according to plan.

5. *The goals and methodologies of the participating agencies must be reconciled with the main objectives of the work.*

The main source of strength of inter-agency cooperation is also its vulnerable point. Because inter-agency effort taps the specialized resources and skills of varied entities, it is able to meet the complex problems posed by such a challenge as urban community development. At the same time, however, the more agencies involved in a project, the greater is the likelihood that agency goals and methodologies would be different, making it difficult to reconcile them and to bring about concerted action.

Understanding the main goals of community development, as mentioned in observation 1 above, may help bring about coordinated effort. In addition to this, however, each agency must take pains to understand the objectives and methods of the other agencies engaged with them in this work. It is the duty of every agency representative to find out what specific goals and methods are being used by the others and to find out how these will fit into the general plan of action.

The difference in methodologies is most obvious between public and private agencies. While the broad goals of service to fellow men may be the same between the two types of agencies, differences occur in their approach to this objective.

Lacking the regular fund-sources that government agencies often take for granted in their budget requests, private agencies have to be constantly on the lookout for persons, institutions, and groups that may assist them in their perennial funding difficulties. This search for funds, therefore, influences their approaches. Unlike government agencies, they have to constantly court the good will of would-be contributors. As such, they have to use publicity and other techniques to convince others that it pays to support private charitable organizations.

An example of this difference in viewpoint may be found in the public and private agencies' attitude towards publicity. Early in the Barrio Magsaysay project, it was decided by the staff that there should be no publicity on the efforts in Barrio Magsaysay because of the danger that the project may raise false hopes about the real intention of the government in the place. It was known early that the people were battling for ownership of the land they were squatting on and that they would use any means to improve their claim. If it became widely known that a government agency (PACD) and other entities were working in the area, this might be construed as official sanction for the people's tenure. So, a ban on publication of anything about the pilot project was imposed.

One of the cooperating agencies in the place, however, considered publicity and public relations an essential part of its approach. To Operation Brotherhood International a judicious and skillful use of publicity is necessary for generating support for its projects, for reporting to the public on accomplishments, and even for allowing the people to voice their own opinions on OBI operations. One of the proposals of the head of the OBI team, therefore, was the printing and circulation of a community newspaper.

As proposed, the community newspaper would serve as the voice of the people of Barrio Magsaysay, although it would be run and managed by the pilot project teams. It would contain news of interest to the community, profiles of community leaders, a forum on community problems and proposed solutions as seen by the people. The paper would not only be circulated inside the community but also would be sent to local and national leaders and to other interested persons.

Although the other team members agreed that a community newspaper would have a positive function in the community, they argued that it would violate the ban on publicity. They were also afraid that the people of the community and their leaders may use the paper as a propaganda sheet for their protracted fight for the land. These arguments and counterarguments were threshed out in staff meetings. Finally, the proposal was withdrawn.

Still, the publicity issue focuses on a basic difference in approach. To a private civic organization, it is almost mandatory that publicity be used to achieve support. Many people do not just contribute to private civic efforts out of a generous and magnanimous nature. They have their own particular interests, and publicity is one of them. If there is a need for proof regarding this, the pictures and press releases of company officials and personages handing over checks and cash to various charities, so generously spread all over the newspapers, would be enough. Donations, especially when publicized, are one of the few cases where donors may have their cake and eat it too. They get free publicity and tax deductions.

To the government civil servant, service is considered its own reward. But this is only possible under conditions of an assured budget, a payroll that can be regularly met, and where resources are not the worry of the agency. Where civic volunteers have to scrounge about for resources and often their very maintenance, they have to use all methods considered fit to do their work.

There are other issues on both goals and methods that differentiate public and private agencies. For example, there is the question of office hours. As civil service employees, those in the government service are covered by the eight-hour law. As such, they are entitled to overtime pay when they stay late in the field or when they have to visit the field on weekends to perform their jobs. This issue is not so crucial with private employees, whose organizations are usually small and manageable enough to be flexible.

## Conclusion

In the urban environment, inter-agency cooperation is the most likely administrative process that would yield good results for community development. The resources and skills of the city are just too many to be centralized in one administrative unit, without loss of efficiency and effectiveness. While a government agency (such as the Division of Community Development under the City Government) may be set up to "coordinate" the whole effort, this agency must rely on the cooperation of the many entities in the city if it is to succeed.

As it is, many public and private agencies are engaged in various programs designed to achieve a better urban life. Their services range from health and welfare to purely physical renovations of the urban environment. Because they remain bureaucratic entities, with very little contact with their human clientele, they tend to view the urban problem from their own narrow focus as defined in their formal statement of duties and responsibilities.

Urban community development attempts to "coordinate" these various functions. In achieving this goal, however, certain new administrative concepts and structures are needed. Hence, instead of hierarchical coordination, an urban community development movement must rely on cooperative coordination. Instead of expecting that orders would be self-executing as soon as they are officially issued, the urban community development official must create and hammer out compromise from many agencies that have various aims and different methodologies.

The task of community development becomes more difficult when the elected or chosen leaders of the various urban communities come in. Political by instinct and pragmatic in practice, they are quick to take advantage of urban community development programs to further their own ends. To properly coordinate the efforts of these local leaders, first among themselves, and then in their relationships with the bureaucratic agencies, Urban cd workers require new skills. It is hoped that the various propositions presented here would be useful in the pursuit of their aim.

The job of the Urban cd worker is further made difficult when the sense of community does not exist in his community. In Barrio Magsaysay, the people were united because of the outside threat of eviction. If this was not the case, the Urban cd workers would have had to start from the initial step in Urban cd work—the development of the sense of community itself.

In a way, creating a sense of community is the initial step on the road to cooperative coordination. But locating common goals and finding out organizational techniques that would help him in welding a group of varied persons together, the cd worker may be able to improve his organizational talents. As his efforts go beyond the community and reach the relatively more powerful but no less confusing area of inter-agency cooperation, his initial experiences would be of some help.

It is the ideal of "democratic decision-making" and personal participation so central to community development that makes Urban CD so difficult. There is a great temptation to do something *for* the urban slum people, so difficult is their lot and so pitiful is their condition. However, the greater challenge is how to do something *with* them, through their emotional involvement, their organized efforts, and their joint resolve.

In a similar manner, it is so easy to perform the job of one's organization—the lines of authority are so much clearer, the spheres of responsibility so much more defined. Yet, the greater challenge is how to work *with* other agencies, for, in the long run, this is the only effective way of providing effective services.

# CHAPTER 8

# Urban Community Development Projects

The most important part of an urban community development program involves the various projects that are introduced into a community. Since people judge the effectiveness of a program on the types of projects introduced and on the relative success or failure of each, careful planning and attention must be given to the nature of projects selected, the manner in which they are introduced, the resources needed to achieve them, and the role of the initiators and the community members in their successful completion.

In Barrio Magsaysay, a variety of projects were introduced. Each one of these was carefully planned to fit into a general approach and to fulfill a particular part in a larger design. Such projects may be categorized under the following broad headings: (1) service-impact projects; (2) community organization projects; (3) infra-structure projects; and (4) income-producing projects. Although not all of the projects mentioned here were brought to a successful completion, the rationale and the means used for each one may shed light on its value as part of an integral program.

## Service-Impact Projects

As mentioned in Chapter 6, entry was considered one of the most crucial parts of the action-research pilot project. Because of the welfare orientation of most urban slum dwellers, projects that provide a particular service to the community are easily welcomed by the people. The trust generated by such projects constitute the foothold, from which the Urban CD workers are able to introduce other efforts that foster self-reliance. When the service-impact projects have already resulted in close rapport and cooperation with the people, more ambitious projects that require more community resources and participation may be introduced.

### RELIEF AND CHARITY

The most common service-impact projects are in the form of distribution of relief goods to the most needy members of the slum community. Examples of these are the "rations" of food stuff given by the Social Welfare Administration or the food program administered by the Catholic Relief Service. Because the people entitled to these charity programs are usually almost on the level of starvation, relief is needed. A person with an empty stomach whose children are starving cannot be expected to take interest in community organizations or other developmental activities.

The too-open and sometimes indiscriminate distribution of relief goods, however, sometimes creates a sense of dependence on the Urban CD teams. When this happens, it becomes very difficult to introduce projects that foster self-reliance and personal pride. In fact, where slum dwellers are encouraged to develop dependence, they become extremely hurt when the CD teams demand some sort of contribution from them. The religious connotation of pious giving emphasizes the blessedness of charity. One should not expect something for what one gives; giving is its own reward.

The impact of relief and charity projects as entry wedges into the community may be channeled toward more positive ends if the distribution of such goods is carefully confined to people who are poor. The CD worker may ask the community's leaders for the name of families in the place who are so poor that they are on the verge of starvation. The reasons for the identification of these families should not be divulged. Since most persons are too proud to admit that they are really on the brink of starvation, only a few truly poor people can be identified. Quietly and without fanfare, relief goods should be extended to these really poor families. When this act becomes known in the community, there may be some objections on the part of others who also would want some relief goods. However, the condition of abject poverty required before distribution of relief would discourage others from pressing their claims too aggressively. At the same time, the good act of the Urban CD teams would be known. If the selection of the poor families was correctly done, the people would be impressed with the fairness of the distribution and an impact would be created.

Another way of distributing relief with maximum benefits is to use it as a prize for activities favored by the Urban CD teams. This method may smack of blackmail, but slum families may be given relief goods, *provided* they do such things as setting up their own toilet, cleaning their yards, providing their own garbage can, or showing some such effort or bringing about changes desired by the CD worker. In this way, the relief goods are valued, and the change agents achieve what they want.

Variations on the distribution of relief goods without causing dependence may include giving the goods on a special or timely occasion (Christmas time, inauguration of a community center, opening of a community project, after a disaster, etc.). In this way, the charitable intent of the relief is masked, and the people don't lose too much self-respect in receiving relief goods from local leaders. Where the CD teams want to build up the image of a particular community leader to facilitate social organization, this may be done. However, one danger of distributing goods through leaders is the inevitable jealousies and frictions that this move usually causes. Charges of partisanship aimed against the leader may ricochet on the CD teams, thus, defeating the primary purpose for the distribution of relief in the first place.

The important thing to remember about relief and charity is that while it may create good will on the part of the people, it may also breed a sense of dependence and a feeling that the Urban cd teams may be fooled into giving more goods. The task of the cd worker is to find the right balance between the benefits and the dangers involved in such a project.

## MEDICAL SERVICE

Health and sanitation is usually one of the problems in urban areas that is almost synonymous with slum life. Because of the overcrowding in the slums; the run-down condition of housing; the lack of such basic facilities like water, light, and fuel; and the low income that usually results in malnutrition, the health of the people in a slum community is usually not satisfactory. When the lack of medical, dental, and nursing services is added to all these factors, the problem becomes serious, indeed.

Providing medical service, therefore, is one of the most effective ways of generating cooperation in the community. This is especially true in the Philippines, where people are generally careful about their health. The physician in white is one of the most enduring symbols of goodness in the Philippines. The sight of one in a crowded slum area is usually welcomed by the people.

As in relief and charity, the difficult job of medical service program organizers is how to balance free service with independence. This becomes somewhat serious since, aside from breeding dependence, free medical service is usually equated by the people with poor or even inadequate service. Thus, people want to make sure that full-fledged doctors and not just medical students or interns are giving them service. They grumble about being treated as "human guinea pigs" when they suspect that medical students are "just studying them."

A nominal fee for consultation and full charge for medicine may be introduced as part of the medical service. Aside from keeping the pride of the patients intact, the payment is also some kind of assurance that the people are getting worthwhile service. Even when medicine is donated by drug companies, it may not be wise to give it away free. At the most, discounts should be extended to really needy patients.

Medical service, because of the inter-dependence between health and other aspects of life, may also be used as a means of inducing desirable changes. Thus, preventive medicine should be taught with the curative function. Instead of just effecting cure, a good doctor should know how to relate illness with such things as cleanliness, environmental sanitation, nutritional habits, and even leisure habits. The treatment period may also be used for effective gathering of information related to other programs. This is especially made easy when the doctor is also knowledgeable in social science research methods, interviewing techniques, and methodical means of observation.

Medical service needs a total approach if it is to be effective as an impact program. Health, in all its aspects, must be faced by the medical practitioner. In this way, it facilitates the introduction of new programs and strengthens the meaningfulness of other approaches.

**EDUCATION**

The Filipino's passion for education is almost legendary. Most family heads in urban slums see the bright future of their children in terms of finishing their education. No sacrifice is considered too big to enable children to study. Educational programs are almost always welcomed by people in slum communities.

There are usually two ways of introducing educational projects: (1) setting up nursery or kindergarten schools or (2) tying up with a nearby school for the offering of extension classes in the slum area. Philippine laws prohibit the opening of regular classes without permission from the Department of Education. Nursery or kindergarten classes, however, may be offered anytime by anyone.

Opening a nursery or kindergarten class in a slum area is not new. Dr. Maria Montessori started her famous system of pre-school education in the slums of Rome. Even with the use of teaching techniques less sophisticated than the Montessori system, however, effective results may be obtained.

The nursery or kindergarten school performs many functions. For example, children are cleaned by their mothers before they are allowed to go to school because the mothers know that they would be mingling with other children. Thus, where formerly, children were allowed to wear dirty or tattered clothes, to run around with running noses, and to spend the whole day unwashed and unkempt, the regular attendance at the school forces the mothers to do their duty. When coupled with a school feeding program, the school also supplements the poor nutritional contents of the food children get at home.

It is, however, what the children learn in school, which is the most important aspect of educational projects. Lessons in a nursery or kindergarten class need not be complicated. They may include washing of hands, lacing of shoes, buttoning one's own shirt, sweeping the floor, and other common things that neat, healthy children are supposed to learn. Children's songs, stories, games, and puzzles may also be introduced. The three R's may or may not be attempted, depending on the preparation of the teacher and the readiness of the children.

Another important thing learned in the nursery or kindergarten class is the matter of adjustment to a child's peer group and to a formal learning environment. Just the mere sight of books, of sitting together with other children and doing things with them, or carrying a bag to school and being a student— all these have their own meaning for the child. Where the school atmosphere is warm and friendly and it contrasts sharply with the drab environment of the slum children, the effect on the children's motivations are beyond measure. The school program is also made more meaningful when it is supplemented with occasional field trips and excursions. Aside from normal trips to the zoo and the parks, it is sometimes useful to bring slum children to such modern and new places like the supermarket, the high-class residential areas (like Forbes Park), and other places they would never see otherwise. In this way, the child's horizon is broadened, and the drive to excel is heightened.

The established school system may also be used for educational service projects. The community-school movement, which makes the school the center of community efforts for improvement, is especially helpful in this regard. With the help of teacher-coordinators, adult education and vocational training programs may be introduced as part of the urban CD program.

The Parent Teacher Association (PTA) is also one of the most effective instruments for organized social change in slum communities. When the education of their children is the issue at stake, most Filipino heads of families would be eager to cooperate. Thus, programs may be launched with the cooperation of the PTA, or, at least, the PTA may be one of the sources of funds and resources for urban CD projects.

In Manila, the use of regular schoolhouses at night for vocational instruction is one of the most inspired programs of the education authorities. There is really no reason why the physical plant of the school, which is paid for by public funds, should be left idle during times when it can be effectively used for beneficial programs. Thus, in many high schools or even elementary schools, night classes in electronics, stenography and typing, cooking, automotive skills, tailoring and dressmaking, and other useful skills are taught. Where an Urban CD program can be tied up with such opportunity classes, they provide long-range solutions to the problems of slum dwellers and squatters.

## Community Organization Projects

Another type of Urban CD project that is helpful in achieving the aims of community development involves the aggregation and mobilization of the people's efforts for the achievement of worthwhile goals. A sense of community is the primary requisite for the success of urban community development. Thus, where it is present, it should be nurtured and channeled to more productive ends. Where it is not too apparent, the Urban CD worker must create it and make it functional.

### THE FIESTA AND OTHER SOCIAL ACTIVITIES

One indication of the strength of a sense of community in any area is the way in which people celebrate the fiesta, or the annual feast of the community's patron saint. Originally started as a religious observance, the fiesta has become an almost purely social activity characterized by much feasting, drinking, brass bands, and shows. Two days every year, it is said, the Filipino buys his status and prestige in the community in the way he celebrates the fiesta.

The fiesta is important because it is a community effort. In the slum areas, especially, people feel that they have to celebrate the fiesta even in the midst of poverty. As a community effort, the fiesta is an excellent test of leadership qualities among local leaders. Since it involves collection of money, planning of activities, implementation of plans, auditing of expenses, and evaluation of success or failure, the fiesta is a good practice ground for community-wide activities.

The cooperative efforts shown in the fiesta need only some minor nudging on the part of Urban CD workers for it to be transferred to other group activities. Thus, the cooperative spirit may be extended to mutual-aid societies in case of illness or death on the part of community members. It may be used for the setting up of mutual-protection societies as the *ronda* (volunteer guard) system or the fire-fighting brigades. The leaders in the fiesta may be the ones tapped for these other activities. In such a way, the people's willingness to join group efforts may be redirected to other desirable ends.

The most common reason for the demise of community organizations is lack of funds. Thus, the fiesta and other social activities (including community dances and balls) may be used for fund-raising purposes. People in the slums, using their poverty as a ready excuse, usually resent contributions and assessments where they cannot see the direct benefits that their money brings about. It is thus next to impossible to charge each family with a general contribution for the association's treasury. If the collection is earmarked for the fiesta or some other community activity, then the people pay willingly. These feasts may be held, therefore, but their lavishness may be curtailed. In this way, savings from the social activities may be used for other projects.

## COMMUNITY-MAPPING AND HOUSE-NUMBERING

In most slum areas, people are aware of the natural boundaries of their communities, but they seldom care to formally define such boundary lines. Community-mapping, when done by the Urban CD teams, with the help of community leaders and the public, serve to foster community organization because it enhances community identification and solidarity. House-numbering has the same effect of fostering identification and pride in a person's home. The location of one's home in a community map has a very concrete way of symbolizing one's membership in that community. Where the map, with the homes is prominently displayed in the headquarters of the community organization, it serves to remind the people of their belonging to the community. This is quite aside from the pragmatic benefits that having a locator map of the community gives to the CD teams, visitors, the postman, and other people who wish to know more about the place. Finally, because the community-mapping and house-numbering may naturally be extended to the preparation of a community directory, this additional project provides the community leaders with an assessment of their numerical strength and enables the different community members to know each other by full names and not just by nicknames or faces. This fosters community solidarity.

## COMMUNITY ASSEMBLIES, MEETINGS, AND SEMINARS

The most important badge of a unified and well-functioning urban community is the number of successful meetings, assemblies, and seminars conducted by the leaders and the CD teams. Where a community is able to gather together its citizens and discuss common problems and propose solutions like the Athenians of old, then that community is indeed well organized. The theory of local governments that so impressed de Tocqueville is symbolized in these activities—the town meeting, the community assembly, and the local council—which gather together citizens and enable them to participate directly in the job of policy formulation and implementation.

Because of their training, some CD personnel tend to overemphasize the use of community assemblies and meetings in their operations. It is so tempting to conclude that a community that meets together acts together. cd workers often go to the extent of forcing such group activities on the people. When this is done, community assemblies defeat their very purpose, because the element of spontaneity is lost, the voluntary character of the community meeting is hampered, and the real will of the people does not get truly reflected. After several forced meetings, the people usually resent the nagging of the cd worker and turn against him.

One good way of making meetings work without taxing the patience of the people too much is through the use of the leaders' caucus. After the community organization has been set up and the real leaders that count are identified, the cd worker must help them develop a way of arriving at important decisions through frequent small meetings or caucuses. The really important decisions, therefore, would be only the ones presented to the community assembly. Such assemblies may also be held on special occasions so that the people would have a good motivation for attending. In this way, the leadership in the community is able to exercise influence, while the people do not get fed up with too much time wasted on meetings.

### Infra-Structure Projects

The projects where slum dwellers and squatters need the most help are usually infra-structures that require resources that far exceed the best that they can do. Roads, bridges (including catwalks), playgrounds, and buildings for public use (schools, health centers, and toilets) are much needed in urban slums. Since slums are usually reached only by narrow and muddy alleys, they are often inaccessible to police, fire-fighting, and other services available to other parts of the city. Since they are usually located in low-lying areas or even in places traversed by smelly *esteros,* they need bridges. The children, which seem to be the most marked characteristics of slums in the Philippines, need playgrounds, schools, and other facilities. The congestion makes it almost impossible for people to have their own toilets. Thus, they rely on public toilets, which are often so ill-maintained that they give the slum area its characteristic stink.

One main barrier to the provision of infra-structure projects to slum and squatter areas is land ownership. Where squatters are on public land (as in Barrio Magsaysay), the indeterminacy of their tenure makes both national and local governments refuse to set up relatively permanent construction and structures in the place. The long drawn-out negotiations for the roads in Barrio Magsaysay as well as the big controversy about the construction of a schoolhouse were all the results of the public nature of the land. Because the squatters were not welcome in the place, the government refused to set up any infra-structure projects that would have the effect of giving official approval to their illegal acts.

To the Urban CD worker desirous of setting up infra-structure projects, one good incentive is the usual willingness of the people to assist in the project. In their eagerness to avail of infra-structure projects, squatters and slum dwellers usually offer their free labor and other forms of assistance in the implementation of such projects. Thus, in Barrio Magsaysay, labor was always assured by the people whenever road repairs, building of catwalks, or the digging of drainage canals were called for.

One especially constructive way of making infra-structure projects possible is the use of Catholic Relief Service goods as "payments in kind" for work in infra-structure projects. By supplying the daily protein and other nutritional needs of the squatter family, his worry about not being able to look for money and other resources while engaged in the community project is taken away. He is thus able to save his pride by working for the relief goods he receives. At the same time, he is directly benefitted by the infra-structure projects cooperatively done by the community.

Infra-structures, interestingly enough, are the main needs of the slum and squatter areas. In fact, in most cases, they spell the difference between a really run-down community and a place where even poor people enjoy some degree of comfort. By the narrow policy that prohibits the setting up of infrastructures in public and private lands, the government is only making the slum problem worse. For neglect will never solve the problem; neither will indifference and hostility. What needs to be done is to make life in the slums and squatter areas as comfortable as is humanly possible under the circumstances. Then, perhaps, by providing the infra-structure facilities that are so needed by these areas, their conditions will improve, and, with such progress, people in these areas would contribute to the growth of the city.

## Income-producing Projects

Providing services, organizing the people and assisting them in the construction of much-needed infra-structure projects are all necessary for the improvement of life in the slums. For more lasting benefits, however, income-producing projects are needed. Without the additional income that makes economic and social mobility possible, all the projects mentioned above would only result in the perpetuation of slums and the stifling of urban growth.

Income-producing projects may be broadly divided into those that generate income by training, by the organized utilization of locally available resources, by the introduction of new jobs and sources of livelihood, and by the use of projects that enable slum dwellers to cut down on expenditures and, thereby, save.

### TRAINING

The teaching of specialized skills is one of the most effective ways of generating additional income for people in the community. In Barrio Magsaysay, training in such skills as dressmaking, beauty culture, bag-making, tailoring, and those skills necessary for working as a waiter, maid, or nursemaid were introduced successfully in the area. By getting teachers from the outside or by tapping the skills of people already in the community who were good enough to volunteer their services, the Urban CD teams were able to turn out skilled residents who were able to pursue their trades.

Training is also enhanced by the willingness of some business firms to contribute in cash or in kind to the training program. Thus, sewing machine companies are often willing to lend their machines in the hope that, when the slum dwellers or squatters learn how to sew, they would buy the machines on an installment basis. Restaurants are often willing to send trainers for waiters to assure them of a steady source of men. Most middle- or upper-class families have maid problems, and they are quite willing to contribute something to a training program that turns out honest and responsible maids and *yayas*. Considering that maids and *yayas* usually are given free board and lodging, they sometimes actually earn more than ordinary employees or factory workers because their earnings are net incomes in the first place, and they don't have to spend too much for dresses, food, transportation, and other things that a regular employee or factory worker has to pay for.

A program of apprenticeship training managed by the Urban CD team is often one of the best ways of setting up a self-sustaining program. In this effort, the CD teams identify companies and agencies that require a certain type of skill. An apprenticeship agreement is then set up between this entity and the CD team, by which selected young adults in the community would be trained in a particular skill until they learn and are employed by the company. For making the apprenticeship arrangement, the CD team may get a percentage of the income of the apprentice. Such income may be plowed back into the project, for stationery, stamps, telephone bills, and other expediting arrangements. In this way, the continuity of the project is assured, and many more benefit.

### ORGANIZING THE USE OF LOCAL RESOURCES

Where the community is rich in human resources that are not fully tapped, the CD team may actually set up an organization that would tap these resources effectively. One good way of doing this is by setting up a non-profit employment agency. By acting as a broker between the job seeker and the employer, the project organizers are able to find jobs for their clients and to assure the work continuity of companies and persons in need of services.

Employment agencies may be set up for such jobs as

domestic help, laborers, construction gangs, carpenters, and white-collar workers. All that they have to do is conduct a comprehensive survey of the skills and talents in the community and prepare an updated file on this. Then, the CD teams may write or personally ask companies and agencies for possible vacancies. By matching vacancies with skills, they are able to find employment for their clientele.

To make the organizational work self-sustaining, a service fee may be charged the employer and the employee. A percentage of the salary, payable in long-term installments, may be taken from the employee while a lump-sum service charge may be levied against the employer. If this money so earned is used for expanding and improving the service, it would be able to improve the lot of many poor people.

Another way of making organized effort work is by utilizing the income of those who are able to save, through the use of credit unions, savings and loans associations, and other means of stretching the income of people who don't have enough. In spite of the difficulty of selling the idea of credit unions to Filipinos in general and slum dwellers and squatters in particular, there are some ways of realizing this. The traditional system of the *paluwagan*—by which a group of people agree to contribute a certain amount to a fund regularly, which fund is given to one member on a special occasion (usually his birthday)—may be used as the initial step in a credit union. When the benefits of this traditional system of savings and rewards become proven, a full-blown credit union or savings and loan association may then be established.

### HANDICRAFTS

Projects that combine both the training and the organized aspect of income generation usually take the form of handicrafts or cottage industries. Too often, people assume that such sources of income are good only for rural dwellers. Even in the city, especially in the slums, a large number of people are either unemployed or underemployed. By training them in such skills as bag-making, sewing of placemats and baby dresses, making of doormats from old rubber tires, woodcarving, basket-weaving, and other forms of cottage industries, squatters and slum dwellers are able to augment their income.

Once a significant number of people in the community become skilled and are able to perform work of an acceptable standard of quality, the CD teams may organize them into producers cooperatives, marketing associations, or just an association of producers. In this way, pricing, distribution outlets, design, and other specifications for the handicrafts may be arrived at as a group. By acting together, the participants are able to maximize the benefits that would otherwise be lost to them if they acted individually. The CD teams, therefore, have a large role to play both in the training and organizational aspects of handicrafts work.

### FACTORY-EXTENSION WORK

It is often found necessary by certain manufacturers and factories to farm out some of their jobs to organized groups because it is much cheaper to have jobs performed this way where no overheads in terms of buildings and utilities are needed. Good examples of such factory jobs that are done through contractual arrangements with leaders in certain communities are the sewing and ironing of baby dresses, embroidery work, snipping of excess parts of rubber sandals, and the assembly of certain simple toys and contraptions. By farming out these jobs through organized groups, the factory is able to avail of cheap labor and, therefore, incur less expense.

In the making of baby dresses for local sale or export, big factories usually cut out the patterns and shape the dresses mechanically. These are then distributed to skilled dressmakers and seamstresses, in slum or squatter communities, who are paid by the piece. Sometimes, finished dresses are just given finishing work, such as the sewing of hems, buttonholes, lace, and the like. There are also some factories that require only ironing or laundering; they also pay by the piece accepted on the basis of specified standards.

If an Urban Community Development team is able to get in touch with such factories needing service, take care of the training, and then organize the people to allocate work properly, it would be helping the people earn a great deal more than what they usually get. These factory-extension jobs have the added advantage of being done at home. As such, mothers need not be far from their homes and their children. They don't have to spend for transportation, dressing up, and *merienda* or lunch, because the work may be done at home. In this way, the income of poor people may be effectively increased.

### EXPENSE-REDUCING PROJECTS

One category of projects that enables slum dwellers and squatters to save more money involves ways and means of reducing their expenses. Such projects, for example, include community kitchens, consumer cooperatives, clothing exchanges, and thrift shops. They tend to increase the real income of people because they make living expenses cheaper.

In many slum communities, families don't bother to cook elaborate meals anymore. The mother, because she is too busy or too lazy, usually just cooks rice and buys ready-to-eat viands from the corner store. Normally, she has to pay quite a high price for the type of food she gets, because the storekeeper naturally has to make a profit.

A community kitchen designed to provide this service may be set up by an Urban CD team not only to make life easier for the housewife but also to provide nutritious and well-balanced food items at minimum cost. The initial capitalization may come from the community members themselves or from some civic-minded groups. After some study about the food preferences of the community and a survey into their willingness to buy ready-to-eat food, the community kitchen may be started. It must be made clear, however, that the kitchen is not meant to make profit. Instead, the food should be sold at a cost where the CD team recoups all expenses involved in operating the kitchen, including cost of the food ingredients, transportation, utilities, and the like. Since the element of profit is taken out, the community kitchen is able to sell food at a much lower cost. In this way, people are able to save, and their real income goes up.

Another expense-reducing project is the setting up of a consumer cooperative. Since most slum dwellers buy their food and other needs from small *sari-sari* stores, their expenses for such items may be reduced if they cooperatively owned such a store and shared in the profits they earned. As in the community kitchen, capitalization for the store may be obtained from contributions of the members of the community or from outside sources. Moreover, instead of being after profit, the store would be for service.

The benefits from the consumer cooperative may be spread either through yearly declaration of dividends or by immediate discounts upon purchase. In any case, the people who are members of the cooperative are able to save some money.

Clothing exchanges and thrift shops are effective ways of reducing the cost of clothing and other needs. In these shops, second-hand goods that are usually donated by well-off people are sold at nominal rates by the operators. Because the goods sold are not bought, all the proceeds from the sale are profits. Where such profits are used for projects that benefit the community, the clothing exchange or thrift shops perform a doubly useful purpose. They make available to the people still usable clothes and goods at cheap prices, and they enable the community to finance certain worthwhile projects. Again, because they reduce expenses, they add to the real income of the people.

## Conclusion

In almost all of the projects mentioned and described in this chapter, the benefits that should accrue to the community are fully explored. These benefits, however, would bear lasting results only if certain things are kept in mind by the Urban Community Development teams that may introduce any or a combination of them.

First, the importance of induced self-help should not be forgotten. Just because the role of the CD teams is emphasized in the discussions above, it does not mean that initiation, planning, and implementation should be the responsibility of the teams. If this is done, the squatters and slum dwellers may be able to augment their income or derive some partial benefits, but the most important thing they can possibly obtain from the projects—the important matter of pride and self-reliance—would be lost.

A good Urban CD worker works as if the people themselves are the ones that originate and implement the project. This does not require manipulative or deceitful skills. On the other hand, a proper respect for the skills and knowledge of his clientele should be the guiding spirit for every CD worker. For only if he respects squatters and slum dwellers as persons will a CD worker be able to bring his projects to successful completion.

Another thing that a CD worker has to remember is the importance of people's participation and improvement. Even if a project is fully launched and carried out, if this was due to the efforts of the CD teams alone and to the passive acceptance of the people, it would be considered a failure. For true urban community development has different standards of success. Efficiency in the achievement of programmed results, if not tempered with the need for participation and involvement, would be of little use to it.

Finally, the importance of emphasizing the proper methodology in the pursuance of urban CD projects should be mentioned. Each project must be thoroughly thought out and planned carefully; and such plan must be put into writing. In the planning process, the participation and involvement of other members of the CD team must be sought. The plan, in turn, must be properly programmed, with each line of activity phased according to time and function. There must be standards set for success or failure for each phase so that, in the final analysis, such standards may be used in a correct evaluation of the project.

The importance of methodology is heightened by the need for replication of the project in other places at other times. An urban community development program will tend to be more successful if it is big enough to make allowances for experimentation and innovation. Testing of methodologies under varying circumstances tends to isolate their weaknesses and strengths. In this way, the exact contribution of each project to the total urban CD effort may be defined.

# CHAPTER 9

# Savings and Slum Life

Most middle-class persons find it hard to understand why people flock to the slums. Slums are overcrowded, smelly, unsanitary, and full of trouble. They do not allow privacy. They lack the conveniences so necessary for good city living. So these middle-class persons conclude that slum dwellers live there because they have no other place to go to. They have reached a dead end, financially and psychologically. Some middle-class individuals may attribute this lack of fortune to Fate or Luck, but many of them will trace it to a character taint or personality flaw such as irresponsibility, laziness, and lack of drive, if not, indeed, immorality itself.

Not willing to accept middle-class norms at their face value, the research staff of the Barrio Magsaysay pilot project decided to ask the squatters and slum dwellers in the area themselves. First, the 2,625 family heads interviewed in the Barrio were asked if they would be willing to leave the place if the government asked them to. A resounding 72.5 per cent of them said no.

There may be many reasons why people get attracted to slums, reasons too subtle or abstract to be appreciated either by moral middle-class persons or the slum dwellers themselves. There is the fact, for example, that a slum community in Manila is usually composed of primary groups. Members of these groups identify with their place, find social and economic se-

---

This chapter is based on a special study conducted by Belinda Aquino and Roberto San Juan. See "Income and Expenditure Patterns in Barrio Magsaysay," May 1967. (Mimeographed MS), 35 pp.

curity in it, and are psychologically relaxed in the familiar nature of their environment. It may be also that the rural migrant finds solace in the traditional behavior patterns still found in the slums—the *damayan* and wakes; the *kapisanan* and the fiesta; and the *kumpadres* and feasts.

The most important reason for wanting to live in slums, of course, may still be economic. Indeed, the slum area makes urban life possible at bargain-basement rates. In the first place being a squatter or slum dweller means little or no rent at all. Food may be bought, rather quickly and cheaply, either from the ubiquitous *sari-sari* store or from the itinerant peddler. During hard times, the accommodating storekeeper may be convinced of giving food on credit. Clothing need not be too expensive—neighbors have a nasty habit of commenting on how pretty one's clothes are when all they smell from one's kitchen are *tuyo* and *daing*. And so, with food, clothing, and shelter all taken care of, who can blame the poor slum dweller for refusing to budge?

## The Study

To look into the economic attractions of slum dwelling, this special study was conducted in Barrio Magsaysay in September 1966. The methodology used was simple. A number of housewives were given notebooks and ballpens and then asked to note down every single item of expenditure incurred every day for forty-five days. It was explained to the housewives that this study was connected with the Barrio Magsaysay survey, and they agreed to cooperate. They were visited twice a week by research team members to make sure that they did not lag in their note-taking.

The sample from the study was drawn from the complete survey done in the Barrio the previous March. An original sample of 120 was drawn, 40 each from the three areas of the Barrio. The 40 respondents in each area were further divided according to income brackets: 10 for Group A (income below ₱ 100 a month); 20 for Group B (₱ 100 to ₱ 199 a month); and 10 for Group C (more than ₱ 200 a month).

For various reasons, roughly half of the original sample

was not able to complete the notebooks. The greatest mortality was in Area II of Barrio Magsaysay. During the course of the special study, certain misunderstandings occurred between the Barrio people and the pilot project staff regarding the desire of the Don Bosco Technical School to get a piece of land in the area. The Barrio people thought that the pilot project staff members were sympathetic to the idea of Don Bosco; because of this, they ceased to cooperate in all aspects of the project, including the special study.

In spite of the dropouts, however, a total of 62 notebooks were recovered. These were distributed roughly according to the income groupings: 18 for Group A; 28 for Group B; and 16 for Group C.

The items of expenditures noted down by the respondents were divided into three major categories: necessities, semi-optionals, and optionals. Necessities were items that were needed for the basic functions of life. Some of the items categorized under this were food, clothing, fuel, transportation fare, and medicine. Semi-optionals were those that were needed to supplement the basic needs. Such items as snacks, allowances, extra food ingredients, and others were classed in this category. Finally, optionals were those items that were not considered necessary for basic consumption. They included cigarettes, comic books, liquor, ornaments, movies, toys, and other recreational expenses. The survey results using these categories are seen in Table 12.

A SAMPLE FAMILY—THE RESONABLES

To get a qualitative feel of how the study worked, we cite the case of the Resonable family. From depth interviews and from day to day observations and conversations with Filoteo and Maria Resonable, the circumstances of the family's way of life were studied. The family, upon closer look, reveals why it is not too bad to live in the slums.

Filoteo Resonable comes from Irosin, Sorsogon, while Maria Cuison hails from Cebu City. They met in a slum area in Remedios, Malate in 1959 and decided to live together as husband and wife shortly afterwards. When they got married in 1963, they already had three children. They moved to Bar-

TABLE 12
BREAKDOWN OF EXPENDITURES ACCORDING TO RELATIVE UTILITY

| | Group A (less than ₱100) | | Group B (₱100–₱199) | | Group C (₱200 and above) | |
| | Amount | Per Cent | Amount | Per Cent | Amount | Per Cent |
|---|---|---|---|---|---|---|
| Necessities | ₱2,618.10 | 83.82 | ₱6,198.75 | 83.44 | ₱3,928.95 | 84.46 |
| | 174.54 | | 213.75 | | 392.90 | |
| Semi-optionals | 336.60 | 10.77 | 866.25 | 11.66 | 536.85 | 11.54 |
| | 22.44 | | 29.87 | | 53.69 | |
| Optionals | 168.95 | 5.41 | 363.60 | 4.90 | 185.85 | 4.00 |
| | 11.26 | | 12.54 | | 18.59 | |
| Total | ₱3,123.65 | 100.00 | ₱7,428.60 | 100.00 | ₱4,651.65 | 100.00 |

NOTE: Numbers in italics represent total amounts or percentages; numbers not in italics represent average amounts.

rio Magsaysay in the same year because their *barong barong* was torn down by the Mayor's wrecker crews.

The main earner in the family is Filoteo, who earns about ₱ 144 a month as laborer at North Harbor. He also augments this amount by fishing in Manila Bay, sometimes alone but often in the company of other friends and neighbors. Maria sells his catch at the nearby *talipapa* or sometimes even in Divisoria. Husband and wife estimate that they get about ₱ 60 additional income a month from this source, which, when added to Filoteo's regular income, puts them in the high-income category (Group C) used in the study.

The Resonable home is made of wood and rusty galvanized iron sheets. Most of it is new, but there are some old boards and GI sheets that came from their former home in Malate. Filoteo himself built the house in two days, with the help of one of his *kumpadres* who lives in Gagalangin and Antonio, Filoteo's sixteen-year-old son by a former marriage. Filoteo estimates that they spent about ₱ 500 for the house, which he borrowed from the trucking firm he works for.

By the standards of the community, the Resonable family is not too poor. Filoteo's job with the trucking company is relatively stable—he is a union member and is on good terms with his foreman. "They would not have lent me the money if they were not sure about me," he proudly says.

The Resonable's main problem seems to be Tony. He is being led astray by his *barkada,* according to Filoteo. He is often drunk and involved in the teenage rumbles in the community. Filoteo thinks that Tony resents his having married Maria. He does not want to elaborate, however, on his previous marriage to Tony's mother, not even when he indulges in "happy-happy" on Sundays, with *tuba* and dried squid with the boys.

Of the total monthly income of ₱ 204 of the Resonable family, about ₱ 170 goes to food, clothing, and other necessities; about ₱ 9 goes to liquor, ornaments, cigarettes, movies, and other non-essentials; and about ₱ 25 to semi-essentials like snacks, food ingredients, allowances, and others. Still, the Resonables have some savings—at the time of the study, Filoteo proudly said that he already had about ₱ 300 saved at the trucking company's *paluwagan,*\* and he was reserving this money for Tony's entering a vocational school so he would be saved from the teenage gang he liked to roam around with. Filoteo also claims that Maria has some money hidden away, but he does not really inquire. "I just give my wages to her," he says, "she is the treasurer."

Maria just smiles and does not contradict her husband. When asked what items she buys and how she buys them, she shows the notebook that the research staff has asked her to fill up daily.

The pattern of expenditures reveals that Maria buys things in small usable amounts from the *sari-sari* store. She does her own cooking, although, for *merienda,* she just buys ready-to-eat things. When asked whether it would be cheaper to buy things in bulk so she would get a discount, Maria admits it has not occurred to her to do things this way. "There is not enough money," she says. Besides, she also adds that storage is a problem and that, when there is food in the house, it gets eaten faster. Moreover, the kids are the ones who do the innumerable errands to the store, and this keeps them busy. A sample of daily entries in Maria's notebook includes:

28 MAY 1967

| | |
|---|---|
| *cafe* (coffee) | ₱ 0.20 |
| *tinapay* (bread) | .40 |
| *lugaw* (gruel) | .05 |
| *pamasahe* (jeepney fare) | .50 |
| *bigas* (rice) | .50 |
| *isda* (fish) | .50 |
| *misua* (thin noodles) | 1.15 |
| *kamatis* (tomatoes) | .05 |
| *sibuyas* (onions) | .05 |
| *luya* (ginger) | .05 |

\* A kind of forced saving. Members of a group in a company voluntarily deduct a certain amount from their salary every month and contribute to a kitty fund. On a specified day, usually a birthday, each member gets the total amount saved.

28 MAY 1967 (*continued*)

| | |
|---|---|
| *asin* (salt) | .05 |
| *tinapay* (bread) | .20 |
| *saguing* (banana) | .10 |
| *bigas* (rice) | .50 |
| *tinapa* (smoked fish) | .45 |
| *saguing* (banana) | .30 |
| gas (kerosene) | .10 |
| | ₱ 5.15 |

29 MAY 1967

| | |
|---|---|
| *cafe* (coffee) | ₱ 0.20 |
| *tinapay* (bread) | .40 |
| *bigas* (rice) | .50 |
| *bangos* (milkfish) | .80 |
| *gulay* (vegetables) | .10 |
| *kamatis* (tomatoes) | .05 |
| *vet-sin* (flavoring) | .05 |
| gas (kerosene) | .10 |
| *biskwit* (biscuits) | .10 |
| aspirin | .10 |
| *bigas* (rice) | .50 |
| *bagoong* (salted fish paste) | .10 |
| Pepsi Cola | .15 |
| 1 gallon *tuba* (coconut toddy) | 1.20 |
| *cafe* (coffee) | .20 |
| *tinapay* (bread) | .20 |
| | ₱ 4.75 |

The buying habits of the Resonable family are typical of how families in the community spend their money. Usually, like Maria, they just send the children several times a day to buy small quantities of food from the nearby stores. It really matters little whether Maria has plenty of money or not—she prefers to buy half a *ganta* of rice for lunch and another half a *ganta* of rice for supper. Instead of asking her son to buy forty *centavos* worth of coffee in the morning so they would not have to buy again in the afternoon for *merienda,* she asks him to buy twenty *centavos* worth each time. Perhaps, this is a habit formed out of living from meal to meal, what the Tagalogs call, *isang kahig, isang tuka.** Or maybe, as Maria says, it is really more rational because if she bought things in big quantities (say a can of coffee), they would be consumed faster and the savings generated from buying in bulk would be eaten up by large consumption.

Families poorer than the Resonables have an even detailed small-scale buying habit. This arises directly from the fact that they get things on credit. The owner of the *sari-sari* store keeps a list of the items they get until he is not willing to give them anything on credit anymore. The family then has to pay the whole amount or just a part of it. Usually, the *sari-sari* store owner has a pretty good estimate of the earning and paying capacity of the debtor family, and he sets the maximum amount based on this.

## THE RESPONDENTS

As mentioned above, the participants in this study were divided on the basis of income into low-, medium-, and high-income families. It was found that common to all these groups was the fact that the income of the family head is the main source of livelihood. Other sources of income include extra jobs of the family head and of the mother and, occasionally, earnings of the children. In the Barrio as a whole, skilled employment predominates. This is followed rather closely by unskilled employment and white-collar jobs.

To get a clear picture of the respondents, a profile of the three groups is included below.

*Low income (Group A).* Of participants from Group A, about 66.6 per cent are engaged in skilled manual labor such as carpentry, automotive mechanics, and factory work. About a quarter of members in this group are vendors, or itinerant peddlers in the nearby market.

One main reason behind the low income of members of

---

* Literally, one scratch, one peck, an allusion to how chicken live.

Group A is lack of education. Only about 17 per cent of the sample have reached high school, with about 50 per cent reaching only primary schooling. Not a single person in the Group A sample had reached college.

Low income has influenced the way of life of the Group A members. Thus, family size among members of this group is largest (average of eight members). Only 58 per cent of Group A members use electricity for lighting; 42 per cent own radios; 67 per cent have to rely on public faucets for water; and only 17 per cent have access to toilet facilities. About 66 per cent of Group A members admit to borrowing to supplement their income. A great majority of them said they would like to remain in Barrio Magsaysay, but then 83 per cent of them said they could only afford a maximum of ₱ 5 a month for amortization of the land.

*Medium income (Group B).* Of people earning from ₱ 100 to ₱ 199 a month, 72.2 per cent are skilled manual workers; 22.2 per cent are unskilled workers; and the rest are office workers or *empleados.* About 28 per cent of the group attained high school education, while a little over 60 per cent attained primary schooling. The average family size in this group is seven members.

Compared to Group A, more people in Group B use electric lights for lighting purposes (72 per cent). Some 44 per cent of the group own radios, and 61 per cent use public faucets for water source. Mostly, people in this category buy water from vendors (*aguadors*). Only 11 per cent of Group B members use public toilets, but about 28 per cent of them have open-pit toilets at home. Some 61 per cent of the respondents in this group borrow money to stretch their income. Still, even with their difficulties, 22 per cent of the Group B members said they would be willing to pay ₱ 10 a month for amortization, while 61 per cent could pay ₱ 5 a month, which brings to about 83 per cent those willing to pay something for the privilege of staying in Barrio Magsaysay.

*High income (Group C).* To members of the sample receiving ₱ 200 and above, skilled employment (about 80 per cent of them are skilled laborers) is the main source of income. One-tenth of the group is composed of vendors, while the other tenth is made up of office workers. Some 20 per cent of Group C have reached high school, 40 per cent have reached primary school, and 10 per cent has had college training. The average family size in this group is six members.

As in Group B, a high percentage of Group C members (about 70 per cent) use electricity for lighting. Some 50 per cent of them own radios, and 70 per cent draw water from public or communal faucets. Twenty per cent use the public toilet facilities, though 20 per cent use open pits and 10 per cent have flush-type toilets.

With the income they have, Group C members do not incur as much debt as other groups (about 40 per cent borrow money "now and then"). Furthermore, more members of Group C are willing to pay something for the land—about 60 per cent of them said they could pay ₱ 10 a month, while all the others said they could pay at least ₱ 5 a month.

## Findings

With the differences in income of the three groups in the study are revealed expenditure habits related to their way of life. Table 13 shows the actual items of expenditures, the amounts spent for each item, and the percentage of each item compared to the total. From the table, there are several noticeable trends worth exploring.

One general trend is the decrease in the percentage of food expenditures as income increases. As seen in Table 13, while the average expenditures for food increased from ₱ 162.52 a family for the 45-day period in Group A to ₱ 224.23 a family for the same period in Group C, the percentage of food to total expenditures went down from 82.56 to 61.39 per cent. If food is the most basic of necessities, the trend shows that with higher income comes higher expenses for food up to a certain point, after which food expenses hit a plateau and decrease in percentage as compared to other items.

cent of their income for clothing, this rose to 2.21 per cent in

The pattern of expenditures for clothing is another interesting one. Whereas in Group A people spent only 1.81 per Group B, and to 10.64 per cent in Group C. With the satisfac-

## TABLE 13
### BREAKDOWN OF EXPENDITURES ACCORDING TO ACTUAL CONSUMPTION

| Item | Group A (less than ₱ 100) Amount | Per Cent | Group B (₱ 100–₱ 199) Amount | Per Cent | Group C (₱ 200 and above) Amount | Per Cent |
|------|------|----------|------|----------|------|----------|
| Food | ₱ 2,112.75 162.52 | 82.56 | ₱ 4,352.85 197.85 | 72.43 | ₱ 1,798.65 224.23 | 61.39 |
| Clothing | 46.20 3.55 | 1.81 | 133.00 6.04 | 2.21 | 311.85 38.98 | 10.64 |
| Medicine | 33.45 2.57 | 1.31 | 160.20 7.28 | 2.67 | 9.45 1.18 | .32 |
| Fuel | 66.90 5.15 | 2.61 | 129.15 5.87 | 2.15 | 42.75 5.34 | 1.46 |
| Lighting | 8.55 .66 | .33 | 68.95 3.13 | 1.14 | 36.00 4.50 | 1.23 |
| Water | 42.30 3.25 | 1.65 | 117.00 5.32 | 1.95 | 27.00 3.38 | .92 |
| Transportation | 51.30 3.95 | 2.00 | 109.10 4.96 | 1.82 | 63.45 7.93 | 2.17 |
| Household needs (Laundry needs, kitchen utensils, etc.) | 38.20 6.78 | 1.49 | 338.40 15.38 | 5.63 | 112.95 14.12 | 3.86 |
| Allowance | 72.00 5.54 | 2.81 | 319.95 14.54 | 5.32 | 438.30 54.79 | 14.96 |
| Recreation | 1.50 .12 | .06 | 11.85 .54 | .20 | 2.70 .34 | .09 |
| Miscellaneous (Cigarettes, liquor, trinkets) | 86.10 6.62 | 3.37 | 269.10 12.23 | 4.48 | 86.85 10.86 | 2.96 |
| Total | ₱ 2,559.25 | 100.00 | ₱ 6,009.55 | 100.00 | ₱ 2,929.95 | 100.00 |

NOTE: Numbers in italics represent total amounts or percentages; numbers not in italics represent average amounts.

tion of a most basic necessity, therefore, income goes to other necessities.

It is noteworthy that the expenses for medicine go down as income goes up. The figures may not be statistically significant, but they nevertheless point to the possibility that as living conditions improve, there are less illnesses and, therefore, less need for medical expenses in a family.

One major difference among the income groups is seen in the percentage of income going to allowances. In Group A, about 2.81 per cent of expenses went to allowances. For Group B, this went up to 5.32; while for Group C, it reached a high of 14.96 per cent of expenditures. This trend shows that with basic necessities in life paid for, those with higher income tend to spend a higher percentage for semi-optionals. In terms of savings, the higher income makes it possible for more savings because the semi-optionals can be dispensed with if necessary.

### EXTENT OF SAVINGS

From a case-by-case study of the incomes and expenditures of respondents, it was possible to set, on the average, at what point savings were possible. For the 18 individuals with incomes of less than ₱ 100, it was found that the range was from a family that spent 59 per cent more than it earned to another family that spent only 66.6 per cent of its income. On the whole, those belonging to Group A generally spent more than they earned.

With members of Group B, the range was from a family that spent 94 per cent more than its income to a family that saved 46.4 per cent of its income. As a whole, however, the average point of savings was at ₱ 170 for the 45-day period, which is well within the ₱ 199 maximum income level.

For Group C, the families ranged from one that saved 13.5 per cent of its income to another that saved 22.2 per cent of its income. With higher income, therefore, savings are possible. For people in this category, savings accumulation is set at the monthly income of ₱ 310. Considering the pattern of expenditures of people in this category, anyone earning ₱ 310 and above is most likely to have savings all the time.

With members of Group A generally spending more than what they are actually earning, it is worth exploring how these families are able to survive. What reasons enable these families to go into deficit spending? What factors are there in slum life that make it possible for them to survive?

One very important reason for the ability of those belonging to Group A to make a living is the possibility of hidden income. In Barrio Magsaysay, it is possible that some members of the sample refused to reveal income from illegal sources, such as smuggling, theft, selling of property rights, and the like. Since it is highly unlikely that a respondent would openly admit the presence of such income, it must be admitted that income data for such people would most likely be incomplete.

Another less difficult factor to find out in an income and expenditure study such as this is the availability of loans. To most people in Group A and to some extent to those in other groups as well, borrowing money is a common recourse when there is financial lack. Borrowing may be from friends, neighbors, relatives, or from any combination of these. It may be in cash or in kind. A favorite source of borrowing is the *sari-sari* store. The storeowner usually has a list of items that a family gets on credit. As such, most families are actually eating the food they will still have to pay for in the future. In this way, however, their income is extended.

Finally, there is the possibility of getting food from the sea, from friends and neighbors, and even from the market, garbage dumps, and gardens. Because this food is not paid for in cash, it does not enter into the computation of income and expenditures. We have noticed in the case of the Resonables that when Filoteo catches fish, it is either sold or consumed by the family. Obviously, Maria would not enter the fish they ate as an income or expenditure. As such, income in kind from whatever source is a hidden income that helps the family with their basic needs.

#### USE OF SAVINGS

To find out the values and aspirations of the respondents in this study, they were asked what they would apply their savings to, in the event that their income exceeded their expenditures. Although to some of the respondents with no savings this sounded like a hypothetical case, they still gave very definite items on which they would like to spend their future savings.

As revealed in Table 14, the most common items of expenditure for money saved were furniture and household appliances (33.8 per cent), followed by children's needs (22.5 per cent), and repair or improvement of the house (17.7 per cent). Other items of future expense were clothing, investments, and food.

Of great interest to the analyst is the variation found among the three groups represented in the study. To high-income families, the most important item of expenditures for extra money is children's needs, by which is meant mainly expenses for education. A full 50 per cent of Group C respondents gave this item as future expenditures. To both Group A and Group B respondents, however, the most important items for which they were reserving their savings were furniture and household appliances (38.89 and 39.29 per cent respectively).

Interestingly enough, repair and improvement of house is ranked as second among Group A and Group B members, while not a single respondent in Group C thought of this as an item of future expense. One reason for this may be the fact that the houses of Group C respondents are already comfortable enough. In fact, the distinction among persons in Barrio Magsaysay is most obvious in their houses. The people with higher income tend to have houses of heavy materials (galvanized iron sheets for roofing, adobe stones and wood for sidings, and heavy wood for floors), while those with lower income tend to have houses made of light or mixed materials (rusty galvanized iron sheets for roofing and siding; wood and even cardboard for walls, internal partitions, and divisions).

One trend that is a continuation of the findings reflected in Table 13 is the fact that with Group A, food is still a problem, while for Groups B and C, not a single respondent mentioned food as an item of expenditure for money saved. This is in sharp contrast with the findings concerning children's needs (education), where not a single respondent in Group A men-

TABLE 14
PROJECTED USE OF SAVINGS OR EXPECTED ADDITIONAL INCOME

| Use | Group A (less than ₱ 100) | | Group B (₱ 100–₱ 199) | | Group C (₱ 200 and above) | | Total Number |
|---|---|---|---|---|---|---|---|
| | No. | % | No. | % | No. | % | |
| Furniture and household appliances | 7 | 38.89 | 11 | 39.29 | 3 | 18.75 | 21 |
| Repair or improvement of house | 4 | 22.22 | 7 | 25.00 | | | 11 |
| Food | 4 | 22.22 | | | | | 4 |
| Clothing | 3 | 16.67 | 4 | 14.28 | | | 7 |
| Children's needs; e.g., education | | | 6 | 21.43 | 8 | 50.00 | 14 |
| Investment in business | | | | | 5 | 31.25 | 5 |
| Total | 18 | 100.00 | 28 | 100.00 | 16 | 100.00 | 62 |

tioned it, but those in Groups B and C placed a great deal of emphasis on it. This finding suggests the hypothesis that with higher income, attention of slum dwellers shifts from basic needs of foods to future needs such as the education and other needs of children. This trend from basic necessities to semi-optionals and optionals as related to increasing income is also borne out by the expenditures for clothing. While those in Groups A and B stressed clothing as an item of future expenditure, not a respondent in Group C considered this important.

Finally, the difference in viewpoint may be seen in the fact that only respondents from Group C thought of investment in business as an item for future expenditure. In fact, 31.25 per cent of Group C respondents thought this a necessary item, the second ranking item for expense in their estimation. This may suggest the theory that with increased income, people incur savings, which in turn are reserved for investments in business.

## Conclusion

Even with the small sample involved in this study and the generality of the findings, there are certain trends and suggestions that are important to the whole question of slums and squatters. The general hypothesis that living in slums enables people to save and, thereby, improve their chances for economic and social mobility is greatly suggested by the findings of this small study. More comprehensive studies involving more people and employing more rigorous methodology are needed to find out the truth or falsity of this assertion, but at least this study has defined some of the conditions that characterize slum life—and they seem to point to this general direction.

Indeed, to recapitulate, there are many factors in squatter and slum life that make savings possible. For one, squatters do not have to pay rent for the land they are using. After the initial expense of building a house (the simple design and materials which are not too expensive), the squatter does not have to worry about rent. The lighting the squatter family needs can be obtained at low rates—through the flat rate (usually ₱ 2 a month) or the *tarifa* system of the Manila Electric Company. In fact, there are squatter areas where little or no expense is incurred for electricity through the simple expedient of the "jumper" or the flying connection. Through this device, people steal electricity by tapping on to the main line and by-passing (jumping) the electric meter.

Water is also available quite cheaply to most squatters and dwellers because the city government usually provides communal faucets or artesian wells. Even where piped water is available, the ingenuity of the squatters often makes it possible to duplicate the electric jumper. In one squatter area leveled by bulldozers at one time (not Barrio Magsaysay), many underground pipes clandestinely connected to the main line were found.

This relative dishonesty is not too traumatic to many squatters and slum dwellers because, usually, everybody is doing it. The folkways and values of the people in the slum or squatter area tolerate (and even encourage) this type of behavior. It is debatable whether such types of social behavior are indices to social disorganization and thus contribute to social costs. On the contrary, they may suggest exactly the opposite.

As seen in the case of the Resonable family, life in the squatter area is so simple that it does not encourage too much unnecessary expenditures just "to keep up with the Cruzes." This is one incentive for saving. There are also many means that help to stretch a squatter family's *peso*. Buying on credit is one. Purchasing ready-to-eat food is another. And then, there are always free sources of food such as the ocean, backyard gardens, garbage dumps, relief, and other things associated with slum life. They all contribute, somehow, to make a small income last and enable a mother to make both ends meet.

One interesting finding in this study is the proposed manner of spending savings or future income. For one, the emphasis on education of children and investment in business mentioned by the high-income respondents was very encouraging. It indicated the longer-range viewpoint of these people—the fact that they were not really contented with life in the slums and wanted, in fact, to improve it. What is more, the people wanted to improve their houses, buy more things for the home, and generally make life in the slums more tolerable. They usually don't want to move out of the slum area but are instead thinking of improving life there.

If the good people who can achieve social and economic mobility would all leave the slums, what would happen there? Jane Jacobs, in writing about the problem in American cities, provides one answer. To her, the slum is precisely a place left by the people in the community who are economically and socially able to do so, to the extent that only the apathetic and the dispirited are the ones who remain.[1] This is the real slum. Provided, however, that a number of people who care enough about the neighborhood will stay and do something about it and provided that life in the slum takes on a spirit of community and a character of its own, then, although the physical surroundings may be characterized by decay and deterioration and houses may be old or makeshift, the place is not really a slum.

Perhaps, we have here the ultimate solution to the slum problem. What is needed is not to improve the life of the people in the community so that they would be able to leave the place. The main thing needed is to improve the spirit of community among the people so that they may develop a pride and identity with their neighborhood strong enough to make them want to improve it and continue living in it.

This, then, is the challenge to urban community development. There are many ways of improving the lives of people in the cities. However, if such improvement is tied in with a sense of community and a desire to continue improving that community, then, perhaps, we would have less slums and more happy neighborhoods.

# CHAPTER 10

# The Future of Urban Slums

The year's experience in Barrio Magsaysay has resulted in the formulation of certain propositions and generalizations about life in slums and squatter areas that embody the insights and impressions of those involved in the research and action phases of the pilot project. It is too early to say that urban community development as a concept and an approach is the correct solution to slum and squatter problems. This work has attempted to explain what urban community development is, described how it was introduced into a pilot community, and analyzed how its introduction affected the relationships between the people and the CD advocates as well as those from the government and civic agencies that participated in the program. Based on this experience, the work suggests the initiation of more urban community development projects in other areas, and, if possible, the adoption of a larger (regional or national) program in urban community development.

The research findings in Barrio Magsaysay reveal the existence of a sense of community among urban squatters and slum dwellers. In the pilot area, this was especially significant because it is a relatively young squatter colony—most of the people there migrated to the reclaimed lands in 1963, when the relocation program of the City of Manila was intensified. It is true that the threat of eviction has been instrumental in the people's organizing themselves at neighborhood and community-wide levels. However, even before the threat really became serious, many organizations already existed in response to the need to maintain peace and order in the place, to device a mutual assistance system, and to have a satisfying social life. These are indications that factors other than external threat are responsible for this growth of community feeling, that there are indeed certain variables within slum life that account for it.

Research surveys in Barrio Magsaysay and elsewhere point to the fact that slums are the real "transitional societies" that social scientists have been describing in their analytical models. For most slum dwellers are rural migrants in the process of becoming urban men. They still retain some of their old ways and values, even as they adapt to the demands of a faster-paced and more dynamic urban environment. As such, slum communities have the best (and the worst) aspects of both worlds. On the positive side, they have a closely knit society characterized by face-to-face relationships that provides them with personal and psychological security amidst the bewildering complexity of the city. Life in the slums is more warm, people know each other, they assist each other in many traditional ways, and above all, it is cheaper than living in apartments or other middle-class environment. On the negative side, slums are also continually troubled by criminal elements that get attracted to them, and they are run down and dilapidated, which often pose direct hazards to health and even physical well-being.

This enumeration of the advantages and disadvantages provided by slums, however, becomes academic in the light of the fact that slums now exist and something must be done about them. The 600,000 or so individuals in Metropolitan Manila who live as squatters or under slum conditions require the immediate attention, not only of public officials, but also of all people concerned about the fate of the city and its role in the country's modernizing efforts.

The time is past when city and national officials can pretend that the slum and squatter problems do not exist or that, if they are just ignored, they will go away like a bad dream. The crying need is for a definite urban policy that will effectively tackle the worsening urban situation. Such a policy, first of all, should include a population policy that is based on the present situation in the Philippines. Obviously, the overconcentration of more than 10 per cent of the national population into an area that is less than .15 per cent of the national territory (Metropolitan Manila) is unhealthy for future growth. The government has to decide that other population centers must be consciously developed to serve as counter-magnets to population shifts and movements.

It is relatively easy to decide, based on economic and population data, just which areas in the Philippines have the potential for further development. The government should then set up a table of priorities, however politically painful it might be, as to which parts of the Philippines should have a higher priority in the allocation of scarce resources. Through government expenditures, administrative action, and economic programs, a conscious plan of action must be evolved to bolster development in these other places.

The slum and squatter problem, as of now, is not dependent on overpopulation. The main cause is the maldistribution of the population into certain growth points. Perhaps, if there is not as much concentration in certain areas, the squatter and slum problems would not be such big headaches.

Policies and action programs are most urgently needed at this time because the rural programs of the government are already bearing fruit, and one side effect of their success would be rural-urban migration. As the "rice and roads" program of the Marcos administration gains headway, for example, production efficiency would require less people on the soil. With roads improved, the people displaced from agricultural employment would surely find their way to the cities. Thus, solving one set of problems creates another. The task of government is always in need of basic answers to questions.

## Urban Community Development as an Answer

The Barrio Magsaysay pilot project provides some proof that urban community development is especially relevant to the problem of slums and squatting. To be effective, however, its basic meaning must be understood.

Urban community development, first of all, is a comprehensive approach. It does not attempt to change the physical environment of the slum area through infra-structure projects, provision of utilities, and community beautification. It is not confined to social welfare projects such as community organization, relief, training, counseling, and skill-development. Its most important contributions are in the field of social change, especially regarding attitudes, opinions, and action-changes on the part of the community members. All other aspects of the community development effort are geared to this. Even when physical improvements in the community are introduced and even when life there has been made more comfortable materially, if the basic internal make-up of the individual has not been affected, if the people have not participated and gotten involved in the process of changing the community— in other words, if they themselves have not changed with the changes around them—the work of urban community development has not been completed.

Thus, this basic nature of urban community development should be an integral part of whatever approach is used for the solution of urban slum and squatter problems.

### PHYSICAL IMPROVEMENTS

The ultimate solution for the problems of slums and squatting would require financial and other resources too heavy for the already precarious financial state of most developing countries. Urban community development may be used as an interim solution, to do something that is within the means of underdeveloped economies and, at the same time, prevent the slum and squatter problem from becoming worse and even from blowing up—into riots.

Physical improvement projects such as road construction and road improvement; the provision of water, light, electricity, toilets, and garbage disposal; the construction of schools, health centers, community centers; and other services should be the concern of the government. When such projects are done with the full cooperation of the people (and urban community development has the responsibility of mobilizing such community effort), then the projects come out cheaper and they produce the additional advantage of achieving the less tangible benefits of community solidarity, community pride, and self-respect, which the slum and squatter areas sorely need.

One may even go to the extent of proposing that instead of outlawing slums and meeting them with punitive action, they should be met with "planned slums." The government should start planning its own slum and squatter areas, laying them out rationally and specifying exactly what purposes they are intended to fulfill. For example, why can't marginal government land be used for low-cost housing? This can be easily done by subdividing the land into very small parcels (say 100 square meters each); laying out the streets; providing the basic necessities of water, light, toilets, garbage disposal, fire-fighting, and others; and then selling these lands to slum dwellers and squatters on long-term payment periods. The squatters, in other words, would be allowed to build their own shanties, following certain minimum standards as to type of construction, size, proximity to adjoining shanties, etc. In this way, slums do not just grow haphazardly, they can be controlled as "planned slum neighborhoods."

This scheme of planned slums is not new. The *"barrio obrero"* concept that started as early as the time of President Quezon started it. Had these *barrios* been better planned and better managed, they could have achieved the benefits expected from this physical improvement scheme. By just providing the lands, and allocating them haphazardly, the maximum benefits from these projects have not been achieved. If only the government shouldered the meager additional expense of setting up rational street layouts, of providing the basic services, and of putting the planned slum under an urban community development program, then the *barrio obrero* neighborhoods would not have become the problems they are today.

## COMMUNITY ORGANIZATION AND PLANNED SLUMS

The idea of planned slums will not work if such areas are conceived only in terms of physical structures—rational street layouts, sub-standard housing, fire hydrants, schools, medical centers, drainage facilities, water and electric services, etc.

Without the human component of community organization, neighborhood activities, local identity, and all the other social aspects that differentiate a disorganized slum from a viable community, the places will only become worse slums. A program of urban community development, therefore, should be planned hand in hand with the development of an "organized slum." [1]

Essentially, then, the program for making a place a really low-cost housing area would follow the steps carried out in the Barrio Magsaysay pilot project in urban community development. For slums already existing, the Urban CD teams must enter an area, mobilize the people for community self-help, get them interested in doing something about improving their environment and way of life, and then rehabilitate the community to make available to it the services and amenities needed for urban living (roads, water, electricity, health and sanitation, employment, etc.). Such efforts must be done by motivating the people, not by substituting the will and authority of the CD workers for those of the community.

Since providing the services and amenities would need the assistance and financing of the city and the national government, however, it is necessary that a positive policy for urban community development and an official endorsement of it by public entities be clearly enunciated. Much as squatters and slum dwellers would like to realize through their own efforts the laying out of good roads and the provision of other services, their combined resources would not be enough. The government must come in and provide these heavy capital expenditures if the program is to succeed.

For planned slums set up on government or private land formerly devoted to other purposes, several things have to be cleared first before starting the project. First, there must be good reasons for allocating such land for planned slum neighborhoods—proximity to work, marginal utility of the land, land zoned as a residential area, etc. Second, there must be a planned program of social welfare services and community development assistance along with the physical-structural schemes.

In selecting tenants for planned slums, utmost care must be exercised in finding out those people who would be willing to do their share in community activities and efforts. Here, social welfare and research facilities are needed, whether the tenants of such slums are individual families or whole communities formerly inhabiting unplanned or disorganized slums. The family case study is a most necessary aid in the selection of tenants. The community survey and profile, too, is a needed tool. When these two research aids are joined and when their findings are made available to trained Urban CD workers who have worked in the older slums before, they contribute to the success of the project.

In the long run, it would be the human element and not the physical characteristics that would determine the quality of life in planned or organized slums. If the people are organized so that they take care of peace and order, health and sanitation, fire-fighting, and road repairs, then the government's efforts to provide these things adequately and efficiently would be complemented to such an extent that they would achieve their goals. If the people are organized so that they have social activities, community identity, self-pride and if they find a sense of belonging and personal worth in community activities they are all involved in, then the place ceases to be a slum area and instead becomes a livable and responsive urban community.

## TRAINING AND SKILL-DEVELOPMENT

The governmental approach to the slum and squatter problems often neglects to see the common benefits that may accrue with joint efforts between communities and private entities, such as business concerns and civic groups. For example, one of the most obvious ways out for the people of Barrio Magsaysay in their struggle for the good life may very well be the opening of a technical school in the area. The Don Bosco Training School and Boys Center, a project proposed by the Salesian Fathers and the Tondo Youth Foundation, has planned the setting up of free vocational training for out-of-school young adults in the community. And yet, the efforts to establish this school has been hampered by misunderstanding between the community and the initiators of the projects, as well as the lukewarm support from the government.

As proposed, the Don Bosco Training School and Boys Center would be able to accommodate about 300 students between the ages of 15 and 19. The only requirement for entrance is the ability to read and write and do simple arithmetic. There will be no tuition fees involved. Courses offered are carpentry, auto-mechanics, electronics, radio-television, and other household-appliances repair. After graduation, the school will take care of placing the students in a job that will assure a minimum income of ₱8 a day. Some 35 of the biggest industrial firms in the Philippines regularly accept Don Bosco graduates, sometimes, even before they finish their formal schooling.

Aside from being a training school, Don Bosco also is planned to be a community center. Thus, the complex will include a gymnasium, an auditorium, a swimming pool, basketball courts, and a health center. All these facilities would be made available to citizens of Tondo to serve their recreational needs.

To the people of Barrio Magsaysay, all these proposed benefits are too good to be believed. From the start, therefore, they vehemently opposed the setting up of the Don Bosco school. Their main immediate complaint was that the Salesian Fathers were asking for the long-term lease of five hectares of the reclaimed land, which would result in the relocation of certain squatters who have already settled on the land. Some 200 families, according to the tenants federation, would be affected. While there were other places in Barrio Magsaysay still available for housing them, they were not too eager to transfer without some material assistance.

Another suspicion of the squatters arose from their fear that the land grants to Don Bosco would only be the start of other requests for the land they have fought so long for. They closely scrutinized the list of people identified with the Tondo Youth Foundation, found some big businessmen among them, and concluded that these big businessmen would grab some lands for their projects later on. They felt that if they allowed one agency—even if it was a religious, charitable organization —to start getting land, this would be the hole in the dike that would weaken their position and result in the erosion of their claim to the land.

The controversy about Don Bosco plagued the pilot project in Barrio Magsaysay throughout its one year of existence because both sides were suspicious of the presence of the action-research teams in the area. The squatters, especially, were suspicious that the data gathered by the researchers and action team members were being fed back to Don Bosco to bolster the latter's claims. There was even one time when no member of the Barrio Magsaysay project staff was allowed to enter a certain area in the community because of direct threats of physical harm. Luckily, communications opened again, and understanding between the teams and the people was established.

The experience with Don Bosco shows the characteristic tendency among squatters and slum dwellers to take "first things first" and to stick to what is already available rather than to risk it for more long-range gains. This attitude is one of the main concerns of an Urban CD worker. All sorts of physical improvements may be set up in a community, but, if attitudes, such as this one held by the residents are not changed, the urban CD program will not succeed.

## SLUMS AND TENEMENTS

One advantage of an urban community development program is that it is compatible with other programs to alleviate urban problems. It is, for example, a logical first step in a tenement housing program, if and when the national and local governments already have the technical and financial capacity to embark on it.

The main danger to tenement housing is the lapsing of these projects into conditions of dilapidation, anarchy, and restlessness that generally reflect the worst characteristics of urban slums. Usually, these disorganized conditions may be traced directly to the lack of a sense of community spirit among the tenement dwellers. And this is not at all surprising. Where people are drawn from many disparate slum neighborhoods and dumped into concrete and glass cubicles, they are supposed to call home; they react like caged animals and start tearing away at each other and at their environment. It takes a great deal of time, allowing for social interactions and human relationships, before a feeling of community and belonging comes about. Without any institutionalized way of providing for this, it takes longer to grow, if, indeed, it gets a chance to grow at all.

With an urban community development program in old slum areas, tenement housing projects may be planned so that most, if not all the members of this slum area, could be accommodated in tenements. When this is done, and friends and neighbors are transferred together, the sense of community and oneness travels with the relocated people. The social relationships that grew up in the old slum would then help the people in adjusting to their new surroundings. The patterns of mutual assistance built through the years of being slum neighbors come in handy under the new conditions of stress in the tenements. Where the administrative support that brought about urban community development in the slums is transferred along to the tenement project, the chances for a smoother adjustment are enhanced.

This idea of transferring whole closely knit neighborhoods, in fact, may be the missing ingredient that would make more successful the government's relocation program. Thus, there are indications in Sapang Palay that the families who remained in the place where those who had friends and neighbors transferred along with them. Instead of transferring families and individuals, the government should try relocating whole neighborhoods, making sure that such friends and neighbors are given lots adjacent to each other in the new area.

The influence of the change agent in helping to bring about unity in the old slum is all the more needed in the new site. In Sapang Palay, the whole cohesive community tended to be the one composed of parents and children from Intramuros who were helped by the Sisters of the Immaculate Concepcion. Prior to relocation to Sapang Palay, these people were already being assisted by the religious order. The main nucleus of this assistance was a primary-grade school for the children. When the Intramuros families were moved to Sapang Palay, the school and the sisters went along with them. In the early days of Sapang Palay, the thatched schoolhouse was the first public building to be set up in the area, with the labor and assistance of the parents who were relocated in the area. Even at this time of writing when only 20 per cent or so of the former relocated squatters and slum dwellers still remain in Sapang Palay, the community of these former Intramuros squatters is still intact.

This aspect of community organization by an external change agent, then, is of utmost importance in the programs for on-site tenement housing projects or relocation schemes. If the community development worker, the social worker, the medical workers and other people engaged in an Urban Community Development Program would work with them in the slums and then move along with them in the tenements or the relocation site, the probability of success is greatly enhanced. If the old patterns of mutually beneficial relationships can be maintained between the change agents and the people, on the one hand, and among the people, on the other, then the assurance of success is greatly helped.

## Towards a Wider Program

One problem with introducing schemes of urban community development solely in the Metropolitan Manila area is the possibility that with the improvement of life in this primate city, in-migration from other places would be encouraged. If this happens, the gains achieved through the program would easily be lost.

For urban community development to succeed, there is a need for the introduction of programs in other regions of the Philippines. As already mentioned, some cities in the country have a worse squatter and slum problem than Manila. As long as these problems are not solved or alleviated, the problems of the central city will not be adequately met because the people pushed from these other cities find their way to Metropolitan Manila.

Urban community development programs, to succeed in other cities, must have the full backing of the national and the local governments. As the national agency for community development, the PACD may take the lead in introducing such programs. Owing to lack of personnel and financial resources, however, the PACD should only take the initiating role. The full support of the local governments would be needed to bring these projects to completion.

Luckily, there already exists in the local governments the basic machinery for the setting up of urban CD programs. In the first place, the officials of most cities are acutely aware of the slum and squatter problem. Moreover, almost all cities have local planning boards, composed of civic spirited citizens and public officials. These planning boards, though many of them are inactive, may be used as the proper agencies to carry projects on urban improvement. With the support of the local executives and councils, their plans may be widely broadcast to achieve support and then formally adopted by the proper local government officials for policy execution.

Initially, of course, the concept of urban community development must first be known and understood. It is hoped that the Barrio Magsaysay pilot project, by breaking the ground, has contributed to this process of discussion that leads to understanding. The experience during the past year of work in the community may have been characterized by trial and error. But at least, the first faltering steps have been taken toward a better city life.

Third Congress of the )
  Republic of the Philippines)       H. No. 5738
Third Session                    S. No. 486

## REPUBLIC ACT NO. 1597

AN ACT PROVIDING FOR THE SUBDIVISION OF THE
TONDO FORESHORE LAND INTO LOTS AND THE SALE
OF SAID LOTS TO THEM OR TO BONA FIDE OCCU-
PANTS OF SAID LAND, AND FOR OTHER PURPOSES.

Be it enacted by the Senate and House of Representatives of
the Philippines in Congress assembled:

Sec. 1. This Act shall be known as the "Tondo Foreshore
Land Act of 1956."

Sec. 2. Notwithstanding the provisions of Public Land Act,
as amended, and Proclamation numbered one hundred eighty-
seven of the President of the Philippines, dated June seventeen,
nineteen hundred fifty, the Director of Lands, under the direction
of the Secretary of Agriculture and Natural Resources, is hereby
authorized and directed to survey and subdivide immediately the
land in the district of Tondo, City of Manila, comprising what is
known as the "Tondo Foreshore Land," which is bounded on the
North by the Philippine Manufacturing Company compound up
to Vitas (Government Tenement Houses); on the East by privately
owned parcels of land from the present Azcarraga Street Extension; and on the West by that portion of land three hundred meters
from the pier line to the East, with the exception of such areas as
are reserved by the Government for port facilities, roads and

other public uses, into lots in such a manner that every lessee of any lot in said land or bona fide occupant of any parcel thereof will not be deprived of any part of the same, should he decide to buy it under this Act. The Director of Lands is hereby further directed to complete such survey and subdivision within one year from the date of the approval of this Act, after which said Director shall turn over all the pertinent records or papers of said survey and subdivision to the Land Tenure Administration which is hereby authorized and directed to sell without delay and without the necessity of public bidding the lots as subdivided to their respective lessee and bona fide occupants if they are duly qualified to acquire lands at the time of the approval of Republic Act numbered five hundred fifty-nine, or, in the case of vacant lots, to persons who are not disqualified to acquire public lands: Provided, That those lessees and bona fide occupants who will be deprived of their lots or parcels of land by reason of the opening or widening of streets and alleys by virtue of the subdivision herein provided, shall be given preference in the order mentioned, in the award or sale of the vacant lots: Provided, further, That if said vacant lots are not enough to accommodate all such lessees and occupants, the award or sale thereof be by lot: Provided, further, That if there are lessees or bona fide occupants who, after going through the above procedures, still are unaccommodated, the same shall be given preference to acquire lots on the reclaimed area towards the East of Bangkusay Street, in the district of Tondo, City of Manila, and/or occupying or buy houses in the housing projects of the People's Homesite Corporation to be established in the district of Tondo, City of Manila.

No person shall be entitled to purchase more than one lot in the Tondo Foreshore Land, and any person purchasing two or more lots therein shall lose his rights and interests in said lots and forfeit all amounts paid on account of the same.

The selling price of each lot shall not be more than five pesos per square meter: Provided, That expenses for the opening or widening or repairs of the streets and alleys, the laying of sewage system, and the costs of the survey and subdivision shall not be added to the selling price of each lot as herein fixed.

All streets and alleys existing on the date of the approval of this Act within the Tondo Foreshore Land shall not be changed either by the city Government of Manila or by the National Government, unless the public interests demand that they be changed.

Sec. 3. The purchases shall be allowed, with no down payment whatsoever, fifteen years from the date of purchase within which to pay the purchase price in one hundred eighty equal monthly installments with an annual interest at the rate of four per centum on all installments due and payable. They may also pay the price in cash or more than one installment at one time.

Sec. 4. Lands acquired under this Act shall not, except in favor of the government or any of its branches or institutions, or legally constituted banking corporations, be subject to encumbrance or alienation within fifteen years after the date of the issuance of the transfer of certificate of title to the purchaser, nor shall they become liable to the satisfaction of any debt contracted prior to the expiration of such period: Provided, however, That such lands may be mortgaged even before said period has expired.

Every conveyance shall be subject to repurchase by the original purchaser or his legal heirs within a period of five years from the date of the conveyance.

Sec. 5. Any contract or agreement made or executed in violation of this Act shall cause the reversion of the property and its improvements and the forfeiture of all payments made on account of the purchase price thereof to the Government.

Sec. 6. In the event of the death of a purchaser prior to the complete payment of the price of the lot purchased by him, his widow and children shall succeed in all his rights and obligations with respect to his lot. In the event said purchaser or his successors in interest should fail to pay six consecutive or cumulative installment on the purchase price and the interest therein or on any installment, when and as the same mature, it shall be the duty of the Chairman of the Land Tenure Administration at once to bring suit for the recovery of such installments and interest due, or of the total amount of the purchase price unpaid, with interest thereon, and also to enforce the lien of the Government against the lot by selling the same in the manner provided by law for the foreclosure of mortgages: Provided, That only persons who do not own any residential lot in the cities of Manila, Quezon City, Pasay or their suburbs and are qualified to acquire public lands, can take part in the sale by auction. In the event of such sale the purchases at such rate shall acquire a good and indefeasible title.

Sec. 7. The Land Tenure Administration shall, upon proper consultation with the "Federation of Tondo Foreshore Land Tenants Association," implement and carry out the provisions of this

Act. To this end, the Chairman of said administration may promulgate such rules and regulations as may be necessary to carry out said provisions.

Sec. 8.   The sum of four hundred thousand pesos is appropriated, out of any fund in the National Treasury not otherwise appropriated to carry out the purpose of this Act.

Sec. 9.   All laws or part of laws inconsistent with this Act are repealed or modified accordingly.

Sec. 10.   This Act shall take effect upon its approval.

Approved, June 16, 1956.

# APPENDIX B: SQUATTING AND SLUM-DWELLING IN METROPOLITAN MANILA

(*Note: In a meeting held at Malacañang Palace on March 19, 1968, the officers and members of the National Housing Council as well as government and private individuals concerned over the growing problem of squatters and slum-dwellers voiced the need for accurate information that would serve as basis for policies and programs. Executive Secretary Rafael M. Salas, in response to this need, created a Special Committee that would make a survey of the squatter and slum-dwelling problem, define its scope, analyze its nature and draw up specific recommendations. Secretary Esteban Bernido, Presidential Assistant on Housing and Resettlement Agency and Chairman and General Manager of the People's Homesite and Housing Corporation, was named head of the Special Committee. Other members included: Felix D. Abesamis, Central Institute for the Training and Rehabilitation of Urban Squatters; Sylvia P. Montes, Social Welfare Administration; Jose G. Narcelles, Presidential Assistant on Housing and Resettlement Agency; Vicente T. Paterno, Management Association of the Philippines; Tomas Testa, Jr., Bankers Association of the Philippines and Aprodicio A. Laquian, College of Public Administration, UP, secretary of the committee. The Special Committee immediately embarked on the actual survey of squatters and slum-dwellers in Metropolitan Manila. The survey was the cooperative effort of the SWA, PAHRA, PHHC, the City of Manila and all other local governments in the Metropolitan Manila area. Rather than wait for the completed survey, the Special Committee decided that a report based on available secondary information and surveys be prepared. This comprehensive report is a result of that decision.*)

**THE PROBLEM**

(1)    Squatting and slum-dwelling are twin aspects of the housing problem. They are indications that the supply of houses has been greatly outrun by the growth of households. Squatting and slum-dwelling, however, cannot be solved merely by making houses available. For the two are only symptoms of greater economic, social and political problems that go with urbanization.

(2)    Based on the most recent data available, there are about 127,852 squatter families (767,112 persons) and 55,907 families (335,442 persons) living in slum conditions in Metropolitan Manila, a total of 183,759 families or 1,102,554 persons.[1]

(3)    A distinction must be made between squatting and slum-dwelling if these problems are to be effectively solved. Squatting is primarily a legal concept and involves the occupancy of a piece of land or building without the permission of the owner. As a violation of property rights, it is punishable under our laws. Slum-dwelling, on the other hand, is more of a socio-economic concept. It is living in homes that are so dilapidated and congested that the condition poses a health, fire, vice and crime hazard not only to those who live in the slums but to the whole urban community as well. In Metropolitan Manila, squatting and slum-dwelling usually occur together, that is, slums are usually squatter areas and vice versa. There are some notable exceptions, however. Thus, in Magsaysay Village, Tondo, many squatter homes are built of strong materials. Slums in Malate and Pasay are usually peopled by home-owners who pay rent to private landowners and who, therefore, cannot be technically called squatters.

(4)    The problems of squatting and slum-dwelling are usually closely related to other problems:

  1. The presence of slums and squatter areas is generally related to the incidence and type of crimes found in a place. Thus, the district of Tondo, which has 57.5 per cent of Manila's squatters and slum-dwellers, had 35.8 per cent of reported

---

[1] See Table I for the breakdown. Metropolitan Manila, in this report is defined as the built-up area (conurbation) with the city of Manila as its core and with the following other local units included: the cities of Caloocan, Quezon and Pasay and the towns of Malabon, Navotas, San Juan, Mandaluyong, Marikina, Makati, Cainta, Pasig, Taguig, Parañaque and Las Piñas, in Rizal province.

crime victims in 1965.[2] Tondo also has the highest percentage of "crime against persons" cases among the districts of Manila.

2. Big and costly fires usually originate from slum and squatter areas. This is shown by the Pasay and Binondo fires.

3. The incidence and type of diseases are usually related to slum and squatter areas. The predominance of respiratory diseases and gastro-intestinal diseases is closely linked to the presence of slum and squatter areas.

4. Breakdown in morals and socially accepted behavior is related to the presence of slums and squatter areas. Thus, crimes against chastity and crimes against morals and order are highest in areas that have slums and squatter areas.

5. Low property values and the concomitant low income from real property taxes are also related to slums and squatter areas.

(5) Aside from these specific problems related to slums and squatters, there are others, more difficult to assess and quantify. The physical disorganization of the slum, though a frequent subject of paintings, jars the aesthetic sensibilities of many people. Squatting as a way of life, when tolerated and even encouraged for political and selfish ends by government officials, contributes to the incidence of more serious crimes. And the personal and social disorganization brought about by life in the slums may be hard to document but it is nevertheless a growing threat.

### THE PRESENT SITUATION: GEOGRAPHICAL DISTRIBUTION

(6) While the whole Metropolitan Manila area is faced with the problems of squatters and slum-dwellers, the situation is especially grave in the city of Manila itself, Quezon City and Caloocan City. These cities have 43.8%, 17.8% and 13.1% of the total squatter and slum population of the metropolitan area respectively.

(7) In Manila, the biggest problem is in Tondo, where an estimated 46,297 of the City's 80,436 households that make up the total squatter and slum population are concentrated. The biggest squatter-slum colonies are found in Barrio Magsaysay, Barrio Magdaragat, the railroad tracks from Tayuman to Barrio Obrero and

2 City of Manila and National Science Development Board, *Manila: Its Needs and Resources.* (Manila: Manila Social Welfare Department, 1967), Ch. IX.

TABLE NO. 1

ESTIMATED NUMBER OF SQUATTERS AND SLUM-DWELLERS
IN METROPOLITAN MANILA, 1968 (FAMILIES)

| Location | Squatters | % | Slum-Dwellers | % | Total | % |
|---|---|---|---|---|---|---|
| Manila | 35,329 | 27.6 | 45,107 | 80.7 | 80,436 | 43.8 |
| Malabon | 9,000 | 7.1 | — | — | 9,000 | 4.9 |
| Navotas | 4,000 | 3.1 | — | — | 4,000 | 2.2 |
| Caloocan | 21,650 | 16.9 | 2,350 | 4.2 | 24,000 | 13.1 |
| Quezon City | 31,297 | 24.5 | 1,450 | 2.6 | 32,747 | 17.8 |
| Mandaluyong | 15,250 | 11.9 | 6,000 | 10.7 | 21,250 | 11.7 |
| San Juan | 3,384 | 2.7 | — | — | 3,384 | 1.8 |
| Marikina | 456 | .4 | — | — | 456 | .2 |
| Pasig | 196 | .2 | — | — | 196 | .1 |
| Taguig | 200 | .2 | — | — | 200 | .1 |
| Cainta | 80 | .0 | — | — | 80 | .0 |
| Makati | 971 | .8 | 200 | .4 | 1,171 | .6 |
| Pasay | 1,939 | 1.5 | 800 | 1.4 | 2,739 | 1.5 |
| Parañaque | 3,600 | 2.7 | — | — | 3,600 | 1.9 |
| Las Piñas | 500 | .4 | — | — | 500 | .3 |
| Metropolitan Manila | 127,852 | 100.0 | 55,907 | 100.0 | 183,759 | 100.0 |

the notorious Isla Puting Bato. The physical conditions in Tondo are especially bad. Many squatters live along the district's many esteros (Canal de la Reina, Estero de Vitas, Estero de San Lazaro, Estero Sunog Apog, Fishermen's Wharf, etc.). The streets in the district are small, winding and narrow, with numerous pockets (*looban*) not accessible to motorized vehicles.

(8) Squatters and slum-dwellers congregate in the Tondo district because there are job opportunities there for unskilled and uneducated people. North Harbor employs many stevedores and laborers. Divisoria and other markets in the area provide livelihood to many *kargadores* and small vendors. The thousands of factories and little shops also provide job opportunities. The district's proximity to the Sta. Cruz and Quiapo downtown sections, coupled with the cheapness of jeepney transportation, also encour-

ages many poor people who live off the commercial bustle of downtown (sidewalk vendors, scavengers, watch-your-car boys) to live in Tondo.[3]

(9)   The squatter and slum problem in Manila is also bad in the district of Sampaloc, (12,914 squatter and slum families) a lower to lower-middle class community also made attractive by its proximity to the downtown area. In Sampaloc, squatters are mostly concentrated along the railroad tracks right-of-way and in the low-lying formerly swampy areas (*kangkungan*), just off BalicBalic. There are also squatter colonies along Dimasalang and Dapitan streets and along G. Tuazon. Smaller colonies of about 800 families each are found along Dapitan to España and from España to Lealtad.

(10)   The difficulty with Sampaloc is that there is little by way of an economic base to support communities of low-income people. Aside from the markets and some small commercial establishments, Sampaloc has little to offer. It is primarily a residential community serving the downtown section.

(11)   The third area in Manila troubled by slum-dwellers and squatters is the Fourth District, with 13,360 squatters and slum families located around Sta. Ana, Pandacan, Paco, Intramuros, Malate and Ermita. Slums and squatters in this area are the outcome of the fact that Manila south of the Pasig was the most devastated section during the Second World War. The availability of public lands (Fabie Estate, the railroad tracks), big private estates, and marginal lands formerly devoted to agriculture and to fishponds has also attracted squatters and slum-dwellers.

(12)   The district of Pandacan has the highest concentration of squatters in the Fourth District (2,370 families). Pandacan is an industrial area, with almost all of the oil depots and the main gas company plants located there. As such, it has attracted both skilled and unskilled workers, who naturally want to live close to their jobs. Combining squatters and slum-dwellers, however, Sta. Ana, especially that sector known as San Andres Bukid, has the largest concentration (about 5,559 families). The low and formerly flooded portions of San Andres (along Esguerra and Dagonoy streets) have invited squatters and slum-dwellers. The presence of markets in the area and the easy transportation between San An-

---

[3] For more on Tondo squatters, see Aprodicio A. Laquian, *Slums Are For People: The Barrio Magsaysay Pilot Project in Urban Community Development* (Manila: College of Public Administration, UP, 1968).

dres and South Harbor, combine to make the place a favorite for low-income people.

(13)   Among the suburban cities and towns, Quezon City has the worst squatter (not slum) problem. The biggest headache of city and national officials is the Quezon Memorial Park site, especially areas along E. de los Santos Avenue, North Triangle, Elliptical Avenue, Quezon Boulevard and the UP campus. The park site contains close to 4,000 squatter families. Though they are widely distributed throughout the large park, the squatters have managed to discourage developments in the area.

(14)   One problem with Quezon City squatters is the fact that they are well organized and therefore an important political bloc that local politicians have to contend with. The capital city, however, does not have the types of industries and commercial concerns that would warrant the concentration of low-income communities. Most of the Quezon City squatters are agricultural persons who make out a marginal living from the often rocky and infertile soil. Some of them were also "builder squatters," people who worked on the many construction projects in the city, built shanties for their families, and then stayed put even after the construction work was done. No doubt the undeveloped public and private lands in the city also contributed a great deal to the coming of squatters. Many of the squatters in the park site contend that they were encouraged to stay in Quezon City by signs put up by the government a long time ago inviting them to "Come and Plant in the Capital City." Now that they have contributed their share in the development of the City, they claim they are being driven away.

(15)   As an old community swallowed up by the urban sprawl, the City of Caloocan has the third worst squatter and slum problem in Metropolitan Manila (about 24,000 families). The largest single concentration of squatters in the place is Bagong Barrio, followed closely by public property owned by the Manila Railroad Company.

(16)   The older sections of Caloocan have deteriorated very fast as more and more migrants concentrated in them. The many small shops and trades in the city attract people of the low-income variety. In addition, the presence of large tracts of public lands and private estates temptingly beckons to squatters. Many of the barrios of Caloocan that have been transformed into subdivisions are plagued by squatters. The presence of squatters and slum-

dwellers, in turn, has greatly affected the peace and order situation in the city.

(17) To sum up, therefore, there are many reasons why certain areas in Greater Manila attract squatters and slum-dwellers. These reasons include the following:

1. Proximity to sources of employment that depend on unskilled labor and which give low pay;
2. Availability of undeveloped or unused public lands or large private estates;
3. Availability of poor or marginal lands not suitable for other development, such as swampy areas, reclaimed land, estero sides and others;
4. In the case of slum-dwellers, they are usually attracted to private lands where the owners are willing to receive low rents because the land is marginal or the owners do not want to invest money into developmental purposes. Slums also grow up in public lands where there are no control measures because of lack of concern or even corruption.

(18) It is seen from the reasons enumerated above that there is some logic in the distribution of squatters and slum-dwellers in the Metropolitan Manila map. Squatters and slum-dwellers are not just randomly distributed all over the place. Their concentration is influenced by employment, political and other factors. It is extremely important that such logic be kept in mind in the preparation of a program to solve the squatter and slum-dwelling problem in Metropolitan Manila.

## THE PRESENT SITUATION: SOCIAL BACKGROUND CHARACTERISTICS

(19) Pending tabulation and analysis of the complete survey results of squatters and slum-dwellers in Metropolitan Manila being done through the cooperative efforts of the Social Welfare Administration, People's Homesite and Housing Corporation, Presidential Assistant on Housing, Presidential Arm on Community Development, the City of Manila, and other national and local government units, secondary data obtained from previous studies have been

used in this report.[4] Such studies, although conducted in various squatter and slum communities, show an amazing comparability of findings.

(20) Some of the more important characteristics of squatters and slum-dwellers are the following:

1. The average family income of squatters and slum-dwellers is between ₱ 100 to ₱ 149 per month. About 51.3 per cent of squatter and slum families earn less than ₱ 150 and about 14.8 per cent claim having no income and income that is so variable one cannot depend on it.

2. The average size of squatters and slum-dwelling household is between five and six members. The degree of dependency is high, with 70 per cent of household members below 18 years of age. About 32 per cent of dependent members are below school age, while 11 per cent of those of school age are out of school.

3. Doubling up in squatter and slum houses is quite frequent. More than 30 per cent of houses in squatter and slum areas have more than one family residing in them. Home ownership, however, is quite high, with 67 per cent of families owning their houses and only about 26 per cent renting (others are even rent free).

4. Utilities are greatly lacking with water and roads being the most serious problems, followed closely by police and fire-fighting facilities. Barely a quarter of squatter and slum-dweller households have toilets and garbage collection is almost non-existent. Only electricity is adequately provided, with about 70 per cent of households using electric lights and 42 per cent using radios.

5. Squatters and slum-dwellers are very organized, with more that 65 per cent of household heads being members of at

---

[4] These studies include: (1) Complete survey of Barrio Magsaysay, Tondo, 2,625 families, conducted by PACD in March 1966; (2) Complete survey of squatter families on Broadway, Quezon City, 203 families, done by the UP through the Manila Complex Study, March 1967; (3) Complete survey of slum families in Tramo, Pasay City, 295 families, conducted by the Asian Social Institute, January 1967; (4) Sample survey of Manila residents, 731 households, conducted by the Manila Department of Social Welfare and National Science Development Board, April 1965; and a (5) Complete survey of Quezon City park squatters, 3,045 families, conducted by the Social Welfare Administration and the PHHC, March 1966.

least one organization. This joining provides not only a sense of community identity but political power as well.

6. Most of the squatter and slum-dwelling families are migrants from the rural areas, with only about 7 per cent being originally from Metropolitan Manila. About a quarter of squatters and slum-dwellers are from Central Luzon, 20 per cent from Western Visayas and 17 per cent from Eastern Visayas. Other regions where they come from are Northern Luzon, 14 per cent, and the Bicol region, 13 per cent.

7. The most important reason given for going to Metropolitan Manila was to improve means of livelihood. Most important reason for staying in the squatter area was "no other place to go to" and "closeness to job." More than three-fourths of squatter and slum-dwellers are unwilling to leave their area. They are almost unanimous in looking up to the government for help.

(21) The findings from the five studies mentioned above provide the baseline data which the complete survey of squatters and slum-dwellers currently being done in Metropolitan Manila will supplement. As soon as more updated information is obtained, a concrete program for solving the squatter and slum-dwelling problem will be prepared.

(22) Even with the tentative information currently available, however, specific proposals can already be made to solve the squatter and slum-dwelling problem.

## THE PRESENT SITUATION: GOVERNMENTAL EFFORTS

(23) The government's effort to solve the problem of squatting and slum-dwelling have been characterized by sporadic campaigns and programs more or less related to specific crises situations. In the absence of a definite policy and program touching on such aspects as the legality of squatting and slum-dwelling, urban development, population allocation, public investments and credit for housing purposes, there have been independent and uncoordinated efforts on the part of many agencies. The result has been organizational confusion marked by overlapping of functions, repetition of efforts, passing the buck and other undesirable bureaucratic practices including corruption.

(24) The primary agency charged with coordinating housing and urban development in the Philippines is the Presidential Assistant on Housing and Resettlement Agency, created in 1964. The

Agency, however, has a small staff, only two of which are technicians. While the Presidential Assistant has cabinet rank, he is also saddled with too many administrative and political details because he is also the Chairman and General Manager of the People's Homesite and Housing Corporation. Though the PAH was created to coordinate the actions of agencies involved in housing, a combination of lack of personnel, funds and political factors has made it ineffective.

(25) The government's main housing agency is the People's Homesite and Housing Corporation, authorized by law to acquire land, build houses, manage housing projects, clear slums, relocate squatters and do research on housing and slum rehabilitation. Since its creation in 1947, however, the PHHC has built only 12,000 dwelling units in 17 projects, 11 of which are in the Greater Manila area. It has not built any dwelling unit during the past five years.

(26) The PHHC's troubles may be traced to specific pressures that result in legislation detrimental to the agency's operations. Thus, Republic Act 3818, passed in 1963, provided for the outright sale of PHHC homes, with rental payments being considered as payments to the purchase price of units. This alone resulted in a ₱ 15 million loss to the PHHC. The landholdings of the PHHC have also been slowly depleted by special housing projects for government employees, veterans, newspapermen, etc. Finally, even landholdings of the agency outside the Greater Manila area have been occupied by squatters or used as relocation sites for squatters. When coupled with specific political pressures for accommodations, patronage and other demands, these problems of the PHHC conspire to make the agency ineffective.

(27) Another agency created in 1956 to help improve housing is the Home Financing Commission. The commission has the power to insure loans up to ₱ 25,500 for individual mortgages, with only a one per cent insurance premium. As of now, however, the volume of HFC-financed mortgages amounts to only ₱ 62 million. The main problem is the interest rate for loans insured by it, which is only 6 per cent. Because the market interest rate is about 12 per cent or more, very few people avail of the funds of the HFC. In fact, of the ₱ 5 million starting fund of the HFC, ₱ 2 million is still available.

(28) Aside from these three main agencies, there are others which are primarily or peripherally connected with housing, squat-

ter and slum programs. Among these are the Social Security System, the Government Service Insurance System, the Social Welfare Administration, National Planning Commission, Presidential Arm on Community Development, Development Bank of the Philippines, regional authorities and, of course, the autonomous local governments. The local autonomy law gave local governments complete jurisdiction over planning. While some of the local units have responded positively to this responsibility, many have totally neglected this function.

(29) All in all, the government's activities in the housing, slum and squatter improvement fields have been ineffective and insufficient. The proliferation of responsibility among national and local units, coupled with the lack of a central agency with the necessary powers, finances and leadership have been the reasons behind this. There is also a crying need for a definite housing policy and an integrated program that would face up to the problem once and for all.

## RECOMMENDATIONS

(30) One serious mistake of previous plans and programs to meet the squatter and slum-dwelling problem was in treating this as primarily involving housing. If having a roof over one's head is the only concern, the problem would be easy to solve. Unfortunately, the problem is much more complex. It is closely tied up with such factors as employment, journey to work, land values, ability to pay and others. As such, a housing program must be seen in the total light of comprehensive urban development, for it affects, and is affected by, the other factors that make for rational urban development.

## LOW-COST HOUSING

(31) It is obvious that a low-cost housing program is called for if the squatting and slum-dwelling problem is to be solved. When coupled with a program of relocation, redevelopment, community development and other schemes, low-cost housing has a better chance to succeed.

(32) Housing policy must depend on the characteristics of the people it serves. One of the most important factors to be considered is the income of the housing clients. The type of housing scheme to be introduced, therefore, may be guided by the following considerations:

| Type of Scheme | Monthly Income of Clients | Per Cent of Clients to be Served |
|---|---|---|
| 1. Government provides social housing practically free; people have little or no capacity to pay. | Below ₱ 100 | 25.6 |
| 2. People pay rental on government houses built on government land to amortize construction and operation cost. Rents from ₱ 10–₱ 50 monthly. | ₱ 100–299 | 63.5 |
| 3. People buy government houses built on government land on 10–30 year repayment plan at 6 per cent interest. | ₱ 300–399 | 6.4 |
| 4. People construct houses on government land, with loans from government lending institutions at 6 per cent interest. | ₱ 400–499 | 2.0 |
| 5. People construct homes on private land, with loans from public or private credit institutions. | ₱ 500 and above | 2.5 |

(33) For the government, the biggest problem involves squatters and slum-dwellers with income less than ₱ 100 per month which make up more than a quarter of the slum and squatter population (about 45,939 families). To set up social housing for these people with no hope of ever recouping the government's investment is a great financial burden. At the lowest rate of ₱ 5,000 per dwelling unit, this will already entail a cost of about ₱ 229,695,000, a sum the government can ill afford.

(34) It is imperative, therefore, that to meet this serious problem, a combination of schemes should be used. Thus, those

among the bottom income squatters and slum-dwellers who have agricultural skills may be encouraged to return to the farm or to migrate as members of agricultural colonies to open up new lands. Others may be relocated to semi-urban lands around metropolitan fringes to go into vegetable gardening, poultry raising or cottage industries, under the government's Food Production Program. Purely social housing should only be provided for the handicapped and the destitute over which society really has an obligation.

(35) For the 115,768 families who are squatters and slum-dwellers in Metropolitan Manila who can afford to pay from ₱ 10 to ₱ 50 per month for housing, various types of low-cost housing ranging from row houses to seven-storey tenements may be built. The location of such low-cost houses, however, must be planned in close coordination with such factors as transportation, employment needs, social amenities and upward economic opportunities. Thus, Tondo, Marikina, Navotas and the Fourth District of Manila should have high priority as locations for such housing because of the factors mentioned above.

(36) For families with capacity to pay, the government must provide the climate for encouraging the private sector to enter the housing field. Aside from such schemes as credit for housing, mortgage insurance, savings and loan associations and the like, the government must also make sure that it will not directly compete with the private sector in programs that can be served effectively by commercial ventures.

## URBAN COMMUNITY DEVELOPMENT

(37) Much as the government would want to provide low-cost housing or relocate urban squatters and slum-dwellers, the expense of pursuing these programs effectively is too much for it to shoulder. Financial realities, therefore, call for a program of urban community development.

(38) As envisioned, urban CD involves toleration of squatters and slum conditions for specific periods of time. Instead of ignoring the squatter and slum problem, the government, through community development workers, should organize the people and ask them to improve their conditions through aided self-help. Under this scheme, the government provides basic infrastructures and amenities such as roads, water, medical help, schools, firefighting equipment and others. The people, in turn, contribute their labor or even funds, in whatever construction or cooperative efforts are needed for the community.

(39)   Sociological studies have shown that squatter and slum communities are usually well organized. The sense of identity among such people is strong. Thus, cooperative efforts such as the *ronda*, community fiesta, pooling of funds and labor resources are quite common. This human resource should be fully tapped by the government for taking care of slum and squatter problems with the main efforts of the people themselves. To this end, the Community Welfare Services program of the Social Welfare Administration as well as the Urban Community Development efforts of the PACD should be expanded and their coverage enlarged to include slum and squatter communities in urban areas. This uniquely human approach to solving basically human problems should be tried to avail of its advantages.

### RESETTLEMENT AND URBAN DISPERSAL

(40)   About 93 per cent of squatters and slum-dwellers are migrants from the rural areas. Of these, 16 per cent arrived from 1946–1955, 14 per cent came to Metropolitan Manila from 1956 to 1960 while 28 per cent came between 1961 and 1965. The increasing rate of migration may be seen in the fact that 9 per cent of squatters migrated to Metropolitan Manila in the two years of 1966 and 1967.

(41)   The pattern of migration indicates that squatters and slum-dwellers first passed through a secondary urban area (e.g., Cebu, Iloilo, Legaspi, Davao) before going to Manila. This two-step migration is of tremendous significance in relocation projects because it explains the reluctance of squatters and slum-dwellers to go back where they came from.

(42)   For squatters and slum-dwellers who moved to Metropolitan Manila during the past two years, and who presumably still have rural attitudes and skills, a program of resettlement and relocation may be recommended. However, to avoid "loss of face" which may occur if these people will be asked to return to their hometowns, they may be resettled in other rural areas either as homesteaders or members of agricultural settler colonies. Relocation may be made more palatable by the government offering free transportation, credit, farm implements and other forms of assistance. An information campaign to make such programs more appealing to squatters and slum-dwellers may be made by the SWA, PACD and other agencies.

(43)   Past experience has shown, however, that programs for encouraging urban squatters and slum-dwellers to return to the

ESTIMATED NUMBER OF SQUATTERS AND SLUM-DWELLERS
IN THE CITY OF MANILA, 1968 (FAMILIES)

| Location | Squatters | % | Slum-Dwellers | % | Total | % |
|---|---|---|---|---|---|---|
| Ermita | 475 | 1.4 | — | — | 475 | .6 |
| Malate | 206 | .6 | 2,810 | 6.2 | 3,016 | 3.7 |
| Intramuros | 73 | .2 | — | — | 73 | .1 |
| Paco | 610 | 1.7 | 950 | 2.1 | 1,560 | 1.9 |
| Sta. Ana | 1,297 | 4.0 | 4,162 | 9.2 | 5,559 | 6.9 |
| Pandacan | 2,370 | 6.7 | 307 | .7 | 2,677 | 3.3 |
| Sampaloc | 7,400 | 20.9 | 5,514 | 12.2 | 12,914 | 16.1 |
| San Miguel | 166 | .5 | 320 | .7 | 486 | .6 |
| Sta. Cruz | 750 | 2.1 | 3,325 | 7.4 | 4,075 | 5.1 |
| Quiapo | 100 | .3 | 291 | .6 | 391 | .6 |
| San Nicolas | — | — | 1,803 | 4.0 | 1,803 | 2.0 |
| Binondo | 900 | 2.5 | 210 | .5 | 1,110 | 1.7 |
| Tondo | 20,882 | 59.1 | 25,415 | 56.4 | 46,297 | 57.5 |
| Total for Manila | 35,329 | 100.0 | 45,107 | 100.0 | 80,436 | 100.0 |

rural areas have not been too successful. A supplementary program of encouraging such people to locate in secondary urban areas or at the fringes of the metropolis is therefore needed. At the personal level, this may require the expansion of the program envisioned by the Central Institute for the Training and Rehabilitation of Urban Squatters (CITRUS). By training squatters and slum-dwellers in new skills that may be useful in urban life, they may be encouraged to move to other areas where such skills would be needed.

(44) At a broader level, dispersal of people to other urban centers may be done by the conscious development of other urbanizing centers so that they will serve as "counter magnets" to Metropolitan Manila. This program may be pursued through the following means: (1) The allocation of public investment in infrastructures and production facilities to other urban centers; (2) The planning of development regions around urban growth points; (3) The encouragement of private business and chambers of com-

merce in their efforts to drum up support for the development of their areas; and (4) The intensification of government operations and development efforts in secondary urban centers. Such a conscious policy of resource allocation and urban dispersal will bring about many advantages. Its most lasting benefit, moreover, is the achievement of balanced growth over the whole country, instead of the present concentration in Metropolitan Manila.

### RELOCATION

(45)    There is a need to take a hard second look at the government's program of relocating squatters and slum-dwellers to such places as Sapang Palay, San Pedro Tunasan and Carmona. More than 55 per cent of the people relocated to Sapang Palay have moved out of the area. Those who remain are trying to eke out a miserable life, with able-bodied males working in Metropolitan Manila and going home only on weekends. Others have built ghost houses only for speculative purposes, with no real intentions of ever occupying them.

(46)    A relocation program is not a simple operation that involves bodily transferring people from the slums to the relocation area. If it is to succeed, the following must be assured first: (*a*) A means of livelihood in the relocation area which is just as good as the one originally enjoyed by the squatter or slum-dweller; (*b*) If there is no immediate means of livelihood, a cheap and convenient transportation system between a person's job and his new home; (*c*) Adequate facilities such as roads, water, medical services, waste disposal and others; and (*d*) Provisions for new housing. The failure of past relocation schemes may be traced to a lack of some, if not all, of the above.

(47)    To assure that future relocation projects are done properly, a standard operating procedure should be devised that would include the following steps: (*a*) Complete survey of persons to be relocated, noting down all personal and social background information that may aid the planners of the project; (*b*) Survey, planning and preparation of the relocation site; (*c*) Provision of basic facilities and amenities before transfer of human beings; (*d*) Specific allocation of lots to families so that the latter would know exactly where they will set up their new homes; (*e*) Clarification of the terms of relocation, such as whether families can hope to own the land and under what manner of payment; (*f*) Assistance during the actual period of relocation in terms of transportation,

core housing, food rations; and (g) Continued follow-up of the progress of people in the relocation site, including programs for community organization, technical assistance and eventually, local governments.

(48) Relocating people in a hurry because of political convenience or other reasons does not really solve the slum and squatter problem. It only postpones the actual solution, with the possibility that the problem would be compounded because of the failure to come up with real solutions. The lack of regard and respect for the plight of human beings that has characterized relocation projects in the past also serves to add fuel to an already heated issue. In a matter as explosive as the squatter and slum problem, the country cannot afford half-way measures.

## ROLE OF PRIVATE INDUSTRY

(49) Governmental efforts alone will not be able to solve the squatter and slum problem. In the Philippines, only 1 per cent of houses are built by the government. Another 20 per cent are financed by the government but the remaining 79 per cent of houses are privately built and privately financed. Yet, taking the country as a whole, 70 per cent of the Philippine population cannot afford to build their own homes nor have enough collaterals to avail of government credit.

(50) Some 2.5 per cent of squatters and slum-dwellers in Metropolitan Manila or about 45,939 families have incomes of ₱ 500 per month or more. When added to the middle and high income level persons in the urban population, this is quite a rich market for housing. Proof of the profitability of housing is the proliferation of subdivision and land development companies in the metropolitan area. What is practically left untouched, however, is the venture of private industry into low-cost housing. Here, it would be unrealistic to expect that this will come about until major revisions are made in governmental program and policies.

## LOW-COST HOUSING

(51) The government's encouragement of low-cost homes that cost from ₱ 5,000 to ₱ 10,000 each as typified by Eternit homes or the Bancom design is laudable but it should be analyzed further. For the main problem in housing today is not the house itself but the land. Uncontrolled land use, speculation, unrealistic tax rates and other factors have combined to send land values soaring in

Manila and suburbs. On the average, land to house and improvement cost ratios are about 60:40. Constructing low-cost houses on expensive land, therefore, will make this situation worse. It is only logical to expect that when land values are extremely high, optimal use of land requires building upward and not horizontal expansion which only leads to undesirable urban sprawl.

## HOME LOAN BANKS

(52)    At present, about 79 per cent of all housing constructions in the Philippines is financed privately. However, credit facilities for housing are very inadequate. Housing has a low priority as far as public and private lending institutions are concerned. The GSIS, SSS, DBP and PNB require big collaterals or a high capacity to pay for housing loans. Such loans, therefore, go to people who need it least because they have enough money to avail of commercial bank loans. The middle-income person does not have ready access to credit for housing. Interest rates in private banks are generally higher than the legal 12 per cent while public funds at 6 per cent are in scarce supply.

(53)    The government should set up Home Loan Banks, with public funds made available solely for housing. Even if such funds are lent at 12 per cent interest, if no collateral is required, people will still borrow. If such home loans are properly administered, there are indications that they will help in increasing the stock of housing in the Philippines.

## MORTGAGE INSURANCE

(54)    Private capital in the Philippines is often not devoted to low-cost housing because there are many ventures where the returns to capital are higher. One way of encouraging private capital to go into housing, therefore, is by reducing the risk through mortgage insurance. This was the main idea behind the Home Financing Commission (HFC). This agency insures house mortgages at the minimal cost of 1 per cent added to the interest of the loan.

(55)    Unfortunately, the HFC has not been able to function effectively because it still insists on using 6 per cent as the interest rate on housing loans, a rate in force in 1956 when the agency was created. Since the current interest rate on housing loans in the open market is about 12 per cent or more, no entrepreneur is willing to have mortgage insured if his interest rate is reduced to 6 per cent. The charter of the HFC, therefore, should be revised to enable it to raise its interest rates closer to the current rates.

### SAVINGS AND LOAN ASSOCIATION

(56)   Another way of encouraging private capital to accumulate so that it could be used for housing is by setting up savings and loan associations. Unfortunately, in the Philippines, savings and loan associations find it more lucrative to grant short-term commercial loans, to be repaid from six months to one year. Under these terms, very few people would be able to devote funds from the associations to housing. If the savings and loan associations would be of help to the housing industry, some basic changes in their concept and operations must be introduced.

### COOPERATIVE AND CONDOMINIUM HOUSING

(57)   Since housing, like other production ventures, benefits from standardization and economies of scale, a group of persons pooling their resources together stands a better chance of solving their problem than just one person. Cooperative housing, therefore, is another way of encouraging private initiative in setting up low-cost housing. A group of persons in a cooperative may buy land together and build their homes much cheaply. The condominium law allows such cooperatives to be composed of individuals with private shares in an existing building. Unfortunately, in the Philippines, the benefits from cooperative and/or condominium housing are not too well appreciated yet. Lack of mutual trust and an understandable fear for something novel get in the way of improved housing through these methods.

### HOUSING FOR EMPLOYEES

(58)   Factories and industrial plants requiring unskilled or cheap labor must be urged by the government to provide low-cost housing for their employees. The advantages to the firm of this arrangement are many. Not only can tardiness and absenteeism be avoided because of the closeness between home and working place, the cost of housing as a fringe benefit may actually be shifted forward to consumers or backward to the workers in terms of lower wages.

(59)   Unfortunately, the high unemployment rate in the country prevents the full implementation of a scheme like this. Where there are many workers eager to work without low-cost housing provided nearby, the company has no real economic reason to go into the additional expense needed by housing. It is often much cheaper to provide shuttle transportation for employees or to give transportation allowances.

## HOUSING POLICY

(60)   In general, there can be no better scheme that the government can introduce than for it to issue a definite policy on housing. The changeable attitude of the government toward all aspects of housing (unrealistic interest rates, toleration of squatters and slum-dwellers, granting of concessions to vested interests and groups in public housing, direct competition with private builders) often discourages the private sector from really doing its best in trying to solve the housing problem. The lack of policy is further highlighted by the absence of a definite government agency in charge of housing and urban development. With the private sector having to contend with almost two dozen agencies when it goes into housing, it cannot be blamed for its reluctance.

## INSTITUTIONAL CHANGES IN GOVERNMENT

(61)   The present government institutions charged with the housing function are in a state of confusion and disarray, with overlapping in jurisdictions and non-coverage of many vital functions. If a comprehensive national housing program is to succeed, it must effect some basic institutional changes in the government.

## A CENTRAL HOUSING AGENCY

(62)   At present, aside from the PHHC, there are other government agencies directly or peripherally concerned with the housing function. Among these are the Presidential Assistant on Housing, Social Welfare Administration, National Planning Commission, Government Service Insurance System, Social Security System, Development Bank of the Philippines, CITRUS, the National Committee for Multi-Storey Tenements and others. The confusion that can arise from a proliferation of so many agencies is typified in the case of Sapang Palay where no less than 19 public and private agencies were involved.

(63)   There is an urgent need for the consolidation of so many agencies and a clarification of their functions. The proposal for the creation of a Department of Housing and Urban Development merits closer attention. As proposed by the bill, there is really a need for the housing function to be elevated to higher status in the Philippine government. By centralizing this function in a single department headed by an official of cabinet rank, the present confused state of affairs may be improved.

## REVISION OF PRIORITIES

(64)  With the government's major success in rice and roads, it is high time that the third basic necessity of roof should be given higher priority. The slum and squatter situation has already been allowed to deteriorate while other seemingly more urgent matters were looked after. The more than a million squatters and slum-dwellers in Metropolitan Manila provide ample evidence that meeting the problem cannot be postponed any longer.

(65)  Giving housing higher priority should bring about major changes in the credit facilities extended by public lending institutions. It should result in increased public expenditures for housing. The Philippine Government is one of the very few entities around the world that does not provide a regular appropriation for low-cost housing. Finally, a revision in priorities should clarify the government's policy toward land.

(66)  In other countries, public policy encourages the purchase of land by the government because of the fact that planning and development are much easier and more rational when the decision-makers are dealing with publicly-owned land. In the Philippines, however, we have embarked on a policy of selling public urban lands to finance land reform and other rural-based functions. The decision to sell Plaza Militar and some parts of Fort Bonifacio to finance the land bank is contrary to international trends in urban development and city planning.

(67)  While the government is disposing of public urban lands by sale, lease or even outright grants to such vested interests like the press, civic organizations and groups of employees with their own housing projects, it refuses to set up regulatory actions that would curb the widespread abuses of private landowners. Everyone recognizes that a punitive tax on idle lands will not only increase government income but will discourage speculation as well. It is also admitted that zoning codes, building regulations, minimum standards and modular coordination are all beneficial in the long run. However, too strong an adherence to the spirit of free enterprise, political opportunism, and plain disregard for the general welfare all combine to prevent the government from exercising its full influence for the common good. The squatter and slum-dwelling problem is only a symptom of the wider and deeper ills that beset the country. It can be solved only by major changes in our society and the revision of certain highly held institutions and beliefs.

# Notes

INTRODUCTION

1. Marshall B. Clinard, *Slums and Community Development* (New York: Free Press, 1966), p. 75.
2. *Ibid.*, pp. 51–54.
3. *Ibid.*, p. 4.
4. T. G. McGee, *The Southeast Asian City* (New York: Frederick A. Praeger, 1967), p. 1961.
5. Philip M. Hauser, ed., *Urbanization in India and the Far East* (Calcutta: UNESCO Research Centre on the Social Implications of Industrialization in Southern Asia, 1957), p. 133.
6. McGee, *op. cit.*, pp. 15–17.
7. Ofelia R. Angangco and Fe R. Arcinas, "Subproject: Urban Adjustment," in "Sociological-Anthropological Studies of Selected Sub-Communities in Manila," Phase 1 of a research project sponsored by the Social Science Research Council, University of the Philippines.
8. See "A Comprehensive Report on Squatting and Slum Dwelling in Metropolitan Manila," a report prepared by a Special Committee created under the Office of the President, April 1968, which is appended to this book.

CHAPTER 1

1. Nels Anderson, *The Urban Community* (New York: Henry Holt and Company, 1959), p. 191.
2. United Nations, *Urban Land Policies*, Document ST/SCA/9 (New York: UN Secretariat, 1952), p. 200.
3. Anderson, *op. cit.*, p. 191.
4. Morris Juppenlatz, *Housing the People of the Philippines*

(Manila: UN Dept. of Social and Economic Affairs, October 1966).

5. Juppenlatz, *op. cit.*, Table 14.
6. Edgar U. Ilarde, "The time-bomb keeps ticking and precious time is running out," *The Manila Times,* 21 April 1967, p. 12–M.
7. Juppenlatz, *op. cit.*
8. Aprodicio A. Laquian, *The City in Nation-Building* (Manila: School of Public Administration, University of the Philippines, 1966).
9. John F. C. Turner, "Uncontrolled Urban Settlement: Problems and Policies," Working Paper No. 11, Agenda Item No. 4, Inter-Regional Seminar on Development Policies and Planning in Relation to Urbanization, organized by the UN Bureau of Technical Assistance Operations and the Bureau of Social Affairs, University of Pittsburgh, 24–27 November 1966, p. 17.
10. Max Millikan and Don Blackmer, eds., *The Emerging Nations* (Boston: Little, Brown and Company, 1961).
11. Aprodicio A. Laquian, "Isla de Kokomo: Politics Among Urban Slum Dwellers," *Philippine Journal of Public Administration,* Vol. 8, No. 2, April 1964.
12. Oscar Lewis, *Five Families: Mexican Case Studies in the Culture of Poverty* (New York: John Wiley and Sons, 1962).

CHAPTER 2

1. Jose V. Abueva, *Focus on the Barrio* (Manila: Institute of Public Administration, 1959), pp. 1–2. The underscored lines are from Executive Order No. 156, 6 January 1956.
2. Buenaventura M. Villanueva, "The Community Development Program of the Philippine Government," *Philippine Journal of Public Administration,* Vol. 1, No. 2, July 1957, p. 145.
3. *Ibid.*, p. 146.
4. Marshall B. Clinard and B. Chatterjee, "Urban Community Development in India: The Delhi Pilot Project," in Roy Turner, ed., *India's Urban Future* (Bombay: Oxford University Press, 1962), pp. 71–93. See also, Aprodicio A. Laquian, "Urban Development: Lessons from the Indian Experience," *Philippine Journal of Public Administration,* Vol. 7, No. 3, July 1963, pp. 175–183.
5. Clinard and Chatterjee, *op. cit.*, p. 76.
6. *Ibid.*, p. 74.

7. "Training of Urban Community Development Workers," mimeographed proposal submitted to the PACD, 10 February 1966.
8. Buenaventura M. Villanueva, *The Training Program of the PACD* (Quezon City: Community Development Research Council, 1966), pp. 12–13.
9. *Ibid.*, p. 14.
10. *Ibid.*, p. 15.

CHAPTER 3

1. Kevin Lynch, *The Image of the City* (Cambridge, Mass.: MIT Press, 1969).
2. *Ibid.*, p. 4.
3. *Ibid.*, pp. 47–48.
4. Carlos L. Castillo, "Planning Aspect of the Manila International Seaport," Ports and Harbor Division, Bureau of Public Works. Undated mimeographed manuscript. See also, Jose A. Cruz, *et. al.*, "Economic and Technical Soundness Analysis of Proposed Port Improvement of the Republic of the Philippines To Be Undertaken with the Assistance of AID Loans," Division of Ports and Harbors, BPW. Undated mimeographed manuscript.

CHAPTER 4

1. See companion report, "Income and Expenditure Patterns in Barrio Magsaysay," by Belinda A. Aquino and Roberto San Juan (Manila: Barrio Magsaysay Urban Community Development Project, May 1967). Mimeographed manuscript.

CHAPTER 6

1. See for example, Buenaventura M. Villanueva, *A Study of the Competence of Barrio People to Conduct Local Self-Government* (Quezon City: Community Development Research Council, 1959).

CHAPTER 7

1. Executive Order No. 156, 6 January 1956.
2. Republic Act 4050, 18 June 1964.
3. Herbert Simon, *Administrative Behavior* (New York: Free Press, 1957).

4. Gelia T. Castillo, "Coordination—Anyone?" Paper presented at the Conference-Workshop on the Improvement of Instruction," Research Extension and Home Economics Programs of ACAP Member Institutions, Community Development Center, College, Laguna, November 1965.
5. *Ibid.*, p. 6.

CHAPTER 9

1. Jane Jacobs, *The Death and Life of Great American Cities* (New York: Vintage Books, 1961), Chapter 6.

CHAPTER 10

1. The term has been used by Bernard Wagner, U.S. AID housing advisor, in several of his papers. Others who share the idea of planned slums, often using other names, are G. F. Faithfull, UN consultant to the UP Institute of Planning, and Jacobo de Veyra, PHHC assistant general manager.

# Glossary

*aguador*   A water carrier or seller of water.

*Ang Tundo Man, May Langit Din*   Even Tondo Has the Sky, the title of a novel by Andres Cristobal Cruz, serialized in the *Liwayway* magazine; it tells about a young man who rose from the slums of Tondo.

Bago Bantay   A slum relocation area in Quezon City, one of the earliest such areas in the Philippines.

*Bahala na*   A common expression of fatalism meaning "What is meant to be, will be." Derived from *"Bathala na,"* or "God will provide."

*barkada*   A group or gang, usually of teenagers, that sometimes has the connotation of "bad company."

*barrio*   A rural community in the Philippines, though it is sometimes used to denote an urban community as in Barrio Magsaysay.

*barong barong*   A makeshift shanty usually made of old galvanized iron sheets, wood, boards, and scrap materials.

*caldereta*   A heavily spiced dish usually made of such meats as lamb, goat, dog, and beef.

*cara y cruz*   A gambling game using two coins, "heads or tails."

*concierto*   Literally, "a concert," though also used to refer to a gambling game such as cards and *mah jong*.

*daing*   Dried salted fish, the usual poor man's fare in the Philippines.

*damayan*   Traditional cooperative voluntary activities similar to the Indonesian *"gotong rojong."*

Damayan ng Nayon     A community organization in Barrio Magsaysay. The name means "Cooperative Society of the Town."

*empleado*     An employee, a white collar worker.

*estero*     A small stream or canal; the traditional drainage system of Manila was made up mainly of such streams and canals.

*fiesta*     A community celebration that has religious origins that is increasingly becoming a secular affair in the Philippines; the feast day of the patron saint for the community celebrating the *fiesta*.

Isla de Kokomo     A slum community in Metropolitan Manila. The name literally means "Island of Crabs," *kokomo*'s being dark salt water crabs commonly found in muddy places.

Islang Puting Bato     A slum community in Manila. The name literally means "Island of the White Stone," an allusion to the fact that this community grew on the stones of the breakwater near the piers.

Iglesia ni Kristo     "Church of Christ," a Philippine sect that split from the dominant Roman Catholicism.

*jeepney*     A reconverted jeep that constitutes Manila's main public transport vehicle.

*junta*     A leadership group for the community.

*kapisanan*     A voluntary association.

Kapisanang Lakas na Pinag-isa     A community association in Barrio Magsaysay; literal translation: "Association of Combined Force."

Kapisanan ng mga taga-Dalampasigan     A community association in Barrio Magsaysay; literal translation: "Association of Those Who Live by the Seashore."

Kapisanang taga-Baybay Dagat     A community association in Barrio Magsaysay; literal translation: "Association of Those Who Live by the Bay."

Kapisanang Tanglaw ng Kababaihan     A women's association in Barrio Magsaysay; literal translation: "Association of Women's Guiding Light."

Kapisanang Tanglaw ng Mahihirap     A community association in Barrio Magsaysay; literal translation: "Association of Poor People's Guiding Light."

*kargador*     A carrier of loads, usually at the piers or in the markets.

*kumpadre*    A ritual kin relationship established by a person acting as the godfather of somebody's child; the feminine form is "*kumadre.*"

*laos*    A has-been; somebody past his prime.

*lider*    A politician's leader in a community; a key member of a political machine.

*looban*    A traditional urban community; literally, "a community with no access to public thoroughfares."

*matadero*    A butcher; also used to refer to a killer.

*merienda*    A snack, usually eaten between meals.

Oxo    The name of a criminal gang in Manila.

*pabasa*    The singing of the life and passion of Jesus Christ traditionally done by the community during Holy Week.

Pagkakaisa ng Kababaihan sa Dalampasigan    A women's association in Barrio Magsaysay; literal translation: "Unity of Women Who Live near the Seashore."

*paluwagan*    A money pool, usually in offices, where members contribute a certain amount and the accumulated money is given to a member on his birthday.

*pook or purok*    The community unit or association under the Philippine community school movement.

Pulong Diablo    "Devil's Island," a community near Barrio Magsaysay known for its tough guys.

*ronda*    A voluntary community organization for maintaining peace and order, fighting fires, and, generally, protecting the community.

Samahan ng Kababaihan ng Baybay Dagat    A women's community association in Barrio Magsaysay; literal translation: "Association of Women Who Live near the Sea."

Samahang Busilak    A community association in Barrio Magsaysay; literal translation: "Association of Purity."

Sangguniang Nayon    A community association in Barrio Magsaysay; literal translation: "Council of the Community."

Sapang Palay    A squatter relocation area about 37 kilometers outside Manila; literal translation: "Brook Where the Rice Is."

*sari sari* store    A small variety store that sells household needs in small quantities; a corner store.

Sigue-Sigue    A criminal gang in Manila that has a running feud with the Oxo gang.

*talipapa*      A small open market, sometimes unlicensed.

*tanching*      A child's game played with coins.

Tanikala ng Pagkakaisa      A community organization in Barrio Magsaysay; literal translation: "Chain of Unity."

*tarifa*      An electrical connection that charges a fixed rate, in contrast to a metered rate.

*tuyo*      Dried anchovies; a poor Filipino's staple food.

*yaya*      An *amah;* a maid that takes care of children.

# Index